VALIANT ENDEAVOURS

ISBN 1 872350 80 1

Published by
GC Book Publishers Ltd
17 North Main Street
Wigtown
Scotland DG8 9HL

Printed by
Cromwell Press
Melksham
Wilts.

VALIANT ENDEAVOURS

Personal experiences recalled by Members of the
Dumfries & Galloway Branch of the Aircrew Association

**On the 75th Anniversary Year
of the Royal Air Force.**

"So many years have passed since then,
The flames of war have died,
The individual paths we chose,
Are scattered far and wide,
But we remember proudly those
Whose lives to our were tied,
When we were young."

Reproduced by the kind permission of Mrs Audrey Grealy from her poem "Bomber Aircrew - Times Past"

Contents

		Page
Foreword by	Air Chief Marshal Sir Kenneth Cross K.C.B., C.B.E, D.S.O., D.F.C., R.A.F. (Retired)	5
Preface		6
Acknowledgements		7
List of plates		8

Part 1
The Gunners' Gallery

Wartime Reminiscences	Donald Irving	10
That's the Way it Went	Daniel Brooks	14
Air Gunner Extraordinary	James Farish	19
Close Encounter	Douglas Coopey	26
The Luck of the Draw	James Carson	29
An Unhappy Birthday	Jim Mitchell	31
Line Shoot of the Month	George Halbert	34
Special Operations from Brindisi	Arthur Lenz	36
And They Called it Manna	Gordon Agnew	43
In Search of an Aircrew Brevet	Frank Armstrong	45
Cook's Tour	Tom Murchie	48
Anoxia And All That	Malcolm Stewart	51
A Tribute to the Resistance	John Waugh	53
Special operations	Donald Whyte	58
Convoy to Russia	Thomas Gibson	61

Part 2
The Signallers' Stories

34 Years in Aircrew	John Snee	67
Good Luck: A Reverie	Charles Munro	74
Lady Luck or But For the Grace of God	Matthew McGinily	79
Taxi Sergeant	Bill Clapperton	82
Wartime Reminiscences	Matthew Cochrane	86
A Bridge Too High	George Purslow	91

Part 3
The Engineers' Boost

Varied Experiences	Angus Cobban	95
Special Operations Europe and the Far East	Eric Till	97
A New Lease of Life	Reginald Eastoe	102
Virgin Airman	George Johnson	107

		Page
Part 4		
The Navigators' Narratives		
Wartime Experiences	Jack Jarmy	114
Every Little Helps	Ken Anderson	118
Service in the Desert	Jack Bisbey	123
A First Operation	Hugh Crawford	126
A Tale of Self Promotion	Robert Combe	131
A Promising Career Cut Short	Desmond Athol	138
From Young Volunteer to Senior Operations Officer	Ted Faulder	142
Maritime Operations	John Wray	146
In Some Quiet Corner	James Fyfe	150
Never Volunteer	Rowland Maddocks	156
The Gulf War	Stevie Tait	166
Part 5		
The Pilots' Perorations		
Naval Incident	Peter Boggis	168
Ten Times Roly	James Rogers	173
How the Mighty Were Fallen	Graham Douglass	178
Royal Air Force Career	John Elder	186
Survival in an Alien Environment	Jack Geekie	189
Monsieur le Commandant	Tim Hannay	192
A Valuable Post-War Career	Tom Manson	196
On Water	Hector Monro	200
The Making of a Glider Pilot	Bertie Moss	202
Ice is Not Nice	Robert Pate	206
Part 6		
Our Belgian Friends		
Belgium Twice Under Invading German Boots	Marcel Wouters	211
I Was Only 8 Years Old At The Time	Georges Wouters	218
Glossary of Service Terms		220
Further reading		222

FOREWORD

In reading these remarkable stories I cannot avoid being impressed by the universal enthusiasm shown for one of the most dangerous occupations in war, that of aircrew. Taking into account that environmental belief amongst these splendid young men that "it couldn't happen to me" it is nevertheless well known, and was known at the time, that the losses in aircrew were very heavy. In war all young men were compelled to join one or other of the Armed Services but there was never any compulsion to become aircrew. All were volunteers and this remained so throughout the War. That there was never any shortage of applicants is a tribute to the British character.

In these stories time and again is recorded tales of courage, ingenuity, devotion to duty and unselfishness and above all comradeship of young men never knowing what might be their last moment. I congratulate the Dumfries and Galloway Branch of the Aircrew Association on their enterprise.

Kenneth Cross,
Air Chief Marshal RAF (Retired)

PREFACE

This volume of stories about service in the Royal Air Force, in both peace and war, is a compilation of the personal experiences of individual members of the Dumfries and Galloway Branch of the Aircrew Association. Hopefully it will serve two purposes, firstly, to inform and interest its readers, particularly those who do not share similar memories, and also to raise funds for R.A.F. charities, the R.A.F. Benevolent Fund in particular. The philosophy behind its production at this time is that it will be a worthwhile addition to the history of military aviation during the 75th anniversary year of the Royal Air Force.

The period covered in this volume spans from 1936 through to the Gulf War of 1991, but, as might be expected, the bulk of the material is drawn from experiences in the war in Europe and the Far East between 1939 and 1945. In that period many thousands of young men from Britain and from the Dominions volunteered for flying duties in the RAF. Sadly, the greatest number of those are no longer with us. The personal stories here related reflect the high standards of skills and efficiency required of RAF aircrews and many recall periods of frustration along the difficult path to gaining the coveted aircrew 'brevet' (flying badge). Although acts of personal heroism are recalled, none of the contributors lays any personal claim to such; indeed, in many instances, it is the almost total reticence by the authors which most impresses.

Another feature which emerges strongly throughout is the unique bond of comradeship existing in individual crews, flights and squadrons. This is never more vividly demonstrated than in the night skies over Germany during W.W.II. The total interdependence of the bomber crew members was an essential feature of survival, this being first engendered by the eminently sensible procedure of allowing crews to assemble themselves from personal choice. This loyalty to one another is clearly shown in the instances where a crew member had to be replaced due to death or injury. In many cases the new crew member would not have completed his full tour of operations at the same time as the rest of the crew; frequently, the original crew members volunteered to continue operations until the new member's tour was completed.

The stories in this book cover a wide range of experiences; some sad, some heroic, some totally philosophical, some slightly hilarious. All are individual, related by survivors either born in or otherwise now residing in the beautiful countryside of Dumfries and Galloway Region. These stories are also a tribute to the 55,000 members of aircrew who were not so fortunate!

ACKNOWLEDGEMENTS

As the Chairman of the Dumfries and Galloway Branch of the A.C.A., it is fitting that I should personally thank all our members who have played such a sterling part in the production of this volume.

First must come KEN ANDERSON, D.F.C., our Honorary Secretary without whose dogged perseverance and 'push' this book would never have been written. Ken has been assisted in his editorial task by GRAHAM DOUGLASS, O.B.E., A.F.C., as both sub-editor and researcher, who has spent countless hours putting it all together. As a third member of the editorial team, I wish to thank PETER BOGGIS, D.F.C., for his assistance as proof reader. Thanks are also due to TOM MURCHIE, a published author in his own right, for always being available for consultation and advice. Thanks are also due to JAMES FYFE, M.A., for translation of the foreign language contributors, and to DAN BROOKS, a very able artist, for his black and white sketches used to illustrate the texts and to ROWLAND MADDOCKS for his splendid design of the front cover.

I also wish to thank all our A.C.A. members for contributing their individual articles, the majority of which have never been in print before. Last, but no means least, all our thanks are due to MAISIE DOUGLASS for her dedication, interpretation and typing of the original manuscripts.

DONALD C. IRVING.

List of Plates

1,2, & 3	"Air Gunner Extraordinary"
4	"The Gulf War"
5	"That's the way it went"
6 & 7	"A new lease of life"
8	"Wartime Experiences"
9	"Maritime Operations"
10	"A Tribute to the Resistance"
11	"Survival in an alien environment"
12	"A bridge to high"
13 & 14	"Service in the desert"

The Gunners' Gallery

Warrant Officer D.C. Irving, (Air Gunner.)

The indefatigable Chairman of our branch of the A.C.A., Donald Irving, was born in Annan on 28th September 1923. Educated at Annan and Dumfries Academies he became an apprentice engineer, volunteering for aircrew duties in the RAF at the age of nineteen. His article below describes his training as an air gunner and gives a vivid picture of both life and death on a wartime bomber squadron.

When Donald completed his voluntarily extended tour of operations he trained as an air armaments instructor both in the air and on the ground. He attended a course at the Empire Air Armaments School at Manby in Lincolnshire, before serving as an instructor at a number of stations including the Central Flying School at Uphavon and Little Rissington. Subsequently, he underwent training as an Armament Fitter at the Central Armaments School at Kirkham in Lancashire, remaining there as an instructor until his demobilisation in August 1951.

Donald married whilst still in the RAF and after leaving the Service became an Engineer Planning Officer. Now retired he and his wife live in his native Annan; they have an adult family of two sons. Donald's hobbies are gardening and a deep involvement in Service Charities.

Wartime Reminiscences

My war, as it was to many airmen, was an experience that I would not have volunteered for, if I had known what it involved, but on hindsight wound not have missed - and so, despite my being a country boy and never seen much at all of the world outside, I was ordered to report to Lord's Cricket Ground to be sworn-in as a member of the RAF.

I cannot ever remember being sworn-in, never mind receiving the King's Shilling. After the usual square-bashing, inoculation, dental treatment etc., I was posted to I.T.W. Bridlington for eight weeks more square-bashing.

I couldn't see what marching everywhere, performing rifle drill and jumping to attention every time a Corporal spoke had to do with flying; however, after what seemed an age I was posted to 7 A.G.S., RAF Morpeth where we flew in Bothas with Polish pilots who had not mastered the English language, but somehow I managed to cope and eventually received my Wing. I was now a Sergeant Air Gunner.

Posted to 16 O.T.U., RAF Upper Heyford to crew up, my first contact was with my navigator, P.A. Andrews (Andy) - how, I cannot tell you! We then chose our W/Op, a little Cockney that I immediately took to; then our Bomb Aimer, Mac McCue. Lastly we picked our pilot, Jack Lett (the best day's work I have ever done!) From then on, we flew together and finished O.T.U.

We were next posted to RAF Swinderby for H.C.U. on Halifaxes, where we picked up our Mid-Upper Gunner Tommy Woods, and our Flight Engineer Darky Morgan.

After converting to Halifaxes, we were then informed that we were going to fly Lancasters. After converting again, we were posted to 49 Squadron, RAF Fiskerton, in No 5 Group.

My first op was to Frankfurt, then we never seemed to go anywhere else except Berlin, with a little break in between to Stettin. After the Berlin battle it was on to Leipzig then Stuttgart, where we were hit by flak after bombing, which blew open the main door. My Flight Engineer Darky Morgan was detailed to go down to try and repair it. On reaching the door, his oxygen bottle gave out and he collapsed in the entrance with his hands on the airframe.

Flying at 25,000ft on a cold February night the temperature was below zero. I could see him lying there and told the Skipper to keep flying straight and level. Sergeant McCue (Mac) then came down and got Darky up to the rest bed. He gave him a shot of morphine and massaged his hands all the way back. We landed at Ford on the South Coast where Darky was taken to hospital and transferred to East Grinstead, where unfortunately he lost all his fingers. He is one of McIndoe's guinea pigs.

The next op on 26th March 1944 again was Berlin. Just after dropping the bombs we were hit and the starboard wing set on fire. The Skipper feathered both engines and stuck the nose down - he remembered from somewhere that doing so would cause a vacuum, therefore the fire would go out - talk about panic stations! All this time I was getting a commentary from Tommy Woods, my Mid-Upper Gunner as I couldn't see anything from the rear turret. We levelled out at around 9,000-10,000 feet with both engines gone and it was quite hairy on the way home, losing height all the way back. Fortunately, the Luftwaffe seemed to be having the rest of the night off.

Decisions about ditching and parachuting were then made by the whole crew, who decided to stick with the Skipper as long as we were airborne. We made it back and were refused permission to land at

Fiskerton; We were directed instead to Swinderby where Jack Lett put her down without mishap. After landing and climbing out on the wing we found no trace of flak, but incendiary bomb casings from another Lanc. (My Skipper still has one of the casings as a souvenir). That piece of flying was rewarded with a D.F.C. to Jack Lett.

On the night of 30th March 1944 we took off at 2200 hours for Nuremberg and were harried all the way to the target by night fighters. The Luftwaffe seemed to know where we were going; I have never seen as many fighter flares as there were that night - there were combats going on to both port and starboard of us, Lancs blowing up etc. We were lucky again, always managing to corkscrew out of trouble. That night, Bomber Command lost 92 aircraft.

On the night of 22nd April 1944, it was Brunswick, where we were attacked from below just after the bombing run (which as all aircrew know is the hairiest part of bombing - running straight and level for the photograph).

After getting out of the target, the Skipper always called up the crew; that night there was no reply from Mac.

We thought his intercom had disconnected. That particular night we had with us, in place of Darky, a new Flight Engineer who went down into the bomb bay to plug in Mac's intercom. We heard him say, "Mac's been hit and just lying here". He was sick and had to come back and let the "Old Man" of our crew, Frank Campbell, go down.

Frank's words across the intercom (I'll never forget) were, "I'm afraid he's gone Skipper, his eyes just like a dead fish's". However, Frank stayed with him all the way home. On arriving back at Fiskerton the M.O. verified that Frank was correct. We had lost a great friend and comrade and to say the least, were shattered.

Mac had come through the Battle of Berlin, had survived Nuremberg and most major targets in Germany. It would have been his twentieth trip. He was 21 years old.

My Mid-Upper Gunner, who blamed himself for not seeing the fighter in time, vowed he would not fly again and to the best of my knowledge, he never did. I met him the following March at E.A.A.S. Manby on an Instructor's Course as a Flight Sergeant.

On 22nd April 1944 the trip we had all been dreading was finally decided: Munich - nine and a half hours in the air.

Until reaching the target area we had been lucky. All of a sudden my turret was as bright as day - we were 'coned' by searchlights, for the first and only time, thank God. How the Skipper got us out, I'll never know, but after three minutes we were clear. I recall the aircraft being flung all over the sky, and feeling disoriented and shit-scared. Once again, B-Baker's luck was with us. It couldn't have been a master searchlight, otherwise I wouldn't be writing this. We went on to bomb the target and were awarded an aiming point. The feeling on arriving home and seeing the damage done to our aircraft by flak and yet still bringing us home, never fails to amaze me.

Group Captain Leonard Cheshire marked this target in a Mosquito and later he was awarded the V.C.

After Munich things got a bit better, and I knew within myself that I would survive. As I had flown operations with other crews earlier on, I should have been screened after thirty operations but my Skipper and the remainder of the original crew still had eight ops to do and asked me to stay with them as Rear Gunner until they finished. This I agreed to do, and we flew our final operation to Beauvoir on the night of 16th June 1944, ten days after D-Day.

I count myself as one of the lucky ones of Bomber Command, to have survived the Battle of Berlin, Nuremberg, Munich and many trips to "Happy Valley" and other major targets in Germany, starting off with seven men and finishing up with four men of the original crew.

Annan

D.C. Irving.

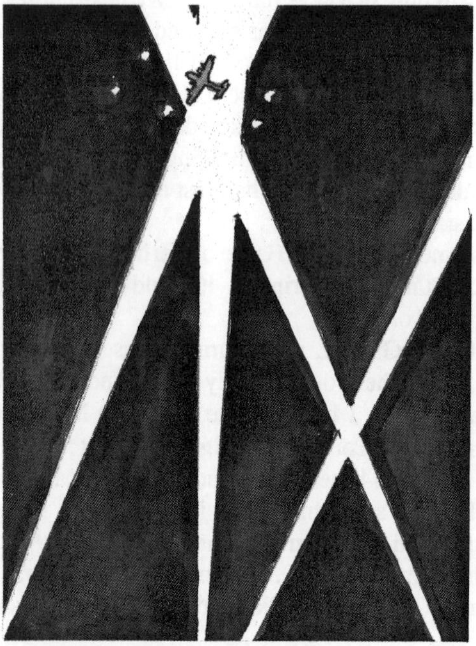

Warrant Officer Dan Brooks.
(Air Gunner)

A native of Lanark born in 1921, Dan Brooks was determined to serve as aircrew in the RAF during the war. After enlistment in 1941 and initially training as a wireless operator, he was injured in a flying accident in a Rapide whilst under training at Yatesbury in Wiltshire. After medical treatment it was concluded that his injury had developed into a chronic condition rendering him unfit for further service and he was discharged. This gloomy prognosis proved wrong and after six months, now fully restored to health, he re-enlisted without saying a word about his previous service and was selected for training as an air gunner. In this he was successful and earned his brevet and sergeant's stripes at Gunnery School, Dalcross near Inverness.

After successfully completing operational training on Wellingtons at Harwell in Oxfordshire, he and his crew were posted to the Far East. Here Dan converted on to Liberator long range bombers at Bangalore in India, the aircraft in which he was to fly 34 operational sorties against the Japanese.

Below he gives a vivid account of one operation which might have ended very differently.

Demobilised at Blackpool in 1946, Dan entered the Royal Observer Corps and became a Commander. He retired as a Senior Operations Staff Officer from Headquarters Strike Command at RAF Stanmore in Berkshire. He and his wife now lived in Annan and they have one adult son. Dan has an impressive list of hobbies 'Fishing, shooting, swimming, gardening, Speakers Club, Probus Club, painting, wood carving, wild flowers, herbal cures, fly tying and wine making. He is also a representative for the RAF Benevolent Fund.

That's the way it went

I was the front gunner on a B24 Liberator - by choice - as nearly all of my 34 operational trips on this type of aircraft were carried out at low level in daylight, sometimes at 200 feet or less.

The main targets were rolling stock and bridges on the infamous Burma/Siam railway, with occasional forays into Siam and Cambodia. Other major targets were Rangoon, Bangkok and Mandalay, such targets being attacked in daylight in close formation.

At low level the Front gunner was an 'action man' and, armed with 2 point 5 Brownings, one could cause considerable havoc to ground targets.

The common practice was for the front guns to bring a train to a halt when it could be bombed at leisure. The front guns also took on the A.A. guns that defended most of the important bridges when, with tracer and incendiary bullets flashing and sizzling around them, the Japanese gunners lost a lot of enthusiasm for their task.

The Liberator, with 110 feet of wingspan and designed for high level bombing, was never intended to operate like a Mosquito or a Beaufighter, but this was the only aircraft with the range and endurance to fly missions of 12 or even 20 hours duration.

So, my squadron, No.356 Squadron, became the first daylight heavy bomber squadron in S.E. Asia.

The date was 1st January 1945 and the target was random. The area of Operations was S.E. of Bangkok, near the Cambodian border. The objective was to search for and destroy bridges and rolling stock in a pre-planned area.

A 12 hour flight was planned and the bomb load was 8 one thousand pound bombs fitted with 7 second fuses, the all up weight was 58,000 pounds, verging upon maximum for a Liberator.

No serious opposition was anticipated other than a new and disturbing fact that most of the freight trains now carried Flak Wagons. But it was assumed that this was going to be an easy one and time would be left to split a bottle of Carew's gin to celebrate 1945 upon our return to base at Salbani, in the Bogra district of what is now Bangladesh, an airfield in the middle of a steaming nowhere.

Take-off was the usual teeth clenching bounce on the dust at the end of the runway - I never got used to that - and the general direction was South, over the mouths of the Ganges, over the bay of Bengal, over the Gulf of Martaban and into the Gulf of Thailand - and so into the designated area of search, endless flat country with strange outcrops of rock and strewn with palm trees.

A railway line was picked up almost right away and as we flew along it a distant puff of black smoke was spotted and on closer inspection it was seen with some excitement, that a goods train had stopped at what appeared to be an unloading bay.

The train driver spotted us and started to let off steam, so that if the boiler was penetrated, it would not explode. As it was , the white pillar of steam made an excellent aiming point.

As we made our initial attack at treetop level, the whole area in front of us began to disintegrate in a melee of dust, smoke, steam and lumps of concrete and wood, with my own tracer bouncing up past our aircraft in an alarming manner. I could see bodies leaping about all over the place, many of them in uniform, and behind me I heard the tail gunner having his share of the action.

So much for the initial dust up, now for the bombing run. A steep turn to port with the wing skirting the palm trees, and this time with the bomb doors open.

Again the pillar of steam was the aiming point, and as we levelled off, heading direct for the train, which, at this height, appeared to rush towards us at a great rate of knots - as did a stream of what looked like large tennis balls.

It was at that moment that I saw black smoke gouting from the starboard outer engine, and I immediately thought, "The bloody Flak Wagon".

Before anyone had time to react, the Flight Engineer who was acting as beam gunner on the starboard side reported, surprisingly calmly, "Flight Engineer to Pilot, fire in starboard outer". I admired young Dave for his calmness, for unknown to anyone at that moment, some oxygen bottles had exploded and split open one of his eyebrows. In later years he was proud of his three eyebrows.

As it was, we blistered over the train with bomb-doors open, but our new Bomb-aimer, a South American by the name of Pancho, had not let the bombs go - we still had them on board!

From now on a horror story began to unfold. The Second Pilot hit the extinguisher button, and effectively extinguished the starboard inner engine - the wrong one.

The situation now existed where we had no engines on the starboard side, 8,000 pounds of bombs on board and our height was a lopsided 200 feet or thereabouts.

The Pilot immediately dropped the bombs manually, overriding whatever ideas Pancho may have had. Later we learnt that an entire village had been blown to pieces, a village no doubt consisting of men, women and children who were unwilling spectators of a war that was beyond their comprehension. Such are the injustices of war.

It was imperative to get out of our predicament and this meant only one thing - gaining height. I was given the task of making the aircraft lighter and to achieve this I organised the jettisoning of the mid - upper guns and ammunition, the beam guns and ammunition and half of the ammunition in the pans of the front and rear guns, together with anything that could be heaved out of the door in the floor at the rear of the aircraft. Resulting from this we began to claw back some altitude.

All the while, a long trail of black smoke streamed from the damaged engine which was now feathered, and as fate would have it, another aircraft from our own squadron on a similar mission to our own, happened to spot us, and to them it appeared as though we were bailing out, so they came alongside to have a look.

When they saw that we were coping with the situation, they flew in front of us and waggled their wings in salute - and we got caught up in their slipstream.

That was the only time during all of the happenings that I was prepared to admit that we had 'had it', too much was stacked against us.

But, an hour or so later we had achieved 1500 feet in a kind of 'Wun Wing Low' attitude and the Navigator took this opportunity to discuss the next step which he conducted over the intercom. To get home we had to clear a range of mountains reaching up to 5,000 feet and this could not be achieved on two engines.

There were three options open to us. to head out to sea where we'd run out of fuel and be forced to ditch, or to eventually come down in the jungle, which was now underneath us, and was impenetrable.

Both of these options were out of the question - but the third option was to fly through a gap in the mountains at Taungoo. Was this some kind of a joke, it was not, for Taungoo was a vital Japanese airstrip.

So Taungoo it had to be , and Taungoo it was. We blistered over that airstrip at about 500 feet, trailing black smoke and front and rear guns blazing at anything and everything.

There were two Oscar fighters just off the runway, but perhaps the element of surprise and impossibility of the situation weighed heavily on our side.

In due course, and almost in disbelief we eventually approached the American P51 airfield at Cox's Bazaar on the Indian side of the border with Burma and the Pilot apprehensively unfeathered the damaged engine. It again gouted smoke but produced power.

The Americans had been advised of our plight and informed that our emergency arrival was imminent, and they turned out in hundreds to witness the spectacle.

When the runway came into view, the Control Tower offered the following, never to be forgotten welcome "Come on in, the big Jesus, high altitude destruction ship". And that we did!

On return to base by jeep, plane and train, we got a brand new Liberator which was written off a week later when we did a 'wheels up' landing following an attack on a Japanese destroyer.

That's the way it went!

Annan

Dan Brooks.

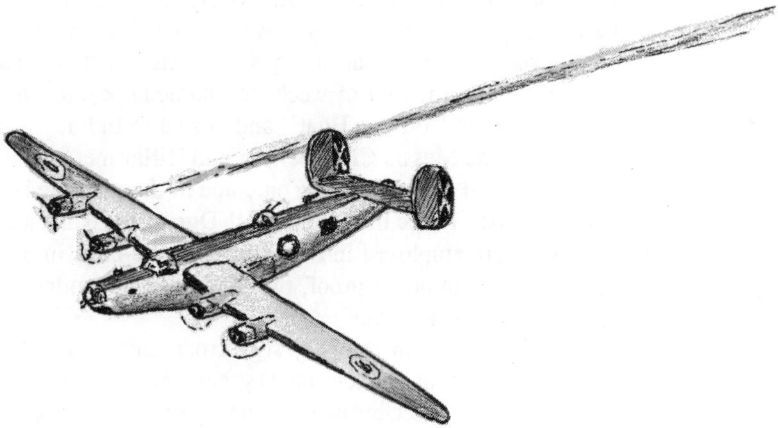

Sergeant James Farish.
(Air Gunner Extraordinary)

I was born at Jenkins Cross, Wigton, Cumbria on 23rd August, 1918. After the death of my father, a farmer, in 1927, the family moved to Annan, and I attended Annan Academy, first at Ednam Street and afterwards at Greenknowe.

What was known as the expansion scheme as applicable to the RAF got into top gear in 1934, and I sat the entrance exam successfully at school for entry in August 1935 as an Aircraft Apprentice at RAF Halton where I became No.568627 A/A Farish. The pay was a shilling a day for the first year and one and sixpence per day for the third year.

The course lasted for three years and I passed out in June 1938 as a qualified Fitter 11 in the exalted rank of A.C.2 !! The 'Best Blue' dress was pantaloons and puttees, the tunic had a choker collar and a swagger cane was carried by all apprentices. My subsequent posting was to No.224 squadron at Thornaby-on-Tees but the squadron was shortly afterwards moved to Leuchars. In a matter of weeks my name appeared on Daily Routine Orders as being "on The Boat" and posted to India.

In the meantime Messrs Chamberlain and Hitler met at Munich. It was panic stations all round until the outcome of the meeting became known and it was to be "Peace In Our Time"!! During the panic all able-bodied personnel were employed in the filling of sand-bags in order to keep the operations room bomb-proof, the Station Commander, Group Captain Brian Baker was not even excused.

Eventually I set sail in His Majesty's troop ship Neuralia from Southampton and arrived at Karachi on 21st November 1938, not what one would call first class travel, but sleeping nose to tail in hammocks was certainly an experience. I was then posted to No.20 A.C. Squadron at Peshawar, North West Frontier Province.

The Squadron was equipped with Hawker Audax aircraft, two-seater, open cockpits, Roll-Royce Kestrel engine and fitted with message picking-up hook to facilitate communications with the army as it was not possible to do so by W.T. A forward firing Vickers gun was fitted. It fired through the airscrew and the air-gunner used a Lewis gun on a swivel mounting in the rear cockpit.

There was a shortage of A.G.s at the time and I immediately volunteered and commenced flying on 16th December 1938. I'd had no instructions on the working of the Lewis gun and the flying I was engaged in was mainly for air experience.

However we were on active service permanently as the tribesmen were always causing trouble. My log book tells me that most of the trips were for proscription, blockade or close support to army columns in tribal territory, the pilot of course doing all the firing and bombing.

The squadron or a flight were frequently detached to a fort called Miranshah in Waziristan, which I believe used to be part of Afghanistan. The camp was surrounded by a 20ft. wall and we were not allowed out during the hours of darkness. The aircraft were pushed out as required and back in at night.

Political agents were appointed to each tribal area and it was from them that the RAF received its orders through a liaison officer from the army. These agents also appointed local natives called Khasidars who were supposed to act as guards or police and also to act as informers as regards the tribesmen's intentions. They wore a sort of uniform and were supplied with rifles and ammunition. A lot of sniping used to go on, always aimed at the camp and the Khadisars were held to be responsible. They were given tracer ammunition and sure enough after that every round fired at the camp was a tracer. The phrase "made redundant" was not in everyday use then but it was applied smartish.

A tribesmen with the title "The Fakir of Ipi" was the major trouble rouser on the Frontier, he had all the tribes on his side in Waziristan and we in the RAF were always on his trail but similar to the present day Mafia leaders he was a slippery customer and was never brought to account.

The political agents would be the first to get information regarding the miss-deeds of the tribes in a certain area such as the looting of a local bus or the stealing of livestock or whatever. A fine would then be imposed on the guilty tribe but they didn't believe in paying up. Next, leaflets were dropped on them to put a time limit on the date for payment, still no response, so more leaflets were dropped to inform them that after a certain date anything moving in their area would be a legitimate target for the RAF be it human being, camel, sheep, goat or dog.

I was still of course not permitted to use the rear gun, but I remember on one occasion the pilot dived down on a tribesman in a prohibited area who was ploughing a plot of land using a bullock as a means of traction for his wooden plough. The pilot released a twenty pound bomb which landed slap on top of the plough. The result was a cloud of dust, a ploughman running in one direction and a bullock running the other........so much for the twenty pound bomb!!!!

At this stage I was often called on to do photography, sometimes with a camera gun but more often with a hand held camera for oblique photography in the tribal areas.

In August 1939 it was decided that all unqualified A.G.s should attend a course on the subject. This was carried out at RAF Kohat, also on the frontier. The course lasted 16 days and for this purpose a flight of Wapitis of No.5 Squadron was attached to Kohat. The Wapitis provided a more stable gun platform then the Audax of 20 Squadron and it was deemed less likely that the elevators and rudders would be shot off an aircraft of larger dimensions. We started with instruction on the use of camera guns using ground targets and eventually air to air. Then the real thing using Lewis guns after having instruction in the armoury on their behaviour with the accent on stoppage procedures.

I had been re-classified A.C.1 by this time and although I was still not fully qualified as an A.G., I was paid an extra one and sixpence a day over and above my trade pay, this would put me in the three pounds a week bracket!!!!

In India Command, A.G.s had to be proficient in level bombing. This instruction was carried out back at Peshawar with 20 Squadron using practice bombs. First of all, the wind speed and direction had to be ascertained using a triangular course system in conjunction with a Mark something or other bombsight and was mostly carried out at 6,000ft.

Further training in bombing was carried out using the camera obscura. A W.T. set had to be installed for this purpose, having a Morse key available to the A.G. in the horizontal position below the pilot. The key had to be in the transmit position on approach to the target and at the bomb release point it had to be freed. The camera obscura operators also had a W.T. set and the aircraft image showed up on a chart in the camera obscura. Thus the accuracy or otherwise of the bombing was worked out.

After passing the bombing tests I was a fully qualified A.G. and was allowed to wear the Flying Bullet brass badge. Most trades were allowed to be A.G.s then, with the exception of cooks and clerks. I still had my aircraft to maintain between flying duties, this was Audax K4854 and I was responsible for the serviceability of both the engine and the air frame. In August 1939 I was reclassified again to L.A.C. No scrambled egg on my hat yet, but you never know!!!

Our various detachments to Miranshah were carried out by air using the Vickers Valentias (bomber transport) of 31 Squadron, Ambala. All the flight equipment including tail trolleys, oil drums, tool boxes and even two locally recruited coolies who were mainly employed in the pushing and shoving of aircraft and the general cleanliness of hangars, cowlings and drip trays. They were usually air sick on the journeys and the atmosphere got a bit thick at times.

September, October, and November 1939 were the months when operations against the tribes was most concentrated during my time there. Reference to my log book again shows that I put my bombing course into practice for real. The 22 H.E. bombs I released, each preceded by 2 practice sighters, were 112 pounders. The target was a cave at the bottom of a sheer cliff in which the Fakir of Ipi was supposed to be in hiding. 31 Squadron was brought in to drop 250 pounders on the same cave, it was bombed for days with no positive results.

On several occasions our aircraft would land with bullet holes in the fuselage and control surfaces, the tribesmen were excellent shots and were always well camouflaged in the rocky terrain. They shot two of our aircraft down during my time, one pilot having been killed outright and the other had lost consciousness due to loss of blood, both gunners were also killed.

In 1941 A.G.s were given the chance to re-muster to full time A.G.s with the rank of Sergeant. I was then a Corporal fitter, part time A.G. I weighed the situation up (finance wise) and decided to stay as a fitter, since promotion to Sergeant in the trade was due in the near future. I was called on to fly on many occasions after this and the good old Indian Government kept on supplying the flying pay until the day I left the country.

Later in 1941 the squadron was spread about a bit, "A Flt." to stay on the frontier and to be equipped with Blenheims, "B Flt." to Bombay and "C.Flt.", including myself, to Madras. Our role changed from Army co-op to Indian Navy co-op since Madras had been shelled by a German cruiser in World War 1 and we used to stooge around over the Bay of Bengal looking for non-existent Japanese subs or surface ships.

I passed my one and only civilian driving test on the grass runways at Madras, hand signals had to be used to notify non-existent traffic of my intentions. Provision was made on the licence for the applicant to sign, or supply a thumb print if he was illiterate.

The squadron re-assembled at Secunderabad in June '41. From there we had one detachment to Poona where co-op with the Army Staff College took place. One of our aircraft had to do a low fly past in order to give native riflemen aiming practice, the pilot misjudged his height slightly and wrecked the undercarriage on a stationary lorry, he was able to maintain height and flew over the aerodrome to drop a message bag with the message "Phone officer's mess, won't be back for lunch"!! He landed safely with no injuries to himself or the A.G. At the subsequent court of enquiry, the pilot said he was climbing steeply when he hit the lorry!!!

Back to Secunderabad in August '41 where the squadron was about to be re-equipped with Lysanders. Before that took place, I was posted from the squadron to Bangalore to help form a Staging Post, primarily to service American Fortresses and Liberators on their way to Palem bang in Sumatra. The Japs very soon put an end to that when they occupied the Dutch East Indies. Thereafter batches of Hurricanes would pass through accompanied by a Blenheim to do the navigating. The Hurricanes had been shipped in crates to Takoradi, West Africa, re-assembled and flown in stages to Ceylon. Also, Fleet Air Arm Fulmars were routed similarly on their way to reinforce, and to replace losses on the carriers when the Japs raided Ceylon.

My A.G. days were almost over by this time. I had been promoted to sergeant in May 1942 and was the senior technical N.C.O. at Bangalore. However I was called upon to do vertical line overlap photo's of a lake at Mysore from the back seat of a Hawker Hart. This was to assess the capability of the lake, area wise, to take flying boats.

In air force language I was now "time-ex", having completed a four years tour overseas and I set sail on Christmas Eve 1942 aboard the Union Castle liner "Stirling Castle". A six week voyage ensued with a two day break at Durban and a week in New York where the ship had to go into dry dock.

I was posted to No.1 Group, Bomber Command and served at Waltham near Grimsby, Kelstern, Elsham Wolds, Hemswell and Wickenby. During my time at Hemswell I was able to cadge my one and only flight for social reasons. Nicholsons, the bakers at Annan, were having a staff dance, I was keen to attend and mentioned this to the engineer officer. He fixed it and on 6th October 1944 I was flown in a Lancaster to Crosby-on-Eden.

While at Wickenby on 103 Squadron, I was dispatched to Belgium in a Lancaster, plus a spare aircrew to service a Lancaster which had force landed near Brussels owing to engine trouble. This was during the time of Hitler's final fling in the Ardennes in December '44. Being east of the German rocket sites we were in view of V.2's being launched.

I volunteered for the next detachment which was to Pomigliano near Naples. When the war was over it was decided that Bomber Command should help to bring ex-prisoners of war and bods due for de-mob back from Italy. 30 Lancasters would arrive in Naples about three times a week and return with 30 bods plus luggage, in each. This was called "Operation Dodge" and I was one of the thirty or so ground staff employed on servicing.

A rapid disintegration of the RAF occurred afterwards and I was posted to 63 M.U. a salvage unit based at Montrose. Detachments were the order of the day and I was sent to Prestwick to help dismantle a Lincoln and an Oxford. Then to Wig Bay, Stranraer, to collect a few Bristol Taurus engines. Next to West Freugh to scrap a Mosquito and on to Baldoon where a Lancaster had conveniently pranged in a ditch. I say conveniently because my wife's parents farmed near Whauphill, so I enjoyed the time at Baldoon in possession of a "sleeping-out" pass....not to be confused with a "Passionate Posting".

Back to Montrose for a spell, then to Alness, near Invergordon, to remove engines from a Sunderland.

My next posting was to 61 M.U. near Stockport, a dismal outfit, manned by a shower of bods who had spent all the war years there. They knew nothing about the camaraderie, which existed in the Operational Units. They were mostly all due for de-mob, so I, having still nine months to go, was sent on a Stromberg carburettor course at a factory near Stanmore, Middlesex and to Cosford, for a course on "planned servicing" which had just been invented.

I was demobbed at Lytham on 23rd August 1948 and for a spell worked with the Forestry Commission at New Galloway, then to gain experience in the dairying industry, my wife and daughter and I went to Tarbert, Argyll. In 1952 I was able to buy a small farm near Dunscore, where with my wife's assistance we milked cows and hatched day-old chicks for sale.

Twelve years at Dunscore, then a move to Waterbeck where I had been able to purchase a larger unit, still dairying, but no chickens. Another twelve years at Waterbeck and I retired in 1976. By this time we had three daughters who all started their education at Speddoch School, near Dunscore. Eventually two of them qualified as primary teachers and the youngest a Radiographer. Now all three are married and have two daughters each.

From 1977 until 1988 I was fortunate to be employed by the Regional Council as an animal health inspector. This involved overseeing the dipping of sheep on farms in Annandale and Eskdale, from September to December, the object being to eradicate a contagious disease in sheep, called "Sheep Scab".

I was awarded the North West Frontier Campaign medal for 1935/39, whilst still in India and subsequently, was awarded the usual Pip, Squeak and Wilfred for war service.

In my apprentice days, all were given a twenty minutes trip in an Avro tutor aircraft, and in the following years I flew in Audax, Hart, Lancaster, Boeing B17, Wapiti and Valentia aircraft and logged 286 hours all told.

My present hobbies extend to gardening and crook and walking stick making, using ram horns when available.

Ecclefechan J.Farish

Editor's note:-

The Fakir of Ipi, who was born Mirza Ali Khan, took advantage of the local religious differences among the tribes of the North West Frontier. His insurrections supported by a considerable force, were a constant source of trouble to the British Authorities. So notorious did he become that he was enshrined as a study in the curriculum of the Royal Air Force Staff College.

Flight Sergeant Doug Coopey.
(Air Gunner)

Doug Coopey was born in 1922 in Forest of Dean, Gloucestershire. He was educated in the district and after leaving school was an apprentice Scientific Instrument Maker.

He enlisted in the RAF in 1941 at Birmingham as an Air Gunner and was called up to Padgate and then to A.C.R.C. in London. He was posted to the Armament Course at Creden Hill and then to No.2 Air Gunnery School at Dalcross, near Inverness, where he was awarded his Brevet.

From Dalcross he went to O.T.U. at Marham, in Norfolk, and then to 1657 H.C.U. at Stradishall, in Suffolk. Continuing in Bomber Command he first joined No.149 Squadron at Lakenheath, Suffolk, operating in Stirlings until his 'B' flight, together with other squadron flights were transferred to Chedburgh, near Newmarket, where they formed the new No.620 Squadron, again equipped with Stirlings. Both of those stations formed part of No.3 Group.

In due course Doug was posted into No.5 Group, joining No.50 Squadron at Skellingthorpe in Lincolnshire, operating in Lancasters. In all Doug completed a full tour of 30 bomber operationa.

He was demobbed in 1946 and post war was a photo-journalist with the London Daily Mail and then a Television Film Producer in Current Affairs and Farming.

He retired in 1982 and lists his hobbies as photography and radio construction. He now lives in Hightae, near Lochmaben, in Dumfriesshire.

Doug has related two experiences which could have been "dicey do's" the first one entitled:-

Close Encounter

The 620 Squadron Battle Order for the 23rd September 1943 showed that F/O Hannah and his crew in Stirling 'Z' Zebra would be flying a gardening sortie that night, with take-off at 20.05 hours.

After air testing the aircraft we went to the Mess for lunch and to wait for the briefing at 16.00 hours when the target would be revealed.

On this occasion we would be going on a long haul to the Skagerrak, code named 'Nectarine', with three 'veg' to drop. No flak or fighters to worry about until we were near the dropping zone. A soft target makes a change.

We taxied out and take-off was bang on time and 'Z' Zebra is performing well as we climb on course, and with the guns tested we settle down to the job in hand. Alone in the sky with a great expanse of water below us.

We find the weather forecast not that accurate, there's more cloud than expected at our cruising height, but no one grumbles at that.

Now comes the time for our last change of course and as we could be coming into fighter range vigilance is even more important, but none of us was prepared for the sight that confronted us as we broke cloud cover, for there in the grey steel sky at 10 o'clock, slightly above us at two or three hundred yards range was the rear end view of a four engined Condor. It was obviously not aware of out presence.

Our Skipper throttled back, and slowly losing height we watched as the Condor was lost to sight.

A sharp look-out was maintained as we neared the dropping zone and with the correct height and position achieved we commenced to drop our mines into the allotted positions, the third one exploding on impact. Then it was nose down for a quick run at low level out to the open sea.

The return journey was uneventful and we landed safely at base at 04.20 hours. Another op. completed with a story to tell.

Secondary Target.
or
"You can't please everyone"

On the 24th March, 1944, with P/O Jenning as Skipper, in our 50 Sqn. Lancaster we were briefed to go to Berlin and as we were crossing the Dutch coast on route to the target, the port outer engine packed up and with a full load we were unable to maintain height.

The Skipper decided to abort and asked the navigator for a course back to base and suggestions for a target to receive our bomb load, which we would have to get rid of before we lost much more height.

The navigator gave a course for home and was searching for a possible target when directly ahead of us searchlights suddenly stabbed up and started sweeping the sky. Our presence was noted, but why were they where they were.

The Skipper decided these searchlights would be our target, the bomb-aimer was in position, bomb doors were open and no time, or thought, to go round again - "Bombs away" came the shout as we flew straight through them. The aircraft bucked from the force of the explosions below and we witnessed huge fires behind us as we made for home.

At our de-briefing 3 hours 25 minutes after take-off our Squadron Commander was not too pleased on hearing what we had done, but reports a few days later confirmed we had destroyed a major fuel dump.

Hightae — Doug Coopey.

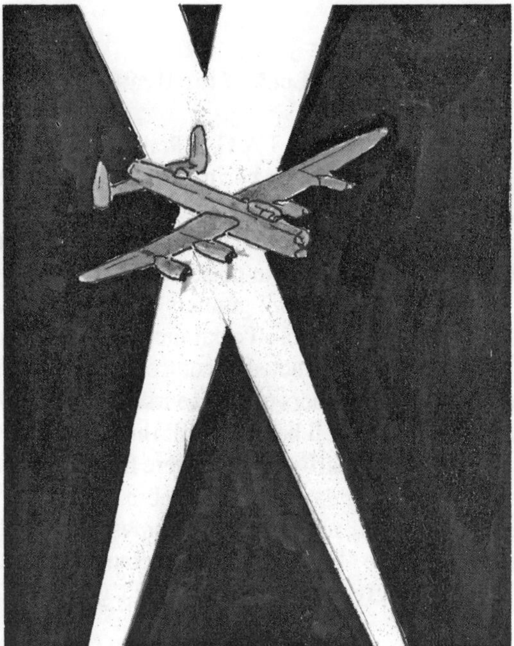

Flight Sergeant James Carson.
(Air Gunner)

Flight Sergeant James Carson, born in June, 1925 and educated at Dalbeattie High School and the De Bear Commercial College he was employed locally in the wages department of I.C.I. The moment he reached the age of eighteen in 1943 he volunteered for air crew duties in the RAF. He qualified as a Sergeant Air Gunner at RAF Pembrey in Wales, passing on to operational training at RAF Abingdon and then to Swinderby in Lincolnshire where his crew converted onto Lancaster Bombers.

After demobilisation in June 1947 James decided on a complete change of civilian occupation and went into transport. Now retired with an adult family of a son and two daughters, he and his wife live in Dalbeattie. His hobbies are walking and reading. He tells a story of a very narrow escape from what might well have been his death whilst under training at RAF Pembrey.

The Luck of the Draw

We were stationed at No.1 A.G.S. Pembrey and we were enjoying the work. Having been on a very boring P.A.C.T. course it was a grand feeling to, at last, be doing something worthwhile.

Our course, No.111, was well in front of schedule and, once more we were waiting to get airborne to do some "air-to-air" firing.

As usual, there were six U/T gunners on board and we were waiting at the end of the runway for take-off clearance. However, instead of being given clearance, we were instructed by control to return to dispersal. This we did and found that members of 110 course were waiting to take over the aircraft as they were well behind in all their work.

I should have said earlier that we were flying Wellingtons and the aircraft on that particular day was Z for Zebra.

Anyway we went back to our classes moaning loudly at having to give up our flying time "just because 110 course was running behind schedule" and , jokingly, wished them all the "gremlins" that could be found.

Later we were outside the class-room having a smoke when we saw Z Zebra come in to land. She came in fast and heavy, bounced very badly and very high. Opening the throttles, the skipper overshot and set off on another circuit and, hopefully, a better and safer landing.

This was not to be. Something went terribly wrong on "finals". Without any warning, that we on the ground could hear, the engines suddenly cut completely dead.

The aircraft dived straight into Kidwelly Flats where it just disintegrated. With the exception of the trainee gunner whose turn it was to land in the rear turret, all lives were lost.

I don't say that the same could have happened to, or would have, to us but it made us feel very humble and lucky that we had been "grounded" for that particular flight.

Eventually we managed to finished our Gunnery Course and the quarters were a hive of industry the night before our passing out parade.

Everyone who knew they had successfully completed the course were busy sewing on their "tapes" and A/G wing. We borrowed tunics from the chaps on the course behind us so after the parade we went to our quarters for a quick change to re-appear proudly sporting our three stripes and A/G wing.

Our course then went on leave and, whilst at home, received posting orders to a new unit.

Many years after the war was over, I was delivering a load of sherry from Bristol to a warehouse in Glasgow. Whilst there, a policeman came into the store.

Nothing unusual in that except that the policeman was named Frank Ford. The sole survivor of Z Zebra!!

Dalbeattie J. Carson.

It was with deep regret that the Dumfries and Galloway Branch of the Aircrew Association was notified of the death of James Carson on 22nd February 1993.

Warrant Officer Jim Mitchell.
(Air Gunner)

Jim Mitchell was born in 1923 in the small mining village of Trabbock in Ayrshire, and was educated at Stair Public School which he left at the age of 14 years. His father and brothers were in the mining industry and two days later after leaving school Jim followed in their footsteps and started work as a belt operator in Mossblown Colliery.

He eventually realised that this mining work was not for him, but unfortunately at that time it was a reserved occupation.

When WWII started Jim was enthusiastically drawn to flying and later when colliery employees were allowed to join the Armed Forces Jim did not hesitate and volunteered for aircrew duties with the RAF and enlisted as an Air Gunner. This was in 1943.

He did his square bashing at Bridgenorth, and then went to Air Gunnery School at Pembrey, flying in Ansons. He was then posted to O.T.U. at Lough Neagh, in Northern Ireland, where he crewed up, flying Catalinas in Coastal Command. From there he and his crew were posted to Oban for further training and were also engaged in anti-submarine patrols and meteorology flights for about three months.

They were then posted to No.240 Squadron at Red Hills Lake, Madras, India, again carrying out anti-submarine patrols and other Maritime duties. he served his RAF career in this area until he was demobbed in December 1947 at Warton, Lancashire, as a Warrant Officer.

After the war, staying in the same area he joined the Bolton Fire Brigade in 1948, and in 1966, transferred to the South West Scotland Fire Brigade, which is now Dumfries and Galloway.

He retired in 1973 and started business on his own account in a Fire Protection Company, being engaged in the sale and maintenance of Fire Fighting equipment, finally retiring in 1988.

Jim is married and lists his hobbies as fishing and bowls.

An Unhappy Birthday.

I was one of those Air Gunners who had a quiet and safe war flying in Catalinas of Coastal Command.

Most of my operations were spent looking at white horses in the hope of seeing a U-boat, but I was always disappointed. Then came the change when my Squadron, No. 240, stationed at Red Hills Lake, Madras, in India, was reformed as a Special Duties Squadron.

In June 1945, we were on Strike Duty, and told we had to pack our kit and set off to Calcutta. The instructions were, pack as though in transit, as you may be away for some time. As Rigger/Air Gunner. I was warned at the briefing to be careful when mooring up , as the River Hooghly was a fast flowing river, and to expect dead bodies floating past. I was led to believe that this river had some religious significance, and was the burial ground for some sect.

After an early morning take-off, we alighted on the Hooghly Estuary, and later after a meal in the camp at Bally, the aircraft was loaded with a large wooden box, guarded by two S.P's who remained on the aircraft until take-off. From then on high security was very much in evidence and the following morning we took off for Trincomalee, in then Ceylon, which was approximately 12 hours flying time away. On landing there the whole crew were escorted to Flying Control, here we ate and slept until the following morning, 26th June 1945.

At briefing, which was very simple, our Skipper, Johnny Freeman, was given a sealed envelope and told to open it when airborne. On opening the envelope it was learned that we were going to the Cocos Islands. I don't think any of the crew had heard of them, but on a makeshift map we saw that they did exist - lying midway between Ceylon and Australia, a journey of some 1,600 miles. Our navigator could then transfer the islands' position onto his plotting charts. I was, until then, surprised at the abundance of goodies we had received for flying rations, and I was glad of them, except for the snag that I had to prepare them. So for the rest of the day my two primus stoves were busy.

The trip was uneventful, and at 00.01 hours over the intercom came a chorus of "Happy Birthday, Jock", 27th June, but no whisky bottles. Shame!!

At approximately 11.00 hours I was up front looking into space when I sighted four little dots on the horizon, which I took to be ships, but eventually we found them to be a small group of islands, yes, the Cocos Islands.

Our navigator was congratulated by every member of the crew for a marvellous piece of navigation, and we prepared for landing. There was no Flying Control and no flare path, just a ship lying stern to anchor, and it did look odd seeing smoke blowing over the sharp end, and after a few flashes on the Aldis lamp we got permission to land.

On our approach, the second pilot pointed out, over the intercom, that we were landing down wind and the Skipper replied "Yes, I know".

Now being an Air Gunner I knew nothing about driving, but I knew enough to get a little worried. I was glad that my landing station was in the blister and not up front, so I sat with my back to the bulkhead with my leg jammed on the gun turret and my Mae West buttoned up. It was worth the trouble, for after the first bounce we dropped like a brick, nose first and then overturned - you pilots must be saying 'I am not surprised', why the hell he continued with the landing no one will ever know.

I must have been knocked out for a few seconds; when I looked up front all was black, and when I looked backwards I saw we were on fire. I tried to open the blister, but I couldn't, it was then that I realised we were upside down and sinking. I managed to squeeze the blister open a few inches, but my Mae West was too bulky, and I had to take it off to get out. There were six of us in the drink and no dinghy, but luckily the Air Rescue boat was soon alongside and we were picked up and taken to a so-called hospital, which was a big tent with some beds, sitting on the sand.

With Bob Short, our Flight Mechanic, the two of us were the only ones to survive; the others were either dead on arrival at the hospital or died the next day. The remaining five crew members, including the pilot, died in the crash.

I only wished I could have found out what was in that wooden box, but the story goes that it was currency in rupees and cents, because on the islands for many weeks there was no change, and if you went to the NAAFI for a cup of tea, your change was in razor blades, no kidding, razor blades were a form of currency, so when you had a shave, you took the blade out, cleaned it, put it back in the carefully preserved packet, and used it to buy your next cup of tea.

While in hospital, Bob and I were visited by Lady Park, and Bob showed some sign of nervous tension, but was relieved when Lady Park admitted that she had blue hair! It put our minds at rest. We also had a visit from Gracie Fields, who called the Islands, the Shangri-La of the RAF, but we didn't agree with her.

It was sad for me to think that after all the long flying hours and discomfort, it was fruitless. The wooden box was never recovered.

Dumfries — Jim Mitchell.

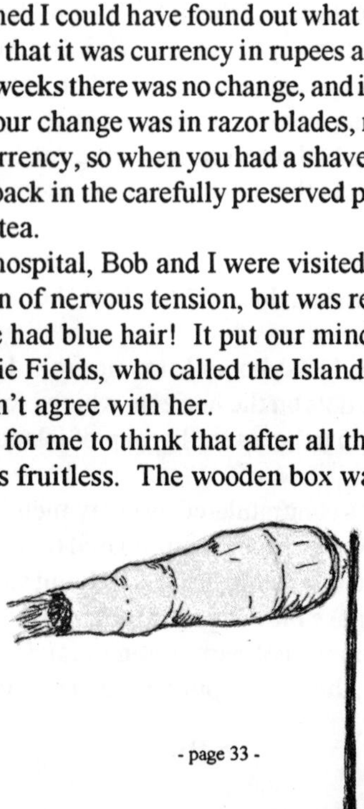

Warrant Officer George B. Halbert, D.F.M.
(Air Gunner)

George Halbert was born in Annan, Dumfriesshire, in 1922 and educated at Annan Academy. Before joining the Royal Air Force, George worked as a Payroll Clerk. He volunteered for aircrew duties at the age of eighteen and was enrolled at A.C.R.C. St. John's Wood, London and was selected for training as an observer. Passing through his initial training course at RAF Shawbury he then attended No.3 Air Observer School at Bobbington, from whence he was posted for operational training on Wellington bombers at No.21 O.T.U. Moreton-in-the-Marsh. Succumbing to the system, as many did, George re-mustered as an air gunner and qualified for his brevet and sergeant's stripes at Llandwrog in Wales.

George joined his first crew at No.1658 Heavy Conversion Unit at Riccal in Yorkshire where they flew Halifax bombers, being then posted to No.76 Squadron, again flying Halifaxes from both Linton-on-Ouse, near York, and from Holme-on-Spalding Moor in Humberside.

Following his first tour of operations George became an instructor at No.20 O.T.U. at Lossiemouth on the Moray coast. George then transferred to the Path Finder Force joining No.35 Squadron at Gravely near Huntingdon, flying Lancasters in that role.

In all, George flew 56 operational sorties about which he is entirely reticent. However he has agreed to contribute one experience which he describes as 'Line-shoot of the Month'. Whilst serving with 35 Squadron his log book records that the role of his crew was 'Deputy Master Bomber' and that they were briefed to mark two separate aiming points on the Brest Peninsula. They took-off from Graveley at 20.10 hours on 25th April 1944, their pilot being Flight Lieutenant "Danny" Everett, D.F.C. and with George flying as mid-upper gunner. Let him now tell his story in his own words.

Line Shoot of the Month

"If I remember correctly we reached our first target on time, and at the briefed height 8,000ft, to find that the target was covered by 10/10ths. cloud.

The Master Bomber instructed us to descend below the cloud base and mark the target, which we did, the Bomb-aimer doing a good job with his Target Indicators. "Right on the Button".

The Master Bomber also brought the main force down below the cloud base to bomb on our T.I's. As a matter of interest, cloud base was about 3,000ft. We did two or three runs over the target area until the raid was completed. The Navigator then gave the Skipper courses to fly over the Bay of Biscay as we had to put off time before marking our second target for another force of bombers coming in from the U.K.

During our last leg over the sea, after a discussion with the Navigator and Bomb-aimer, the Skipper decided to go in at the same height, i.e., 3,000ft. So we flew over the target at that height to find that the clouds had dispersed and the sky was clear.

The Master Bomber was back at the height briefed, along with the rest of the bomber force at 8,000ft.

Needless to say, we stuck out like a sore thumb, with photo flashes bursting all around us. I reckon we had our picture taken a few times that night.

We still had to stooge around until the raid was finished in case something happened to the Master Bomber, thankfully nothing did.

On our last run over the target, a stream of tracer came up at us from a boat in the harbour or somewhere. My immediate reaction being to return fire with a couple of bursts. Needless to say the tracer still came up at us. But all's well that ends well and we made base without anymore trouble.

As you all know the next step was debriefing. the crew sat around a table with the debriefing officer, the first question he asked was. "Did you shoot any fighters down?" The Skipper replied immediately in a very loud voice so everyone would hear. "NO, BUT HAGGIS HERE SHOT DOWN A BATTLESHIP" and burst into uncontrollable laughter. I must say that Danny had a very infectious laugh, and it started everyone in the room joining in.

It took a few minutes before order was restored and the serious business of debriefing continued. I eventually lived it down and went on to finish my tour with Danny Everett in December 1944 making my total of 56 operations.

I was sorry to read in the 1990 Spring edition of "Intercom" that my old Skipper:- Sqdn. Ldr. DANNY EVERETT, D.S.O., D.F.C. AND BAR. was killed on 7.3.1945 on his 99th operation.

"HE WAS INDEED A GENTLEMAN"

Annan G. Halbert

Warrant Officer Arthur Lenz, B.E.M. (Air Gunner)

A native of London, born in March 1920, Arthur Lenz was educated at Osterley Grammar School. At the age of 15 years he entered the aviation industry, training as a press tool setter. After three years, and with the imminence of war now certain, he realised that his occupation would be reserved, precluding him from entry into the armed services. By a medical stratagem, at which the family doctor connived (unfit for night work), he left the industry and later volunteered for aircrew duties.

Called for enlistment to A.C.R.C. London, in the spring of 1940, he was selected for training as an air gunner. In due time he completed a course in gunnery at Stormy Down by Swansea, and was posted for operational training to RAF Kinloss on the Moray Coast. There he joined his first crew, training on twin-engined Whitley bombers. On completion of their course they were retained at Kinloss and employed on anti-submarine patrols over the Firth of Forth and its approaches. Later they converted on to four-engined Halifax bombers at the H.C.U. at Waddington, near Lincoln.

In the winter of 1944, Arthur Lenz was a mid-upper gunner on Halifaxes with No.148 Squadron, then based at Brindisi in Southern Italy, as part of the 'Balkan Air Force'. At that time the squadron was engaged on 'Clandestine Operations' dropping agents and supplies to resistance forces. One such operation was flown from Marseilles in February 1945 on which Arthur Lenz flew as mid-upper gunner and dispatcher, responsible for dispatching by parachute pre-packed loads of equipment at designated dropping zones.

A detailed account of that particular operation has kindly been supplied by his Captain and Squadron Commander, Wing Commander Alan Newitt, D.F.C.

(Editor's note: Subsequently Wing Comander Newitt kindly made available two more accounts of special operations flown by No. 148 Squadron from Brindisi. Arthur Lenz confirms that he flew as mid-upper gunner/dispatcher on both of these operations).

As the allied campaign in Italy moved forward No.148 Squadron moved to Foggia Air Base, where they converted on to long range Liberator aircraft and were subsequently employed in repatriating British Personnel to the United Kingdom, landing at Holmsley South near Bournemouth.

After cessation of hostilities in Europe, Arthur Lenz returned to the U.K. for demobilisation. Deciding to make a career in the RAF he volunteered for further service as aircrew. He was required first to take the armament fitters course at the Armaments School at Kirkham in Lancashire. Qualifying as a Fitter Armourer, Arthur returned to flying duties, joining No. 50 Squadron at Waddington, flying Lincoln bombers.

After the tension and excitement of operations, Arthur found peacetime exercises and continuation training tedious. Being essentially a man of action he elected to transfer into Administrative duties and was sent for training as a Senior NCO to the school of Administration at Hereford. On qualifying he became an instructor in administration at the RAF Apprentices' School at Halton.

For a time Arthur served with the Central Drill Unit at RAF Uxbridge. Later the Central Drill Unit became the Queen's Colour Squadron under the aegis of the RAF Regiment. Arthur's next post was as Station Warrant Officer at the famous fighter station Biggin Hill in Kent. From there he was sent as SWO to Bahrein in the Persian Gulf where he served for three and a half years. His final post in the UK was at RAF Bicester, in Oxfordshire, as SWO where he remained until retirement in 1975.

Arthur is now a resident of Dowding House in Moffat, Dumfriesshire. Arthur lists his hobbies as carpentry, wood-turning and carving, also etching on glass.

A Special Operation.

On the 12th February 1945 I was Squadron Commander on No.148 Squadron based at Brindisi in Italy. The Squadron was equipped with Halifax heavy bombers.

The crew consisted of a Pilot (myself), Bomb-aimer, Navigator, a Wireless Operator, a Flight Engineer, Mid-Upper Gunner/Dispatcher and a Rear-Gunner.

The main task of the Squadron was to supply the insurgents in the Balkans, drop Spies and Military Missions (consisting of five Military Personnel) behind enemy lines.

Just prior to that date I had been briefed to proceed to Marseilles to carry out a special operation from that base over Southern Germany. The instructions required me to collect three bales of wireless sets from the local prison where they had been made ready for collection and prepared for an air-drop, I was told that we would have an Intelligence Officer on board who would issue me with the orders after we had left base, and that I was to obey his commands.

He turned out to be a delightful Frenchman, ex-Maquis, who could hardly speak a word of English, I then realised that this was to be a very highly secret operation, I also knew that the operation had been attempted twice before without success by one of the other squadrons. The 'load' consisted of three huge bales all done up in rope nets and heavily padded for the shock, with parachutes attached. The load was collected and the aircraft was 'Bombed-up' for delivery.

After several days the Frenchman arrived, gave me the co-ordinates of the dropping zone, and said that I could go that night. He mentioned that a white 'T' would be exhibited on the ground and that when the resistance heard the sound of my engines they would flash the letter of the day and illuminate the 'T'. I was told that I had to drop each bale separately and give time between each drop to enable the 'Field' time to collect the bale and clear the area for the next one to avoid any casualties.

I was very dubious about the operation and was not surprised when we arrived over the target to find no reception, little did I know that it was going to take two more tries before achieving success. On the first try we flew along, or adjacent to, the Swiss border and received some 'Flak' which I think was intended as a warning rather than a show of hostility for most of it was well in front of us and appeared to be friendly, one burst however was a little too close and left a few holes in the aircraft which were subsequently repaired without too much trouble. The second try was a bit hairy - for on changing over the fuel tanks we lost both starboard engines; it took a few moments to realise that both engines had cut out before feathering the propellers. As we had plenty of fuel for the rather short trip it was a simple matter to change back to the original tanks and re-start the engines, during the procedure however we lost quite a bit of height and came uncomfortably close to some high ground on our route... Subsequent investigation showed that No.5 tank had been filled with water; I wondered whether it had been done deliberately but was assured that it was due to a leak in the bulk supply tanks on the base.

The third sortie was a great success, I had been intensely annoyed by the attitude of the Frenchman and remonstrated with him about the inefficiency of the reception party in the field. I was mollified when he confided in me, explaining his part of the operation and the difficult task that the 'Field' had to contend with. He was the link man for the operation and had to advise the BBC to send out a coded message such as "Hang out your washing tonight" on their entertainment programme, which would alert the 'field' that the load was ready for delivery. The 'field' in their turn, had to set up the reception. Their task was risky indeed for they had to 'acquire' some German transport, drive out to the rendezvous, set out the lights, collect the goods, return to town, abandon the lorries and secrete the radios without arousing suspicion. The third sortie was uneventful, we arrived over the target, flew round until the 'T' was illuminated and dropped as instructed on receipt of the code letter.

I apologised to the Frenchman and congratulated him on a job well done. I noticed that whenever he operated his radio set he only ever used one ear phone and when he was asked why, he explained that on one occasion he was operating from home and he never heard the Germans arrive to arrest him, and that they had actually broken down his front door before he became aware of what was happening and made his escape. Since that day it was one ear for the radio and one ear for the Germans.

What a man - tall, cadaverous, pale, lanky, clever and brave, he had escaped from France to continue the fight in our country; a hero indeed. I asked him whether we would ever know whether our operation had been a success. To our surprise he said he would find out and came back with the answer that the drop was so accurate that one of their number was struck by one of the bales. They had stolen German transport, collected the load and disposed of it, before the Germans had become aware of anything missing.

Log Book Entry 21st September, 1944. Halifax II JP245 SD Poland (213B)

It was maximum effort for the Squadron on this occasion. The Russians were advancing upon Warsaw, but for some inexplicable reason had stopped outside the City. The Polish People had risen against the Germans, in anticipation of their liberation. The Squadron's task was to supply as much ammunition and small arms as possible to assist the Polish people in their uprising. The Germans, in the meantime, took the opportunity of supressing the rebellion, setting fire to the City and massacreing the Poles in revenge.

We were given the co-ordinates for our target together with the recognition signals for the Dropping Zone (DZ), and took off from our base in Brindisi with a full load. As the DZ was at the extreme range of our endurance, overload tanks were fitted for the flight. The outward journey was uneventful, but on approaching Warsaw, it became obvious from the orange glow in the distance that the City was already in flames. On arrival our worst fears were confirmed for the whole city was a mass of flames with smoke rising to several thousand feet. We descended to a low level in an effort to locate the DZ but soon realised that there would be no reception for us amongst the chaos and confusion on the ground. To drop our load at random was inadvisable in the circumstances as it was unlikely that the Poles would find them and control of the aircraft was difficult in the limited visibility and extreme turbulance created by the fires. We, therefore, reluctantly abandoned the flight and returned to base. The de-briefing was registered as DNCO (Duty not carried out).

Due to the length of the flight we knew that we would still be over enemy territory when dawn broke so dispensed with "weaving". This calculated risk resulted in a well-aimed burst of flak coming uncomfortably close and rocking the aircraft, with some minor damage to the fuselage. The Flight Sergeant in charge of aircraft maintenance was not very happy about the various holes in one of his aeroplanes, for he was very proud of the Squadron's record of serviceability. I thought I should apologise to him, but felt my indiscretion was better than meeting fighters in broad daylight.

Log Book Entry dated 3rd February, 1945 "Icarus".

The Operational Briefing this night was unusual. I was informed that our crew would be dropping a special load which would be delivered to the dispersal point, just prior to take off. Whilst we waited my crew hazarded a guess that it might be a VIP Jo or Jo's (human cargo as opposed to the usual arms, ammunition or supplies). Eventually, a Jeep arrived driven by an Army Major, who asked to speak to the Captain of the aircraft. On presenting myself he asked me to sign a piece of paper by way of receipt for the delivery of the goods which consisted of four kitbags. On my enquiry as to their contents, he reluctantly informed me that they were filled with Golden Sovereigns and Maria Theresa Dollars. I surmised that this money was destined for Marshal Tito and his Partisans for I was aware that this was the only form of currency that the Insurgents would accept by way of remuneration for their services. The kitbags were duly loaded onto the aircraft and placed beside the dispatcher's hatch under the care of the Mid-Upper Gunner, whose secondary task it was to push the load through the hatch over the Dropping Zone (DZ). I noticed that the Jeep remained at the dispersal point until we were airborne.

The flight was normal and the kitbags were delivered over the DZ without incident. We were to make further drops of currency on subsequent operations but, on these occasions, we noticed that the kitbags were containerised with attached parachutes and hoisted into the bomb bays. Whether the containers and parachutes were employed to discourage the crew from "inspecting" the load on the way to the target or, to give the bags a softer landing thereby preventing them from bursting on impact was a theory I preferred to accept despite the local rumours that the odd sovereign was seen in Brindisi.

Some months later, I was fortunate to meet the English Major into whose care we had delivered the kitbags and persuaded him to give a lecture to the Squadron on his experiences behind the lines. This was both interesting and good for morale for we seldom got a feed-back from the field.

He told us that he had managed to recruit a force of some 4000 Partisans onto his payroll and that life was fairly easy for him until the day that the Germans arrived unheralded. It must be said that the Enemy was very thin on the ground in the Balkans and that they were unable to effectively police the whole area. However, when the insurgents became too active in any theatre they would send in a punitive force to burn the villages and shoot the inhabitants.

The Major found a beautiful bungalow and had talked the owner into allowing him to rent it as a billet, in which he kept the kitbags under his personal supervision. The first intimation that the Germans were in the village was conveyed to him by his wireless operator. In the ensuing chaos the Officer and his "WOP" stuffed the kitbags down the toilet, which was a primitive continental type with no pedestal seat but two foot-slabs and a large aperture or hole, and beat a hasty retreat.

After the Germans had done their work, the Major returned to find the Owner still alive, but the bungalow in a shambles. The Owner explained that the Germans had suspected him of being a spy and had ruined his property in their search for incriminating evidence. This he insisted was the reason why the garden had been dug from one end to the other and all the floor boards wrenched up. It was curious, the Major said, for he insisted on following me about like a bloodhound until I got my troops to retrieve the kitbags from their hiding place. The Owner, of course, was well aware that the Major had departed empty handed. When he became a witness to the toilet being broken up, he realised that this was the only place he had failed to search.

The Major dryly observed "It was embarassing really for he fell on my shoulder and wept".

Jersey — Alan Newitt

Flight Sergeant Gordon Agnew, J.P.
(Air Gunner)

Gordon Agnew was born in 1924 in Glasgow and was educated locally. He enlisted in the RAF as an Air Gunner in 1941 and after attending A.C.R.C. in London, was posted to No.4 Air Gunnery School at Morpeth where he was awarded his Brevet. From there he went to Conversion Unit at Woolfox Lodge to fly Wellingtons and then to H.C.U. at Chipping Warden to fly Stirlings.

He was posted to 214 Sqdn. at Chedburgh completing a tour on Stirlings after which he was screened and posted to No.1 School of Aircraft Recognition at Southport.

Later he was posted to 186 Sqdn. at Stradishall, 3 Group, Bomber Command and in Gordon's own words 'did half a tour in Lancasters'. From there he went to Manauri, South East Asia Command eventually returning to the U.K. for demobilisation in 1946 at Kirkby, near Liverpool, via Worli Camp, Bombay.

Post war Gordon was in Insurance and was a Justice of the Peace in the City of Glasgow, he also served for four years in 602 Squadron in the Royal Auxiliary Air Force.

He is married and lives with his wife, Sheila, in Ayr. He has a daughter, and a son, Gordon, who is a Pilot in the RAF with the rank of Wing Commander and is at present stationed with the 8th U.S. Air Force in Louisiana.

Gordon is now retired and lists his hobbies as bowls, angling and Freemasonry.

Not wishing to relate any of his operational trips, he contributes the following :-

And They Called it Manna

The reluctance one feels to launch out in a line shooting gush of nostalgia restricts me, at any rate, to talk about an uneventful trip - the last operation of my one and a half tours in 3 Group of Bomber Command.

All the pundits who write nowadays seem to have known the outcome of the struggle long before it dawned on us.

In May 1945, dog tired, cynical and battle scared we were briefed for what seemed a very dodgy exercise - at low level 200/300 feet or less to the Hook of Holland. Consternation reigned when the Battle Order specifically laid down that guns would not be loaded and that resistance to attack would be frowned on.

We set out for the short trip across the menace of the North Sea - the eerieness of the flight is impossible to describe and the ghost like, silent coast line of Europe loomed ahead just after day break. Jumpiness, the twitters euphemistically called alertness was second nature but usually it was in total darkness at a height of 20,000 feet and the comfort of knowing that if you were hit it would be curtains nearly instantaneously - suddenly was no more.

German troops on armoured carriers, anti-aircraft batteries fully manned, their guns following you all the way. German soldiers on barrack roofs, defence walls, even machine gunners on ambulances silently watched our progress and the feeling was one of absolute conviction that we were remorsely heading for the most ignominious trap and annihilation.

Mosquitos were passing at high speed just above us and we were heading for the target area - an open field already mauled by red flares and smoke canisters. We were on the bombing run, bomb doors open - and we dropped flour, wheat, sugar, bread and climbed away.

Operation 'Manna' remains one of the clearest memories of the war which ended that day - maybe because it was my last - but maybe it was the fact that it could be viewed as a measure in the balance of mercy rather than the destruction we had wrought in the past.

Arriving back home just after breakfast-time to Suffolk we headed for London only to find that the Yanks had known the day before and had drunk the place dry.

Ayr

Gordon Agnew.

Sergeant Frank Armstrong.
(Air Gunner)

In Search of an Aircrew Brevet.

Born in Lockerbie in 1926, Frank Armstrong attended the Corrie Junior School and Lockerbie Academy, before becoming apprenticed as a motor mechanic. He volunteered for aircrew duties at the age of eighteen and was enrolled in the R.A.F. at No.4 Air Crew Reception Centre in Scarborough, Yorkshire, on 5 August 1944. As an apprentice mechanic he had high hopes ofbeing recommended for training as a Flight Engineer but was instead assessed for training as an Air Gunner.

In September 1944 Frank was posted to RAF Hornchurch in Essex for initial training. Here he experienced visits from the German V.1's (Doodle Bugs), both by day and by night, The nearest miss they had dropped some fifty yards away; he and his chums took refuge under a bed when the engine stopped and when the warhead exploded the ceiling of their billet collapsed but fortunately no one was hurt. They manned a Vickers machine gun on top of a bomb shelter and were even given ammunition for it, but, by some extraordinary logic were not permitted to fire it! During the day they would see Spitfires chasing these doodle bugs trying to shoot them down or sometimes tipping their wings to unbalance the gyro-stabilisation which could be similarly effective. A few of the rocket propelled V.2's were also heard, but not too near to Hornchurch.

In November 1944, Frank spent a few weeks at No. 7 A.C.R.C. at Babbacombe, Torquay, billeted in a hotel of the same name next door to a Teachers' Training College with excellent sports facilities, swimming, football, and rugby. From Babbacombe he was sent to the Motor Transport Training School at Melksham in Wiltshire to train as a driver. Being able to drive before joining the RAF this proved to be right up Frank's street and he enjoyed driving all sorts of vehicles including the giant 'Queen Mary', the crashed aircraft recovery vehicle. Following this course Frank was posted as an M.T. driver to RAF North Luffenham where he spent much of his time driving lorries loaded with scrap metal to Wolverhampton Railway Goods Station.

In March 1945 Frank's original air crew assessment finally raised its head and he was posted to the Initial Training Wing at RAF Bridgenorth. He naturally assumed that he was making progress towards the coveted 'Brevet' but once more the overcrowded training scheme defeated him and in April he was transferred to RAF Wickenby in Lincolnshire where he was employed as a 'Bomb Bay Filler' ! The war in Europe had now entered its final stage and 'mercy flights' to assist the starving civilian population commenced. To achieve this object a 'loading hole' was cut through to the bomb bay of the heavy bombers so that food supplies passed from trucks drawn up to the rear fuselage door could be passed through to the three 'fillers' stationed in the bomb bay. For safety, the bomb doors were secured by ropes during the loading of some three tons of food. The ropes were then removed before take-off so that the food, contained in strong medium sized sacks, could be dropped in the designated areas. The 'Bay Fillers' reward for their efforts was to be taken on a ''Cook's Tour'' of places heavily bombed during the offensive.

V.E. Day was celebrated at Wickenby with bonfires and drinking, and with dancing in the hangar. The Canadian crews carried out tables, chairs and anything that would burn to keep the bonfires alight!.

Finally, Frank began to make real progress on being posted, with a group of other would-be gunners, to No.2 Air Gunnery School at RAF Dalcross near Inverness. Yet again 'its dogged what does it', having arrived a day late his party had to be held back for absorption into the next course. While waiting Frank was used as an Orderly Room dogsbody, but eventually he qualified on Wellingtons and could at last put up his brevet. V.J. Day was celebrated whilst at Dalcross, but more quietly than V.E. Day at Wickenby! The gunnery course was followed by a Senior N.C.O's course at RAF Locking; Sergeant Armstrong had arrived at last!

In December 1945, Frank was teamed up with his crew at the Heavy Conversion Unit at RAF Cottesmore where they trained on Lancaster bombers. Entertainment at Cottesmore was watching other crews practising circuits and landings which was heightened when one aircraft performed a cartwheel and crashed, fortunately without casualties; the crew could be seen running for their lives from the debacle in case the aircraft blew up.

Finally, eighteen months after enrolment Frank's persistence finally was rewarded with a posting to his operational squadron, No.83 at RAF Coningsby in Lincolnshire, also the home of No.97 Squadron. From Coningsby his crew flew two ferrying trips to Pomigliano in Italy, bringing home 26 soldiers on each return. For reasons known only to themselves some soldiers refused the offer of a ferry back to the UK. via Lancasters - perhaps they preferred Italy.

In the late summer of 1946 No.83 Squadron converted from Lancasters to Lincolns which were to form the only striking force available to Bomber Command for some years to come. Thus, the operational readiness of the Lincoln squadrons was of high importance. Readiness cannot be maintained without continuous and rigorous training and in this programme the air gunners played a vital role - not only are they the aircraft's defence in war but they are its 'eyes' and the aircraft cannot be flown without them. In this role No.83 squadron made two sorties to Shallufa in the Suez Canal zone where advantage could be taken of the better flying conditions to carry out bombing practice and fighters affiliation exercises. In addition to the regular Command exercises flown in the UK. Frank's crew took part in one exercise against the Home Fleet in waters north of Norway where they put on a slightly hairy low flying display at the request of the Navy.

Early in 1947 the squadrons moved from Coningsby to Helmswell, also in Lincolnshire, as the runways at Coningsby were due for strengthening for subsequent use by the future aircraft with much higher wheel loading than Lancasters and Lincolns. Training sorties and Command Exercises continued unabated from Helmswell including fighter affiliation exercises with the newly formed Meteor Jet Fighter Squadrons. Finally, in September 1948, Frank flew his last night operational training exercise code-named 'Operation Dagger', flying a total of over sixteen hours in two sorties, giving him a grand total of 535 hours of flying in operational aircraft. A fitting end to a worthwhile period of service in which his role was perhaps more important that he realised. With due modesty he sums up his period both of frustration and success in these words:-

"My time in the RAF was an experience I shall never forget - for I was only a country boy".

Flight Sergeant Tom Murchie
(Air Gunner)

Tom Murchie was born in Newton Stewart in 1924 and was educated locally at Douglas Ewart High School and on leaving obtained employment as a clerk until he volunteered for aircrew duties with the RAF on the 17th June 1944. He enlisted at No.6 A.C.R.C. at Scarborough and did his training as an Air Gunner at Dalcross.

On obtaining his Brevet he was posted to 81 O.T.U. at Tilstock flying Wellingtons and Dakotas. He was demobbed medically unfit at Northallerton in September 1947.

He was in the Civil Service until retiring in 1963. He is a widower with one son and lists his hobby as writing, he has had two books published, the first entitled 'The Royal Air Force in Galloway', and the second "The Mulberry Harbour Project in Wigtownshire 1942-1944".

Operation Cook's Tour

In autumn 1942 I spent three long days in the former Music Hall building in George Street, Edinburgh. Following a prolonged prodding and probing of my physical and mental proclivities by a series of, to a seventeen and a half years old, elderly gentlemen, in blue uniforms and/or white coats I was pronounced to be acceptable to the Royal Air Force as an aircrew trainee in the Pilot/Navigator/Bomb-aimer category. Having been attested, given a Service number and a highly prized RAF Volunteer Reserve lapel badge (said to have girl-pulling powers second only to a uniform with a brevet) I was sent home on deferred service. Due to large numbers of volunteers who, like me, did not wish to join the P.B.I. training capacity was fully committed for months ahead.

When eventually called eighteen months later my entire entry, sixty in number, were told within hours of arrival that PNB trainees were not required. Alternatives offered were training as Flight Engineer or as Air Gunner or re-muster to a ground trade. Thirty five opted for training as Air Gunner. Almost one year later six of this group who had remained together throughout training graduated as Sergeant Air Gunners at Dalcross, Inverness exactly one week before VE Day.

Clearly operational flying in Europe was now ruled out, however training continued. I was posted to 81 O.T.U. at Tilstock , Shropshire where I joined a crew with a Flying Officer Skipper and three other recently graduated Sergeants as Navigator, Bomb-aimer and Wireless Operator.

We were advised that on completion of O.T.U. training we would convert to Halifaxes to train in glider towing in order to participate in the battle to release Burma and Malaya from Japanese domination. Recognition of Japanese aircraft became a regular feature of ground training in the Gunnery Section.

Intensive flying training on Wellington Xs went ahead. After preliminary routine training flights concentration was on cross-country flying. After several three to four hour flights came a longer trip of over six hours. This exercise was one of two routes the choice being dictated by prevailing weather conditions. On the day in question meteorologists advised that a cold front was approaching from the West which precluded the westerly route. This followed a course from base to the Isle of Skye then to Rockall which is an uninhabited rocky outcrop in the Atlantic Ocean two hundred miles west of the Hebrides, thence back to base via a turning point in Ulster. More than three hours without sight of land no doubt tested the Navigator's skill but this was not a popular exercise.

At 1400 hours on 5th July 1945 we took off in Wellington "C" for Charlie to follow the favoured route. This being our first ''long'' trip each crew member clutched his unaccustomed flying ration consisting of two sixpenny bars of Cadbury's Dairy Milk with a handful of Horlick's Malted Milk Tablets. Climbing to 3,000 feet we set course for North Foreland crossing the Thames Estuary half a mile starboard of a Flak Tower which was firing Bofors guns at a drogue towed by a Martinet. From the Kent coast we headed across the Channel to Blankenberge on the Belgian coast directly on route for Cologne from where we flew along the Rhine over Dusseldorf and Essen to Dortmund.

In the rear turret I had little to do except to take an occasional drift sight to check on wind speed and direction for the Navigator, thus I had a grandstand view of what little remained of Germany's industrial Ruhr. The only substantial building to be seen for many miles was Cologne Cathedral, little transport appeared to be moving except for Army vehicles and a few tramcars which were linked in pairs. The only bridges over the Rhine were Bailey Bridges erected by the occupying forces. With no distractions such as F.W. 190's and flak, flying at fifteen hundred rather than fifteen thousand feet we could see the devastation created by Bomber Command in the preceding five years in a way which would not have been possible on an operational flight.

Leaving the Ruhr we headed north-west to Arnhem, scene of Operation Market Garden, an unsuccessful Allied airborne assault in September 1944. In three days 17th, 18th and 19th September the RAF and

United States Army Air Force flew 1234 missions over Arnhem dropping 593 Horsa and 38 Hamilcar troop carrying gliders together with a large number of Paratroops - a total of over 10,000 men. Aircraft involved were 280 Dakotas, of which 150 were from the USAAF, and 240 other RAF aircraft mainly Stirling, Halifax, and Albemarle glider tugs of 38 Group. Nine months later a considerable number of Horsa and Hamilcar gliders were to be seen lying apparently where they had dropped. Around and amongst the gliders lay wreckage of Dakotas, Stirlings and Halifaxes which had been shot down or crashed. A Stirling rear gunner, now a Flight Sergeant instructor at Tilstock was awarded the Military Medal for his part in action with a group of Paratroopers whom he joined when his glider tug was shot down on 18th September.

Our final view of Holland was of church spires, the only visible sign of the town of Middelburg on Walcheren Island. In May 1940 in an attempt to slow the German advance the dykes surrounding this twelve miles long, low lying island were breached to flood the entire island.

Crossing the North Sea we made landfall near Clacton with the final leg to Tilstock completed at 20.30 hours. Forty five minutes later, as forecast, heavy precipitation, direct from Rockall, commenced. I omitted to mention earlier that our skipper's name was Jim Cook thus we could truthfully claim to have on this day participated in a veritable Cook's Tour.

Newton Stewart, T. Murchie.

Malcolm Stewart.
(Air Gunner)

Born in Blairshinnock Farm, Beeswing, South-West of Dumfries in February 1925, Malcolm Stewart could scarely wait for the day when he could join the RAF in wartime. Volunteering for aircrew duties at the age of 16 and a half years, he was able to enlist in Edinburgh when he became 17 and was sent to A.C.R.C. in London in February 1942; there he was selected for training as an air gunner. Initial Training at Bridgenorth was followed by Gunnery School at Bishopscourt in Northern Ireland, where Malcolm gained his brevet and sergeant's stripes towards the end of 1942.

After operational training at Husband Bosworth in Leicesterhire where Malcolm joined a crew, they proceeded to convert from Wellingtons to Lancasters at 1653 H.C.U., North Luffeham, before joining No.149 Squadron at Methwold in Norfolk. From Methwold, Malcolm and his crew managed only twelve operational sorties, progress through their tour being hampered by sickness, but towards the end of the war in Europe they were able to be employed in dropping food supplies in Holland and in flying ex-P.O.W.'s from France to Britain landing at Tangmere in Sussex.

Post-war squadron training followed from Methwold and an alarming incident during that period is the subject of Malcolm's story below. Malcolm ended his war service in various administrative posts finally ending where it had began five years before, as Orderly Sergeant at Viceroy Court, A.C.R.C., London.

After demobilisation, Malcolm worked with the Forestry Commission for seven years before moving into private woodland management on the Comlongon Estate, South of Annan, the property of Lord Mansfield, where he stayed for twenty-three years. Malcolm ended his working life in an explosives division of I.C.I. before he and his wife retired to Dumfries.

Anoxia - and all that!.

This is not a story of heroics or of medal winning exploits, but of a Lancaster and its crew who almost ended up on the 'Missing, Presumed Lost' roster.

While waiting for demobilisation we were given all sorts of flying programmes to pass the time. This is one of them. On the night of 15th October 1945 at 18.34 hours Flying Officer Shepherd and his crew were assigned to the Lancaster OJ-S of 'C' Flight with 149 Sqn at Methwold. We were to fly a 'Bullseye' which was a cross country flight over land and sea.

OJ-S was the jinx aircraft of the Squadron, odd things happening to it from time to time, nothing serious but just queer little things which occured when the gremlins took over.

She had just had a major overhaul and had been on a test flight earlier in the day so we thought we had no worries.

We took off and climbed to 18,000 feet, set course for our first objective, a position out in the North Sea and before turning towards the land everything seemed to be going well, but then the old jinx struck again, we had an oxygen failure and the next thing most of the crew knew we were at 2,000 feet and seemed to be heading for a very wet landing.

This is where our Flight Engineer, George Alexander, Alex as we called him, came to our rescue. Alex had recovered much sooner than the rest of us and had levelled the old girl out.

Now whether it was with Alex being used as a stooge in the decompression chamber a few times made him re-act that little bit quicker we will never know, but for him we could have been on that long list of 'Comrades Lost'

I think that finished our 'Bullseye' days and helped our Skipper to give flying the go by. You will never know how grateful we were to our Alex. God bless him.

Dumfries. Malcolm Stewart.

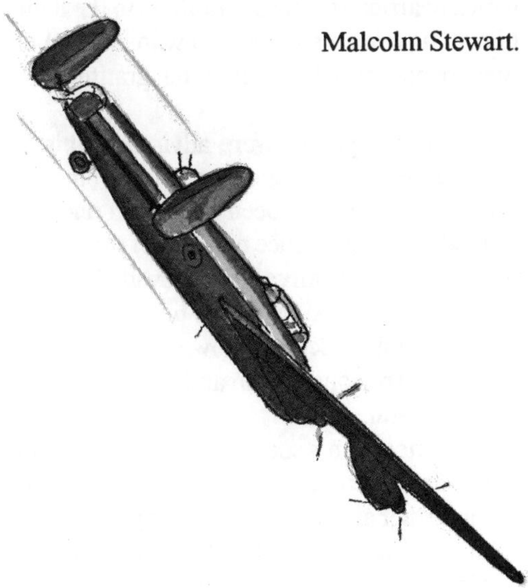

Warrant Officer John Waugh, D.F.M.
(Air Gunner)

Born at Beamish in Co. Durham in 1923 and educated at the Shield Row Intermediate Boys' School, John Waugh was initially employed in the coal industry, working in colliery offices. At the age of eighteen he volunteered for aircrew duties in the Royal Air Force and was enrolled at A.C.R.C. St. John's Wood, London, in January 1942. Selected for training as an Air Gunner he passed through his initial training at RAF Morecambe before being posted to No.2 A.G.S. Dalcross near Inverness, for his air gunnery course. John joined a crew at the Heavy Conversion Unit at RAF Rufforth near York, where they trained on Halifax bombers, before joining No.102 Squadron at Pocklington in Yorkshire for operational duties.

In late June 1944 John's crew were briefed for a raid on the railway yards at Blainville-en-sur near Nancy in Northern France. Of the 202 Halifax bombers from No.'s 4 and 6 Group involved in the raid eleven were lost include John's aircraft in rather strange circumstances. Bailing out successfully John eventually found himself in the friendly hands of the resistance fighters; below he tells a vivid story of his experiences, ending with a heartfelt tribute of gratitude to the many French people who helped him. Those men and women who, at peril of their lives, kept the escape lines open earned the undying gratitude of many thousands of allied airmen.

John's parent were advised by his Station Commander that he was posted as missing on operations but emphasising that there was no evidence that he had been killed. In due time information was received through the intelligence network of the Special Operations Executive that John was not only alive but had evaded capture. His parent were given the good news by the Air Ministry but strongly advised to keep it to themselves since, should it become known to the enemy, it might well result in John becoming a prisoner of war and the summary execution of any found to have sheltered him.

After John's successful return to the U.K. he was sent to the Aircrew Assessment Centre at Brackla in the north of Scotland. Being assessed as fit for further aircrew duties (some people are never satisfied) early in 1945 John was posted to the Far East where he joined No.356 Squadron based on Cocos Island in the Indian Ocean. From there he flew as a rear gunner in Liberators operating against the Japanese in Indonesia, until V.J. Day when he could finally hang up his guns.

Since demobilisation in January 1947, John has pursued various occupations including that of inn-keeper. Married, with a grown-up family of two daughters and one son, he and his wife now live in retirement in Annan, Dumfriesshire.

A Tribute to the Resistance Movement.

The 28th June 1944 was the night of our operation on Blainville-en-sur, and please remember, things are a bit hazy after all these years. We hadn't reached the target and the flak was fairly light with one or two searchlights flashing about. I was a little edgy worrying whether we'd be lucky once again and get back to Pocklington, for there was a party organised at Betty's bar in York the next night.

Suddenly tracers were flying in a thick stream past the rear turret and they were coming from in front of our kite. I knew it was very rarely an attack cam from the front, so I thought it must be some super kite. Just then the Skipper and the bomb-aimer began shouting and swearing and I qoute:- "Them bastards in front are firing at us and it's a bloody Hali".

The skipper came on the intercom and said we were rapidly losing height and we were to prepare to bale out. I opened the turret door to reach for my parachute to find the fuselage a mass of flames. Fixing the 'chute on to my harness I realised I would be unable to use the mid-hatch, so I swung the turret around and waited for instructions, SUDDENLY - "Bale out". I struggled to go out backwards, but something was holding me back, I'd forgotten to unplug the intercom, so I slung my helmet off and I think it was the slipstream that pulled me free. I can't remember pulling the rip-cord, and the next thing I'm floating around in the darkness....then a great flash of light and an explosion down below me. I must have got out just in time, and then I landed in a wood.

It was very dark, and I was in a strange land and was really scared. I heard something or someone moving stealthily through the undergrowth and could see shadows of soldiers and they were searching for me, but it was my imagination, of course. There was no one there. Remembering my instructions to hide in daytime and walk by night, I did just that, but a couple of nights or so, made me realise that airmen were not made to move through woods and fields in darkness, drinking from streams and eating that horrible escape stuff, so I decided to head down a country lane, and after a mile or two I heard the noise of motors coming nearer. I looked round and saw an army vehicle coming towards me and as it was too late to hide, I slung my flying jacket over my arm and kept on walking. Three German wagons passed me without so much as a glance.....what a bloody relief. I decided the best thing to do would be to approach the first civvy I saw. This happened a few miles further on, a lady was standing at a gateway leading to a farm. I approached her and said, pointing to my brevet ''R.A.F.'' I made signs to indicate that I had been shot down. She looked up and down the lane and motioned me to follow her, we entered the farmhouse to be met by the farmer and his wife. No one spoke English and me being a 'Geordie' made little difference.

These good people gave me food and drink, for which I will always be grateful. Using signs and gestures I was given to understand that I was to sleep in a room at the back of the house, until the door was closed I thought it was very cosy, but when the door was closed, I saw chalked on the back was the word ''Swastika''........oh Hell!!! What should I do now, have they gone for the cops or Jerry? I couldn't sleep and kept watch from the window, and later I found that it was the farm kids playing with chalk. After some hours I was brought some civvy clothing. They took my uniform and flying jacket, saying they would bury them. I got my flying jacket back after being liberated.

Some time later I was taken outside, introduced to a man and shown a bicycle. The man indicated to me to follow him, he would take me to the nearest Maquis camp. This camp was near Anghes. I think.

I stayed a few days with this group, there were a few other evaders there, and it was great to be with the lads again. After a few more days I was moved on again to a village called Soulaines-Dhys. Here I was looked after very well by a Madame Claudia Bertin and her family.

I was moved on again to a village called Nieuly, and here I was taken very good care of by Monsieur and Madame Henri Harmand. He owned the cafe in the town, and I was hiding in an upstairs room overlooking the market square and the main road through the town. I often saw German soldiers stopping, taking a break, and looking around and luckily moving on again. There was a young man, a friend of the family, his name was Roger Deprez from Comines in Belgium. (He later joined the Army and was posted to England where he spent a couple of weeks leave with my parents). He could speak good English and was able to bring me up to date with what was happening.

I was again moved to another safe house, in Sommevoire, and here I was very well looked after by Monsieur and Madame Maurice Comte, they did in fact look after me as if I was one of their family, indeed, I took on the role of his nephew from Dijon, and was supposed to be deaf and dumb. The Jerries came nosing around the village on a couple of occasions when

I had to hide under some hay in the chicken house until they left.

Moving again.....The Comtes were moving to Levigny, I was taken to the Maquis camp nearby. Here I met my Navigator, Danny Merrill and Flight Engineer, Bill Craydon again, and it was like meeting long lost relatives. We were quite a happy group here, sometimes it was a little boring and someone suggested a game of cards, Brag, I remember losing all my Escape money.

I felt I should do something in return for my keep and volunteered to do look out duties on the edge of the camp and also help in a couple of supply drops, holding a torch in the delivery area and helping to move the dropped supplies, some were for other groups in the area. The Resistance Group was led by a Captain Jacques Taschereau and Lieutenant Paul Thibeault which were under S.O.E. control. Their Wireless Operator for the Group, which was known as the "Jedburgh Team" was an American Naval Ensign, but I forget his name.

Whilst I was with this team another thing happened which showed me the true feelings of the French people. A Frenchman was brought to the camp and kept under constant guard and we were told that he had been posing as the leader of a Resistance Group a few miles away, but was no more than a gangster, and he and his band had been robbing local people, and had, in fact, turned a couple of RAF evaders over to the Germans for the reward of, I think, 25,000 francs. He was to be Court Martialled, with the Captain and Lieutenant acting as "Watch and Brief" of the proceedings. The Maquisards found him guilty on an overall vote and he was sentenced to death. Everyone was present when he was shot a few feet from where I was standing. It was a horrible sensation, but it showed me the true French feelings towards traitors.

Suddenly, on Sunday morning, 13th August, lying comfortable in my bed of parachute silk, I was startled by someone shouting very excitedly, then the sound of machine gun fire, a few dozen holes appeared in the roof of the tent above my head. I moved quickly onto the floor, then under the tent flap into the wood and saw someone lying in the bushes firing a gun. I moved over and lay beside him to see what he was shooting at. I gave him a nudge to ask him what was going on. He turned to me and it was one of Laval's Malice - he was pointing his gun at me. That was the worst moment of my life and my imagination was playing tricks on me again, I was wondering where I might get some new pants from...I put my arms in the air and shouted "RAF, RAF". A few more of the bastards came and then a German N.C.O. They escorted me away. I didn't care very much for them or their hospitality and was able to go A.W.O.L. The

German SS took me to a police station near Dijon for interrogation, and then I was put on a train to be transported to a POW camp....I jumped out of the train window when it was on the move, and I just kept running. I eventually got back to the Maquis and my friends.

As the war news was greatly improving I was taken back to Sommevoire and stayed once again with Maurice and Madame Comte, and here I lived in luxury until the Americans came and we were liberated.

There were some great parties. I went to the different places where I had sheltered and each one threw a party - champagne and a drink called, I think, Eau-de-Ver, and that believe me is some drink.

After all the festivities Lt. Paul Thibeault decided to get a car, the driver was one of the Resistance lads and came originally from Paris and he would act as our guide there. We had some cash which had accumulated from the supply drops. What a time we had in Paris, a beautiful city even though there was no electricity. We were there for a few days then reported to the British Authorities that we had just been liberated. We were put aboard a Dakota from Paris Airport to London and then interrogated at Air Ministry by M.I.9.

My thanks to all the French Ladies and Gentlemen, the members of the Maquis, S.O.E. and F.F.I. A great many thanks to people like Marcel Wouters and his Escape Line, and I am very sorry that I was unable to meet him before his death. These were all valiant people who could have been executed along with their families for harbouring the lads of the RAF. Thank you. Thank you all.

Annan

John Waugh

Flight Sergeant Donald Whyte.
(Air Gunner)

Donald Whyte was born in Inverness in 1924. Educated there at the Central and High Schools, he became an apprenticed electrician at the age of sixteen, an occupation he followed through to retirement in 1989. He transferred from employment by the local authority in Inverness in 1963 and came to Dumfries to take up the post of foreman of the Dumfries Lighting Department. He and his wife now live in retirement in Dumfries, they have two adult sons and are blessed with two grandchildren.

Donald volunteered for aircrew duties in the Royal Air Force and was enrolled for training as an air gunner at A.C.R.C., St. John's Wood, London, in October 1943. He passed through initial training at RAF Bridgenorth in Shropshire, before undertaking gunnery training at No.1 A.G.S. RAF. Pembrey in South Wales. There he trained on Anson Aircraft and at the end of his course received both his aircrew brevet and Sergeant's stripes.

On posting to No.81 O.T.U. at RAF Sleap in Shropshire, Donald joined his crew and they completed operational training on twin-engined Whitley bombers. Moving on to No.1665 Heavy Conversion Unit at Tilstock, also in Shropshire, where they converted on to four engined Halifax bombers, before joining No.298 Squadron at Tarrant Rushton in Dorset. 298 Squadron formed part of No.38 Group, the Group with special responsibility for airborne transport operations. Below, Donald records his experiences with 38 Group and subsequently in the Far East.

Special Operations with No.38 Group and in the Far East.

Our crew of which I was rear gunner joined 298 Squadron at Tarrant Rushton, an airfield in the South of England not too far from Bournemouth. It was towards the end of the war in Europe and so we did not take part in many "ops" but did manage some S.O.E. (Special Operations Executive) jobs dropping supplies to the underground forces in Holland, and also glider towing and paratroop exercises. The squadron, being part of 38 Group, had taken part in the "D"Day operations and also the operation at Arnhem and the Rhine crossing.

The S.O.E. operations involved quite a lot of low flying and pretty accurate navigation was required to find an open field "somewhere in Europe" and look out for a pre-arranged flashing signal - for our bomb aimer to make an accurate drop so that our supplies would not fall into the wrong hands. Glider towing was quite a hair raising experience at times - the gliders were mainly Horsas and Hamilcars - a mass take-off of Halifax-Hamilcar combinations was quite an experience. The gliders were stationed along the runway while the aircraft were positioned on each side of the runway connected by their tow-ropes to their individual gliders. When clearance was given the Halifax moved on to the runway and took up slack on the tow-rope - checked that the Glider Pilot was ready and with the green for off the Halifax started to roll with the glider lifting off and moving into high tow, with the next combination moving into position and starting to roll, quite a spectacle watching from my rear turret - one unit just airborne - another halfway along the runway and a third just lining up ready to roll. On an average each take-off was about 45 seconds - but sometimes this was not even quick enough for the ''Wingco''. The 'dropping zone' was quite a 'dodgy' place to be, with the mass release of gliders and 'tugs' getting out of the area with tow-ropes flapping behind them.

At the end of the war in Europe the squadron flew some 7,000 troops and equipment to Norway and also helped in the repatriation of P.O.W. from Belgium.

Although the war in Europe was over there was still the ''Far East Situation'' to be taken care of so the powers that be in their wisdom decided that airborne operations were the way to bring the war to an end, and so 298 Squadron left for 'Eastern Climes'.

Our crew set out in July, 1945, and staged from Tarrant Rushton to Castel Benito in North Africa, to Lydda in Palestine, to Shaibah (that place of the well known Blues song) and from there to Mauripur aerodrome at Karachi, now in Pakistan, a total of some 25 hours flying time. From Karachi we flew to Raipur in the Central Provinces of India, which was to be our base while in the Far East. Although one's memory does tend to play tricks after forty-odd years, all the squadron's aircraft arrived safely without too many mishaps ''en route''.

The first few weeks in Raipur were taken up with familiarisation flights and training, with trips to Calcutta and Delhi etc., but in August the Japanese decided to surrender - some do say they had heard that 298 Squadron had arrived in the Far East, but officially it was ''The Bomb''.

So, what to do with a squadron of four engined aircraft - all sorts of jobs were undertaken - troops were repatriated from Burma, freight was carried to Rangoon, Ceylon and Singapore, some aircraft even flew 'over the hump' to China. We even did bombing details on the ranges at

Peshawar and 'showed the flag' flying over the Khyber Pass on the North West Frontier on the borders of Afghanistan.

One of the last jobs the squadron did took us to Burma. It seems that during hostilities in that country the British Government had promised the native Burmese hill people that in return for helping in the fight against the Japanese, they would be helped when the war was over. Now it seemed that what the Hill people needed most of all was rice, but it had to be got to some of the most inaccessible places in the hills and jungles of Burma. So, how to get it there? Fly it in! Who to do it?? A squadron with low flying experience and bomb-aimers who could direct the drop - in short 298 Squadron. So a detachment of aircraft flew to a place called Meiktila. a name well known to Burma Star veterans, which was to be our base during the operation. The rice was packed in sacks, approximate weight 2 cwts. and this was enclosed in a larger loose sack , the idea being that when the sack landed and burst on impact the rice would escape into the loose sack and not be lost, that was the theory and I must say it worked - most times. Each morning the aircraft were loaded by Japanese P.O.W., each carrying a sack and stacking it all round the paratroops exit hatch, in the floor of the aircraft. Memory cannot recall how much each aircraft carried but it would have made quite a few rice puddings! Away we went flying very low most of the way, sometimes below the tops of the surrounding hills. On reaching the dropping zone with the bomb aimer giving directions and then giving us the green light it was all hands to the pumps as we pushed the sacks out through the hatch and watched them thunder down to villages below, hoping that our bomb-aimer was 'spot on' and none of the bags crashed through the roofs of the village huts. That is not to say we were accurate every drop and no doubts there are rice fields growing in some strange places in Burma. On the whole the operation went on for about a month and although none of our aircraft came to grief the flying was quite hair-raising at times. In-fact, three Dakota aircraft doing a similar job crashed in the jungle with no survivors. I hope that our little effort repaid the Burmese people in some way for their help during the war and that my little story tells of some of the tasks of the RAF and answers the question "What did you do in the war, Grandpa??"

Dumfries D.Whyte.

Flight Sergeant Thomas C. S. Gibson
(Air Gunner)

Tom Gibson was born in Lanark in June 1925, where his parents owned a pharmacy. Educated in the town Tom attended both Primary and Higher Grade Schools before leaving at the age of 16. Tom was something of an ebullient spirit and by the age of twelve was delivering newspapers in the mornings and evenings, and attending school during the day. On leaving school he attempted to join both the Royal Air Force and the Royal Navy. Being under age the RAF could not accept him; on the other hand, the Navy would have taken him as a boy entrant for an engagement of 21 years, perhaps fortunately, his mother talked him out of so serious a commitment.

Undaunted by his lack of success with the Armed Forces Tom applied to a shipping company and was signed on as a cabin-boy aboard the SS Empire Baffin, which he joined at Greenock on the Clyde. What followed was an experience Tom will never forget. Returning to Britain and docking at Liverpool, the Captain dismissed the young crew members, saying "Go home, and stay home, you will be in the armed forces soon enough".

Immediately he reached 18 years Tom volunteered for aircrew duties in the RAF. Called to ACRC London, in December 1943, he was selected for training as an Air Gunner. Going through the usual mill of initial training at Bridgenorth and Bridlington, Tom progressed to the Air Gunnery School at Pembrey in South Wales, where he earned both his Brevet and his Sergeant's stripes. Moving on to No. 302 Flying Training Unit at Alness in Ross-shire, where he joined a crew, and where they were prepared for duties in Ferry Command. Joining the Ferry Unit at Oban they commenced the task of ferrying planes right through from Oban to Karangi Creek near Karachi, in then India, flying both Sunderland and Catalina flying boats. From India they were ferried back to the UK by BOAC, prepared their next aircraft for delivery and so back to India once more. Finally, ending in Ceylon, they became members of No. 230 Squadron, and commenced maritime operations, flying Sunderlands.

Finally posted home from Seletar, Singapore, for demobilisation, Tom entered the building industry mastering both building and carpentry skills. Marrying his wife Jean in 1948, a move which has so far led to 44 years of happiness for them both, they have two daughters, Linda and Jane. Shortly after his marriage Tom made good use of his experiences in the Far East and wrote to a friend in Tasmania, who nominated them as New Australians. Emigrating to Australia Tom continued in the building trade and made quite a success in business. After 9½ years abroad it was only the illness of his parents - Tom is an only son - which brought he and his wife back to Britain.

Starting a building business in Kirkcudbright, Tom moved from success abroad to success at home - the years of housing expansion becoming a bonanza. At 68 Tom is still actively engaged in his business, but has taken up fishing as a hobby to pursue in future retirement. With typical enterprise he is learning to fly, from Carlisle Airport, a light aircraft in which he owns a share. Tom admits he must watch his weight for this last pursuit, and truly he would have difficulty in squeezing into the rear turret of a Sunderland today!

Not only in business has Tom scored success - his passion for competitive shooting is perhaps a legacy from his training as a gunner. Since 1971 Tom has twice been Scottish Champion, and was again runner up in 1982. On one occasion he made a record shoot of one hundred first barrels at clays; the only man in Scotland so far to achieve that feat. More recently he was High Gun in the Castle Douglas Guns and Tackle Championships, held in Kirkcudbright.

A Cabin-boy on Convoy to Russia

In October 1941, Tom joined the SS Empire Baffin at Greenock, full of anticipatory excitement at the prospect of a trip to America, which was where the crew believed they were heading. When the news broke that instead of the USA their ship was to be part of a convoy to Archangel in Northern Russia, there was, understandably, some consternation. So much so that the ship's cook, who had previous experience on that route, promptly jumped off the ship, breaking both ankles on the quayside. The cook had borrowed two pounds from Tom, a not inconsiderable sum in 1941, so quite naturally Tom felt an extra sense of chagrin. However, the cook did much to restore himself in Tom's better graces; when he came out of hospital he got Tom's address from the Shipping Company and sent on the £2 with a covering letter apologising for his cowardice in abandoning his ship!

On the 8th October the Empire Baffin left the Clyde to rendezvous at Scapa Flow with five other merchant ships, the steam ships Harpalian, Temple Arch, Empire Sun, Orient City and Empire Zephyr. At Scapa they were also joined by their escort consisting of the Battle Cruiser HMS

Norfolk plus six destroyers. From Scapa Flow the convoy rendezvoused again at an un-named bay in Iceland before setting course for Russia. Tom describes that part of the voyage as "quite a pleasant trip, a bit rough on some days and certainly getting colder all the way". However, the convoy was attacked by submarines on three occasions. During the attacks, non-essential crew were assigned to the boat deck from where they could hear depth charges exploding, but happily, none of the ships were hit by torpedoes. Again in Tom's own words "It was the first time in my life that my knees were knocking and it wasn't with the cold; quite a scary experience, especially since I was only sixteen and on my first trip away from home".

Finally they reached Russia without serious mishap and entered the embayment, Beloye More, moving up to the mouth of the Dvina near Archangel. The Empire Baffin carried eight Hurricane fighters crated on top of the hatches; below decks they carried Bren Carriers (light armoured fighting vehicles), ammunition and explosives. This cargo was all unloaded and the ship was then reloaded with iron and chrome ores for the return trip.

During their stay they saw prisoners from Estonia and Latvia working on the ships. These poor souls were dressed in sack cloth with only sack cloth around their feet. Two of these wretches stole some boots from the Harpalian, which was carrying such items, presumably for use by Russian troops. The two prisoners were apprehended on the spot and taken behind a shed and shot. The crew did not actually witness the execution, but they heard the shots and saw the bodies being dragged off on a sledge, which sight gave them quite a lot to think about during their stay in Russian waters.

There was snow and ice everywhere and the outlook from the ship was pretty grim. Initially, no one was allowed ashore but after a while special passes were obtained and Tom and two other young cabin-boys managed to get to Archangel by crossing the river by ferry. They found it a strange experience. All the roads were covered with ice on which children were skating, wearing, of all things, wooden skates. No one seemed to speak or understand English, but the children all asked for cigarettes; "Smokin Dobra" was their favourite expression. The houses and shops all looked uniformly dingy and there were no street names to be seen, even had they been able to read them. They visited several shops, looking for souvenirs, before realising that, in the semi-light of the Arctic day, they might have overstepped their time ashore.

Returning to the river they failed to find a ferry so went back into the town and found the Police Station. Entering, they showed their special passes but the police merely shrugged and did nothing to help them. Something of a dilemma! Returning to one of the larger shops they had previously visited, Tom shouted at the top of his voice "Can anyone speak English?"

A Russian officer came forward and said "Yes, I speak very good English", and so it proved, down to the last syllable. Relieved, the boys explained their situation whereupon the officer wrote a note and asked if they knew where the Police Station was. On receiving the affirmative he gave them the note saying "Take this to the Police Station and they will look after you". Back they went, and on showing the police the note were amazed at the immediate and massive change of attitude.

Two guards, with fixed bayonets, were detailed to escort the boys back to the shore where they were put upon a strange vessel, which they assumed was an icebreaker, but it had pigs, goats and other livestock all over it" However, it took them across the river and they managed to get back to their ships.

By the time they were ready to make the voyage home the River Dvina was solidly frozen over, with people walking across it in streams. Their ship was preceded by two Icebreakers, criss-crossing ahead of them. People moved back just far enough for the Breakers and Tom's vessel to pass and almost immediately started walking across again. Tom says, "That'll give you some idea of how cold it was and it is just one of those things you never forget".

Once out to the open sea one of the destroyers came alongside and its Captain called over the ship's Tannoy System "You are on your own now Empire Baffin, good-bye and good luck". That, as Tom says was a "scary thought".

The weather on the return voyage was very different from that on the outward journey. This was the Arctic at its worst, gale force winds, mountainous seas and bitter, bitter cold. All exposed parts of the ship were coated with ice and the decks were treacherous in the extreme.

The only fresh water available was from the after peak from which it had to be brought up by bucket. One of Tom's duties was to draw water and carry it to the ship's galley. Times without number Tom was swept off his feet and only saved from immersion in the icy seas by his feet, providentially making contact with the scupper plates before his body would otherwise have been hurled through the rails. Expectancy of life in those icy waters was no more than three minutes, so had Tom's luck not held he would not be here to put his ordeal on record.

Tom left home, a boy in search of adventure - it may fairly be said that he found it! Post war, people discovering that Tom had served as an Air Gunner have observed with awe that "that was a dangerous job". Tom's own view is that life in the rear turret of a Sunderland was totally "laid back" compared with sea-borne experience in the wartime Arctic winter.

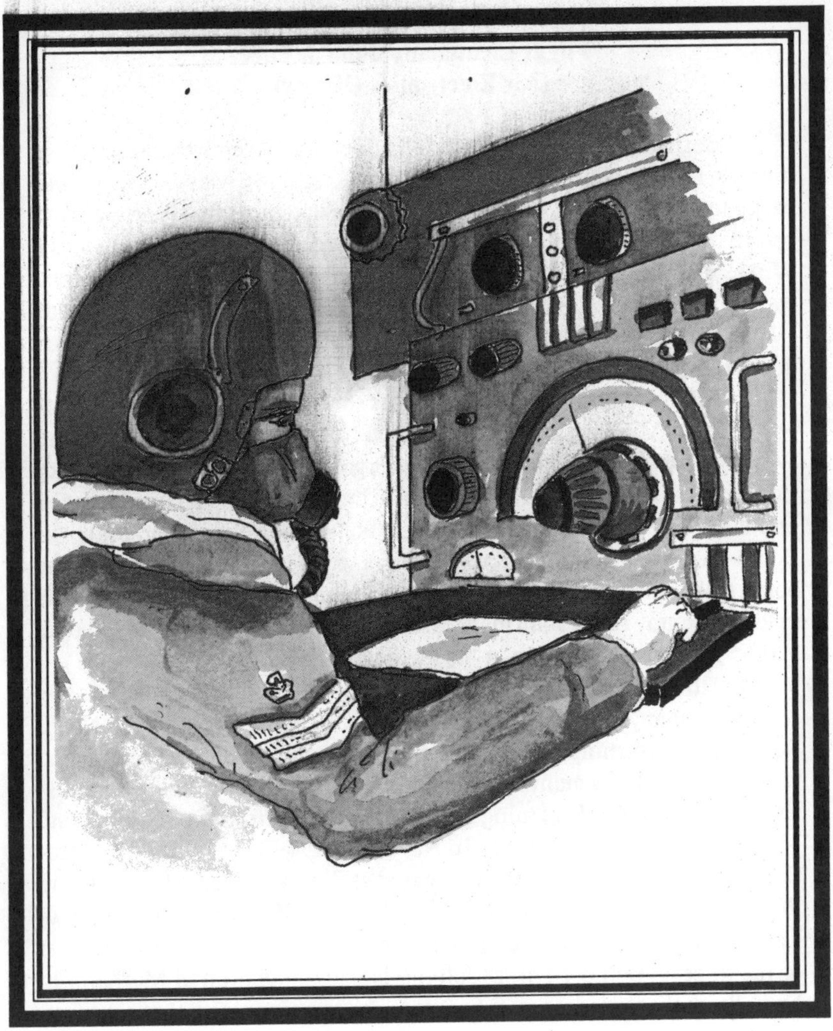

The Signallers' Stories

Flight Lieutenant John J. Snee.
(Air Electronics Officer)

Born and educated in Hull, John Snee was accepted for peace-time training in the Royal Air Force Voluntary Reserve in May 1939. He was called for active service with the RAF on 1st September that year, two days before war on Germany was officially declared. Selected for training as a Wireless Operator his radio training began at Prestwick, in Ayrshire, and was continued at the Electrical and Wireless School at Cranwell. In May 1940 he completed a short course in air gunnery at Jurby, Isle of Man, where gunnery was practised from Blenheim aircraft.

After successfully completing his training John was immediately posted to the Middle East where he joined No.70 Squadron equipped with Wellington bombers. The sophisticated organisation developed in Bomber Command in later years did not pertain in the Desert Air Force in 1940 and on John's first operational flight he flew not as a Wireless Operator but as Bomb-Aimer. Given three days in which to master the intricacies of the bomb sight, and encouraged by the Rear Gunner's threat to kill him if he made a "dummy run ", John made his first night flight with a total of 6 hours and 55 minutes flying time in his log book!

Although completely reticent about his experiences, John actually completed many operations with the Desert Air Force, mostly with No.70 Squadron. Returning to the U.K. he was posted to Bomber Command where he completed many more operational flights before being commissioned in 1944 and becoming an instructor at various Operational and Navigation Training Schools. In November 1949 he rejoined an operational squadron, No.101 Squadron based at Binbrook on the Lincolnshire Wolds, and equipped with Lincoln aircraft. He continued flying in Lincolns until 1956 when he was selected for training on Valiants, the first of the three V-Bomber types. Joining No.207 Squadron at Marham, in Norfolk, as the Squadron A.E.O. Leader he remained with that squadron until 1961. Among the highlights of the post-war flying in Bomber Command John has happy memories of long overseas training flights, (Lone Rangers), Fly-pasts flown over Buckingham Palace on the occasions of the Queen's Birthday and of "Showing the Flag" overseas in the newly commissioned Valiants.

Below, John tells a whimsical and philosophical story of his service experience and the subsequent events of life as a civilian. Surprisingly, now fully retired, his chief interest is as a Licensed Amateur Radio Operator.

34 years in Aircrew - A Philosopher's View of the R.A.F.

"I went to school in Hull, East Yorkshire as it was then called. I always had the usual delay waiting for the bus to come along. Invariably, the weather was wet and cold, but there was a nice Sweet Shop nearby, or as near the bus-stop, where I could shelter from the wind for a few pennies of sweets. Opposite the bus-stop was a large hoarding, advertising such things as Bovril and other adverts which I used to gaze at in my misery. I hated school. To my surprise, one morning the Bovril sign had gone and, in its place was a very attractive poster showing a large bi-plane, banking at an angle of forty-five degrees, with a landscape of green fields below. The large wording was ''SEE LIFE FROM A NEW ANGLE - JOIN THE ROYAL AIR FORCE VOLUNTEER RESERVE''.

I gazed at this with astonishment and knew immediately I had found the very thing for which I had been looking. My excitement was intense and I could hardly wait to obtain further details from the Royal Air Force Volunteer Reserve Centre.

The centre was in an old Manor House and I felt somewhat awed as I walked up the long drive. I rang the bell and was shown into what was once the library, I think. Seated behind a large desk was a Sergeant, and a Corporal asked me to sit down. The Sergeant then began asking me questions and filled up a large green form. I do not remember how much time this took, neither do I remember the questions; but at the end I do remember him saying that ''if this is satisfactory, you will be called forward for an interview'' and, after that he said ''then, all you will require is to pass the medical''. ''Medical?'' I'd never thought of that. My heart sank and, although I had no problems in that respect, I had heard stories of failures for things like flat feet, ingrowing toenails, and eyesight. ''Eyesight?'' you needed good eyesight to fly, that I knew. Oh God, I walked down that driveway with my heart in my stomach, very worried.

My parents were happy for me to do what I wished, and my father gave me great encouragement. However, I was worried about that medical and I made an appointment with the Family Doctor. I told him my intentions and said I would require to pass a Medical. ''Yes, of course'' he said ''but what do you want me to do about it?'' Well, will I pass, or will I fail? Will I be good enough? I'm sure he had a twinkle in his eye as he said ''Well, let's see''. He felt my pulse, opened my shirt and checked my chest, and then looked into my eyes - no instruments of course, he had absolutely no instruments - and said ''You'll pass, young man, and good luck to you." I was once again back on cloud nine.

It seemed an eternity waiting for that interview. Actually it was only about four weeks. In that time, I had gathered much more information about the RAFVR. They paid you! - or so it was said. There was a Retaining Fee, plus Attendance Allowance for Lectures and a Petrol Allowance if you wished to get to the local airfield - in this case it was the airfield at Brough. Unbelievable, I thought and once again, I felt rather worried. The day of the interview came and, some weeks before, my mother had bought me a new suit. I remember it very well from a shop in Hull called Horne Brothers and I changed into this for my interview. I felt very proud, it was very smart and I felt very good. Nevertheless, I was still a little worried and, as I have mentioned, the Volunteer Reserve Centre was in a Manor House the other side of town. I had to catch two buses and went into the Sweet Shop for them, basically, to admire my new suit.

They gave me a small bar of chocolate and wished me luck at the interview. Across the road was the same poster "SEE LIFE FROM A NEW ANGLE". I wondered if they would give me a pair of those nice black flying boots, goggles and a flying helmet, etc. My imagination was running wild.

Then, the walk up the drive again to the Manor House and being shown into another room where two other applicants were seated. After some moments, we spoke and I was told "someone is already in there", pointing to a large, dark, heavy door. Oh gosh - they spoke very posh and I was even more worried with my Yorkshire accent. I had to wait over a half an hour for my turn and was called into a very large room with a desk much bigger than I had ever seen before. Behind this sat a Wing Commander and, I think, a Flight Lieutenant. The Wing Commander smiled at me. He was rather old and, I believe, retired. He asked me to sit down and the questions began.

I was very nervous and I don't remember looking at the Flight Lieutenant at all. School, hobbies, what newspapers I read, etc. All these questions came out and many others. I remember thinking - I'm not doing too well and what shall I tell my parents if I fail? Then sport came up and I cursed my lack of interest in sport. The Australians were in the U.K. that year, 1939, and had played Yorkshire two weeks previously. My father was very keen and insisted I go with him to watch the match, which I reluctantly did. The Wing Commander asked me if I had seen that match and I was truthfully able to say "Yes". I knew the odd names and I knew the score and he looked very pleased about that.

Finally, the interview was over. It was about ten strides to that dark, heavy door. He called my name and said "You will hear in due course if you have been successful, and if you have, remember this, the Air Force is hard work, very hard work, but very rewarding - it's a band of Officers and Men all achieving their aim, but at the same time it's fun" he said "fun is also something else you will enjoy in the Royal Air Force". During my years in the RAF, I often recalled those words.

In-fact, fifty-three occasions in all, especially when the Navigator called out over the intercom "Enemy coast ahead". Oh dear!, the Germans didn't like it and got angry, sometimes they got very, very angry and I wasn't too pleased either!

I was lucky enough to complete two Tours of Operations, mostly with 70 Squadron. I remember flying back from the Middle East, that's from Cairo to Freetown, in a D.C.2, or was it a D.C.3 - I can't remember. The first leg was in a converted Wellington with six seats either side. In-fact, there were twelve of us in all. We sat looking at each other until I couldn't stand it any more. I called the Captain and requested to go into the Rear Gunner's position. At least, I thought, I could see the Desert going by. Permission granted, I unplugged the old Type 29 Intercom.

We were all dressed up to the neck in Irvine jackets, trousers and helmets, etc. and I crawled through the two doors into the Rear Turret and plugged in again to the Intercom, basically to report my position, but all was dead. I spent some time checking connections, but in the end gave up. Chicken that I was, I decided not to turn the turret in case it fell off. I was over an hour in there and became very cold. I tried the Intercom again to report that I was coming forward, but no joy.

Turning round, I opened the two swing doors to return to my position and, to my horror, I saw no-one around. With relief, I saw one person on the rear starboard side - completely covered up and sitting. I moved across and spoke by lifting his helmet and my first question was "Where the hell are they all?" "Forward" was the reply. God, how could they all go forward into the Wireless Operator's compartment - a very, very small compartment? I couldn't understand it. It suddenly dawned on me I was speaking to a W.R.A.C. Officer sitting on the elsan! I had no idea we had a lady on board, no idea at all, but the Captain had, of course and he had called forward all passengers to enable privacy for her to be on the bog! I didn't hear this, of course, and I must admit, this was the first and last time I spoke to a lady sitting in such a private position!

Back to the green fields of England and a trip with a sprog mixed crew to Cologne - the first thousand bomber raid. I was at O.T.U., Abingdon and, if I look much older now than my seventy-three years, I blame it on that trip. Every little light across the North Sea was seen by the Rear Gunner as a Fighter. (Ha, ha, ha, ha, ha) However, I came back and that was something. I was lucky enough to complete two Tours. Most of my pre-war RAF pals 'got the chop' in 1941/42.

There are only two of us left - myself and another, living in Australia. I found him by chance. He is a member of the Royal Air Force Amateur Radio Society - R.A.F.A.R.S. - and so am I. I spotted his letter in the R.A.F.A.R.S.' magazine, with a photograph of myself and others, taken at Monkton House - that's near Prestwick - in 1940 - asking for any information on possible members of the Hull V.R. remaining. I couldn't believe it. I knew him, but thought he had 'bought' it with others. I wrote, and we have had contact ever since via Amateur Radio. I speak to him at 0700 most Mondays.

The war finished and I found myself on Lincolns for many years, until the 'V' Force was formed. I completed No.2 Course at Gaydon and was posted to Marham on Valiants, 207 Squadron. I remained there for nearly four years as Squadron A.E.O. Leader, being crewed up with C.O.'s as they came and went - three in all. They were lucky appointments for them, for all received their Gold Braid on completion of their Tour. We poor old Leaders just pressed on, but it was a bind doing Continuation Training with every new Commanding Officer until he felt competent - many a grumble about that and many a story. Not knowing what to do with me at the end of this Tour, they posted me to Singapore. Singapore? I couldn't believe it. My wife and I had three wonderful years and I enjoyed myself tasking aircraft in Headquarters Far East Air Force. The good life had to come to an end, however, and I found myself in headquarters Strike Command as the Display Controller - that's 'Down the Hole' as it were. My Terms of Reference were to run six close-circuit television channels, one live for a quick reaction alert and intruder contacts, and the others on exercises, aircraft dispositions Worldwide, etc..

This was a new scheme within Strike and I was sent to the B.B.C. and London Weekend T.V. Centres for information. They both gave me lots of advice and I had a good time watching such programmes as "Upstairs, Downstairs" being made, which I thoroughly enjoyed. Back at base in Headquarters Strike Command, it started to work well. I only had six cameras, but with many monitors to the Brass upstairs. There were about 30-35 monitors upstairs in their offices.

Now, what they didn't tell me on appointment was that I had to brief the C. in C. every morning at 0900 hours. He sent for me and asked how things were going T.V.-wise and briefed me on his requirements for the

Morning Brief. He said "Start on time, finish on time, fifteen minutes. I want the weather, exercises - current and future, all the aircraft states, any intruders, results of scrambles, etc.." As I was my own boss, I decided to follow the format of the B.B.C. News at Six. I had the Operations' Clock on line, ticking away until 0900 hours, then the start proper with the Civilian Weather Man giving present and future weather. followed by myself on local events, aircraft states Worldwide, exercises, lone rangers, Russian Bears entering our airspace and results of scrambles, Satellite information - which I could spread out if required to complete the fifteen minutes or chop off as neccessary. This kept me going for nearly three years until my fifty-fifth birthday - my only problem being leave. Nobody wanted my job, talking to the C. in C., who was kindness itself to me, but nobody fancied being on television. I am now living near Moffat with my lovely wife and a lovely young black Labrador, both missing me I understand for, as I write this, I find myself in hospital having the old gentleman's problem - enlargement of the Prostate Gland. I have just been given a pre-med into the bottom. I'm beginning to feel woozy and I'm beginning to get on that cloud nine - lovely. I feel very relaxed now - can't write any more.

So you, gentlemen of the Aircrew Association, remember those wise words spoken to me many, many years ago. Have fun. I hope to see you all soon.

Now sitting up in bed and feeling great - one or two nurses moving about, a scene of great calm and efficiency. You may wonder how I coped with life after being aircrew for 34 years? Some problems.

I completed the 'Bowler Hat' course at the Ministry of Defence and became involved in the care of the Mentally Handicapped (unpaid). This was an enjoyable time for me, and some gentleman in authority was kind enough to say -"he thought this was my vocation". Sadly, I had to leave that environment because I was required to leave our comfortable quarters at Strike Command. Staying as house guests with a very good friend of ours in Kent, I began the process of job hunting. Always on the "short list" for many appointments, but never successful. Reading the small "adverts" in the Telegraph one day I saw a "Kinky Cottage" for sale in Suffolk, with two acres of land and out-houses. A phone call confirmed this and my wife and I travelled to Great Glemham, in East Anglia. What the owner had not told us on the phone was that this cottage was also a Post Office and Shop!!

Problems? After about ten minutes serious consideration (we thought) we decided to buy it on the spot.

The location was in a very small village - a hamlet really, with a 13th century church across the road and a few tithed cottages nearby. 300 yards away was a gorgeous pub and we knew we would both be happy!

It was a great environment. Our nearest neighbour was a retired Air Commodore and next to him was also a retired Air Vice Marshal. I felt somewhat at home if not a little junior!

We were there for 13 years doing a weekly run to the "Cash and Carry" with my wife doing all the accounts for the Post Office. I became a Parish Counciller and eventually the Chairman. At odd times I was also the local Doctor, Dentist, Electrician, Plumber and many other things in an emergency.

However, it all became a little too much and in spite of the many sporting and field invitations received, we decided to "pull the plug". I suppose the garden was the problem, my wife and I are keen gardeners and ours had to be open to the 'locals' twice a year according to records. You can die in a garden!!

We moved to Moffat, in Dumfriesshire, where the RAF language is well understood (being the home of Lord Dowding) and have never regretted it. RAF friends often visit us, bringing cold weather clothing and ear muffs, only to be surprised by the climate and beauty of the Borders.

Moffat John Snee

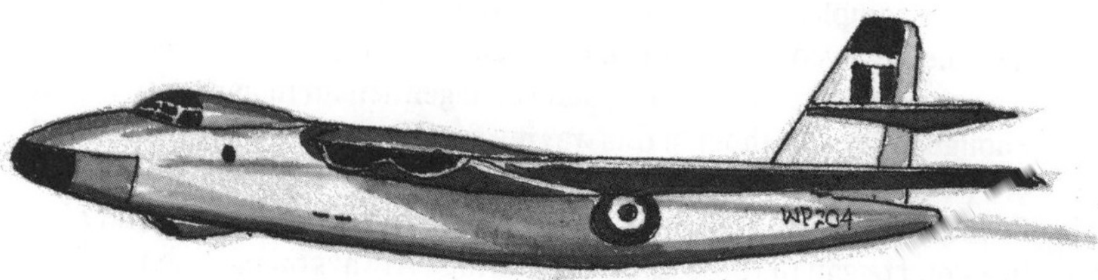

Warrant Officer Charles Munro.
(Wireless Operator/Air Gunner)

Charles Munro was born at Gateshead-on-Tyne on 2nd June 1921, the elder (by 45 minutes) of twin boys. He was educated at three establishments in North Shields, leaving at the age of 15 to become a copy-boy on the local evening newspaper. A rewarding job with a salary of 7s.6d (37½ pence) per week plus a free daily newspaper! Charles continued his education at Commercial College, attending evening classes for two years learning shorthand, typing and book-keeping. In 1938 he became a cub reporter and at the age of 19 he volunteered for aircrew duties in the Royal Air Force. He was attested at Padgate in March 1941 and was selected for training as a Wireless Operator/Air Gunner.

After completing signals training Charles went to Baldoon, south of Wigtown, to complete gunnery training, before entering Coastal Command at the Operational Training Unit at Alness by Invergordon. Below he tells, with becoming modesty, something of his adventures operating in Catalina flying boats from Gibraltar with No.202 Squadron. Having in mind the savagery of the war against the U-boats fought out over the angry waters of the Bay of Biscay, during 1943 in particular, and the proximity of shore based enemy aircraft, adventures there must have been aplenty. Happily his luck held out.

Demobilised at York in April, 1946, Charles became sub-editor on his old pre-war newspaper. From this post he has vivid memories of vetting the reams of Reuter and Associated Press messages about the Nuremberg War Crimes Trials, taking over this task from a Jewish colleague who could not handle the situation as the horrific evidence unfolded.

Charles married in 1947 and after working as a journalist for several years he decided on a complete change of full-time career and took up farming with his father-in-law on his Northumbrian farm, but continued with freelance journalism. After eight years in farming he took a post selling veterinary products to farmers in Northern England and Southern Scotland. After a further three years he obtained a post as Sales Manager with a large distributor of Mercedes-Benz passenger cars. Taking early retirement in 1983, he and his wife now live in Annan, Dumfriesshire. Hobbies which he much enjoys are game-fishing and gardening.

Charles rightly claims that 'luck' played a great part in his wartime survival and it is fitting to concluded this introduction in his own words as he described how luck continued to play an important role in his life. "My "LUCK'' held out until being demobbed, but before that I was LUCKY enough to meet a wonderful girl (ironically, while doing a stint in Air Sea Rescue HSLs). We married in 1947 (a LUCKY man!). Our LUCK extends to having two loveable daughters, one living in France, and the other in Malaysia. The younger, resident in the French Alps, she and her husband are expert skiers, and during the Summer travel the world seeking places where they can enjoy their second-chosen sport - windsurfing. They have done this off the coasts of France, Mexico, Hawaii, Japan and the U.S., but they have their favourite spot - by far!. In the sea off that little Spanish spot of TARIFA! I sometimes think 'If that old Cat had 'bought it' that day in 1944, there may never have been a lovely, suntanned blonde lassie skimming over the same seas that her Dad came down on so long ago!'

And it could so easily have happened over the maelstrom that is Biscay!!"

Good Luck: A Reverie.

On the wall of one of the local hostelries wherein I occasionally partake of a glass of its excellent brew, and enjoy the conversation of friends, hangs a large black and white drawing of a dog. The caption reads : LOST - dog, which looks like the above; has only one eye (it's wearing a black patch) one ear, only three legs and has recently been castrated. It answers to the name of 'LUCKY'.

What a quintessential example of British humour! (I used to toy with the thought of telling this story to certain Germans I used to meet on business trips to Germany, but felt the explanation would take too long!).

No, I refer to REAL GOOD LUCK (neat dictionary definition:- 'fortuitous event affecting one's interest). I feel sure that my ex-flying comrades in the Aircrew Association must look back on their Service careers and recall how luck played an important part in their lives. I feel certain that I am still inhabiting this planet of ours because of the share I was apportioned.

In retrospect perhaps the most important stroke of good LUCK was, when after the necessary signals and gunnery training, I was posted to an O.T.U. of Bomber Command at Moreton-in-the-Marsh, but two days before my two-week leave ended, I received a telegram informing me that, instead, I had to join an O.T.U. of Coastal Command at Alness, near Invergordon, on the Cromarty Firth. (It was here that the Duke of Kent, along with the crew had been killed when a Sunderland flying-boat crashed into high land, before my arrival).

The significance of my changed posting did not immediately sink in, but it didn't take me long to realise - because of the 'name of the game', the fatality/injury risks in Coastal were infinitely smaller than flying in Bombers. To be candid, I think I felt glad, felt LUCKY.

The oldest member of our Catalina crew which formed at this O.T.U. was a chirpy, cheerful sparrow of a man, an ex-miner from Stirling, with crew-cut hair atop of a tough, lined face, bearing also, the blue-black scars ingrained indelibly, through his calling as a pitman. He was a wee terrier of a man, with a blue-eyed twinkling smile, especially after a dram or two in the mess. He was our front gunner/rigger. I was lucky enough to save him from drowning once. He couldn't swim; it was Hogmanay! We (surprise! surprise!) called him Jock.

We flew out to Gibraltar to join No.202 Squadron. Even today that name sounds unfamiliar; it was either 'Gib' or 'The Rock', and we introduced ourselves to the Rock's Barbary apes, learned to fight (and mostly win) against the multitudinous and gluttonous bed-bugs that nightly tried to gorge themselves on our young blood. Soon (very soon) we learned there were no women or children on The Rock, apart from some WAAFs (stories about 'baby-boats back to Blighty abounded!). In addition, there were the guitar-strumming senoritas entertaining in the Main Street drinking spots. All these years later I can still recall the eeriness, in spite of almost constant sun-shine, of not hearing the laughter and shouts of children. They had been evacuated to Madeira, along with their Gibraltarian mothers and other female relatives.

Our flying duties mainly consisted of A/S (anti-submarine) patrols and C/E's (convoy escorts); we got to know the Southern coasts of Spain and Portugal better than an Iberian holiday courier, and Biscay was our 'backyard'. It was especially fascinating at night, watching and identifying the blazing lights of the neutral cities of Cadiz, Lisbon and Oporto, as well as the illuminations of many coastal towns and villages. Lighthouses, too, particularly those at Cape St. Vincent, Cape Roca, Cape Finisterre and Corunna, as we headed north to scour the seemingly ever-savage Biscay seas. Often, gazing out of a side gun-blister of the Cat. I would look at the foaming waters, and think "Thank God I am up here, in the comparative quiet of the skies" - felt pity for the merchant mariners and Naval bods who we were 'one man and his dog-ing' from above, eyes weary from trying, hour after hour, to spot a surfacing periscope/conning tower or snorkel, as we circled the convoy below us.

'The Bay' was a favourite area for menacing Focke-Wulfe Condors with their quite awesome armament. Thinking of them, and how they had claimed the lives of comrades, invariably triggered the thought of our speed (92 knots cruising!). The sitting duck syndrome.

Good old kites, the Cats - tough, dependable, TRUSTWORTHY. I have flown a lot since the war, and although most of the planes I have been in have had Roll-Royce engines - a fact, being British, of which I am very proud - I have never felt any misgivings about Pratt and Witney engines carrying me to foreign parts; through having flown hundreds of hours in the RAF with them I feel no concern.

However, once, I wondered, and didn't like what I felt. I experienced what so many authors describe as a 'frisson of fear'. Early in 1944, at the end of our crew's tour, we were pleased to be going back to Blighty, for six months off flying duties. From May to August, 1943, more U-boats were attacked and more combats took place in the Biscay area than at any other time during World War II.

We were on our way back to the U.K. in a Cat. that had done an awful lot of flying time, so that a major overhaul could be carried out, possibly including engine replacement. In addition to the crew we carried three ground staff as passengers. We didn't have our normal brace of pigeons, though; I have wondered since whether some high-ranking RAF logician worked out that, weightwise, three hefty fitters turned the scales at the same figure as those feathered friends of ours??!! In addition to our 'guests' we had, stowed in the blister ammunition boxes, a considerable number of wrist-watches. I can't remember whose entrepreneurial brain gave birth to this idea! We took off smoothly enough, planning to take our usual route off the Southern coast of Spain, and Portugal's coastline, warmly excited at the prospect of being back home. Between Gib. and Cape Trafalgar is the little town of TARIFA, and it was off there that our port engine began to sound rough and then very rough - it seemed only a second or two before it was enveloped in smoke and flames. After all the years since, I can still hear one of the fitter/passengers (a Cockney) saying "Cor, crikey, this flying lark is bloody dangerous!". Our skipper decided to make a landing (our first, in the sea). Surface conditions had been described as 'moderate'. As we descended - I was seated at the port blister - watching the smoke and flames past the perspex - I was relieved to see the fire lessen in intensity and eventually die, thanks, I learned later by quick thinking and action on our flight engineer's part. My co-radio oppo, had got his Mayday message our smartly. It was a rough landing, on one engine, but the skipper did a good job. I was hypnotised looking at the port float, half-expecting it to snap off like a carrot, as we bounced and crashed through the waves.

I began to feel very seasick - in an aeroplane!!, as we waited for our rescuers. Eventually, answering our distress call, an Air Sea Rescue HSL hove into view and wee Jock soon got a thrown line fastened to the nose-bollard, and the HSL managed to slowly tow us back to The Rock. The bottom of the kite, when we saw it later, on the slips, was as wrinkled as a baby's bottom left in the bath water that was too hot, and for too long!

The plane was successfully 'patched up' and we made the second trip safely back to Loch Ryan, at Stranraer, LUCK (good) again.

And yes, the watches got back safely, and yes, they were not spotted by the Customs boyhos who came to meet us in their launch after we had moored to our allotted buoy. In retrospect I feel somebody in our crew had a pal in our squadron who was an armourer who had worked on our kite!

Some of our 'non-operational' flights out of Gib. harbour had been 'most peculiar', to say the least - especially trips to Port Lyautey in Morocco. We carried a 'cargo' of cases of whisky (an action officially approved - I THINK!) from the Officers' and Sergeants' Messes. We used to land on the brown muddy waters of Lyautey river, and taxi to a mooring near the big American base there. We would stay overnight with our U.S. friends, and enjoy rations that were 'out of this world' - sizzling, juicy gigantic T-bone steaks and pork chops that melted as easily as the dairy ice cream that was flown in from the States for these loud, slightly crazy, quite wonderful USAAF guys. We returned to The Rock carrying crates of fresh eggs, so good to have after months of eating dried-egg powder! It was a case of eggs and whisky galore.

So we had our lighter moments, thank goodness.

Annan — Charles Munro.

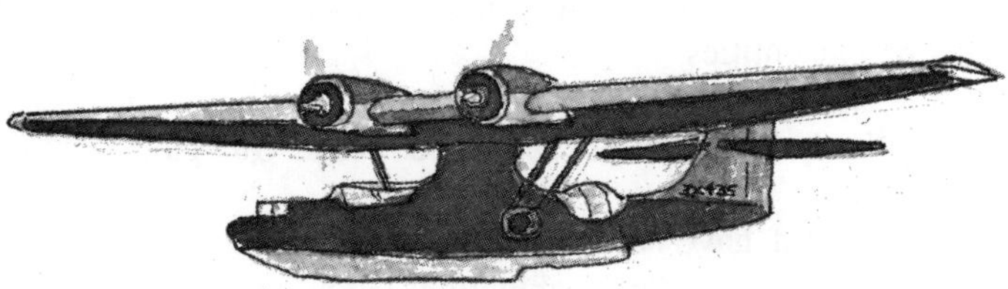

Warrant Officer Matt McGinily (Wireless Operator / Air Gunner)

Matt McGinily was born in New Abbey, Kirkcudbrightshire in 1917 and was educated locally, and after schooling was in farming until he enlisted in the RAF in 1937.

He volunteered as an Aircraft hand General Duties and after basic training at RAF Henlow was posted to RAF Dishforth and subsequently re-mustered to the trade of Wireless Operator. On completion of the W/T Operators course at RAF Cranwell and passing an aircrew medical he was posted to 233 Squadron at Leuchars in December 1938 as a W/T Operator, W/Op (Air) u/t. and A/G u/t.

Training as an Air Gunner was completed on the squadron at Leuchars in the Spring of 1939 and being re-graded as Aircraftman First Class was accepted as aircrew. 233 Sqn. at that time was equipped with Lockheed Hudson Aircraft. In May 1940, together with all other aircrew who were not of Senior NCO rank he was promoted to the rank of Sergeant and awarded his Brevet.

He did a tour of operations from Leuchars with Coastal Command and when resting in 1942 became a W/Op instructor at various Air Observer Schools at Bobbington (re-named Halfpenny Green) Millom and Penrhos. In March 1945 he returned to Coastal Command with 281 Sqn. at Limavady and then went to Transport Command at Dishforth.

In August 1951 he was pronounced medically unfit for flying duties due to Tinnitus, a hearing disability, and was transferred to ground duties as a Telegraphist. He left the RAF in 1972 with the rank of W/O.

He met Mary, who was in the WAAF at Halfpenny Green, and they married and have one son.

In his post-war years Matt joined the Civil Service in the Department of Customs and Excise. He is now retired and lives in Dumfries and enjoys his hobby of fishing.

Matt relates a number of incidents which happened in his RAF career which he entitles,

"Lady Luck, or But for the Grace of God go I".

There must have been few aircrew during WWII who did not believe that Lady Luck, like the ubiquitous Gremlins, accompanied each aircraft and its crew on every flight, whether operational, training, low level hop after an air test or visit to another station. On most she took a benevolent view and saw them safely home. On some she smiled and on some she scowled. Under these two latter headings there can be few aircrew who did not have a tale to tell worth a pint in any "howff" or hotel.

Herewith my contribution. All are authentic though possibly slightly diffused by the ravages of time and some dimness of memory.

In June 1940 when a W/Op with 233 Squadron flying Hudsons with Coastal Command at Leuchars, all leave had been stopped as there was a shortage of aircrews because the Norwegian Campaign was in full swing and all crews were required. Leave was not allowed until July when I headed the leave list.

However, a squadron companion, who was second on the list, asked me if I would change with him as his fiancee was going to take a holiday the week I was due to be off. Since I had no particular ties I agreed and continued on operations. The day my friend returned to the squadron he was detailed for an operational flight from which he did not return.

Lady Luck certainly smiled on the crew of a Bomber Command Wellington, for later in June our Hudson had been on patrol along the Norwegian Coast and we were returning to base in the early light. Roughly halfway between Stavanger and Leuchars our crew saw this Wellington on a northerly course flying towards them. There was no common R/T frequency in those days and the following conversation by Aldis Lamp took place.

Wellington - "Where are you going?"
Hudson - "Home"
Wellington - "Where is that?"
Hudson - "Leuchars"
Wellington - "What course are you flying?"
Hudson - "225"
Wellington - "Are you sure?"
Hudson - "Yes"
Wellington - "How far?"
Hudson - "160 N.M."
Wellington - "Can we follow you?"
Hudson - "Yes"

The Wellington, being some 20 knots faster, continued circling and periodically asked the Hudson if it could increase speed and how far still to fly. He seemed comforted on being told that Coastal Command had been told of his situation and that Air Sea Rescue had been alerted. When the Scottish coast was eventually sighted the Wellington disappeared towards it like the proverbial bat to land at Montrose.

A letter of thanks was received from the Wellington's C.O. to the C.O. of 233 Sqn. explaining that the crew of the Wellington had been on its first operational flight to a target in Northern France and somehow missed England on the way home.

Two or three minutes either way a rendezvous with our Hudson would have been missed. They might have reached Norway, they were going in the right direction, and its coast had just dropped out of sight when we met. I often wonder if that crew completed a full tour.

The above is first hand because I was operating the Aldis Lamp on the Hudson.

In the Spring of 1940 several aircraft were on patrol out of Leuchars. Deteriorating weather conditions caused these aircraft to be recalled. By the time the last aircraft reached landfall the weather was at its worst, a strong westerly gale and lashing rain. Unfortunately W/T contact with this aircraft had been lost, but from previous bearings was thought to be north west of Leuchars.

The next day the aircraft was found south of Edinburgh with only superficial damage, a broken perspex nose cone and bent propellers. The W/T was still active but down on battery power.

No trace of the crew was ever found, and it was thought that they had baled out and because of the strong off shore wind had been blown out to sea.

In July 1940 we had been briefed to bomb Stavanger Harbour and were attacked by an ME 110 and extensively damaged. It took the riggers and fitters over four months to make this aircraft operationally serviceable again. I was wounded in the arm and hospitalised. My mates came in to visit me and told me that one of the Squadron's aircraft had a brief encounter with an ME 115 (seaplane) off Norway. A bullet had hit the astrodrome and no other damage was seen.

However, the rear gunner would not answer the intercom and on investigation he had to be lifted out of the turret as he had been killed instantly, by, it was assumed, the bullet which had damaged the astrodrome. It took the riggers approximately 20 minutes to make this aircraft operational again.

In the Spring of 1941 I was an Instructor at the Gunnery School, Penrhos in North Wales and on one rather foggy day an aircraft was heard flying overhead in a northerly direction. It was subsequently reported that an aircraft had crashed into a hill a few miles north of our airfield. A search party was organised and the crew of the crashed Wellington were found to be dead, but the rear gunner was missing. Single gunshots were heard by the search party coming from lower down the hill and on investigating, the rear gunner was found, still in his turret, with both ankles broken.

In December 1941, at RAF Millom, an Air Observers School, operating Ansons and Bothas, two NCO aircrew, a pilot and a W/Op were posted in for staff flying duties having completed an operational tour with Bomber Command. They had been part of the same crew in Bomber Command and continued to fly together at Millom.

This particular night they were taking off when the tail of their Anson struck a heavy metal runway gooseneck shield. The aircraft did not return to base. The following morning part of tail unit was found on the runway and it was believed that the Anson had crashed into the Irish Sea.

In the Spring of 1944 I was instructing at Halfpenny Green, and on this particular night i/c the section on a night flying exercise across England, with emphasis on map reading. The turning point to the short northern approach track to the airfield was not identified by one crew and the turn was made from a wrong and more westerly point.

Along this new, but wrong track, lay the Clee Hills, two hills approximately two miles apart and of slightly different heights.

The aircraft, quite simply, letting down through broken cloud, did a 'wheels up' landing on the lower hill. No one was injured, and the wireless being OK, base was contacted and the crew set off on foot downhill to look for the nearest habitation. A lucky escape? Yes, for a few feet lower the aircraft would have ploughed into the side of the lower hill, a few higher and it would have missed the lower hill and hit the higher one.

Lastly, an O.T.U. Halifax landed at Halfpenny Green in late 1944 with a minor engine fault, which was repaired and the aircraft took off to continued its flight. Something went wrong and the captain attempted a forced landing.

The aircraft crashed into a copse of mature trees about a mile from the airfield. The tail unit was torn off and the gunner suffered from a broken arm. The rest of the crew were killed.

One mystery, why the copse which was about two acres in extent when there were hundreds of fields all around?

Dumfries — Matt McGinily.

Squadron Leader W.T. (Bill) Clapperton (Wireless Operator)

Bill Clapperton was born in Edinbugh on 17th September 1921. Attending Primary School in the village of Stenton in East Lothian, he qualified for entry to Dunbar Secondary School which he attended until December 1937. During his High School days Bill developed a keen interest in aviation and at the age of 16, encouraged by a Royal Air Force recruiting campaign, he applied for entry to the R.A.F. College at Cranwell as a boy entrant. Required standards of education and health were high but Bill gained entry for training as a Wireless Operator, a category for which there was an urgent need.

Bill had a fascinating career as a Wireless Operator, having many unusual assignments - he was with a V.I.P. Squadron which flew Churchill, members of the War Cabinet and other Allied Leaders. He also served as a member of the King's Flight. On ground duties he served with the Chindits in Burma, and later as an Electronics Officer, he went to help in the development of the electronics systems for the Nimrod reconnaissance aircraft. He was also involved in the development of ground radar systems, and sonar at the air sea warfare unit at Ballykelly in Northern Ireland.

Below, Bill tells an adventurous story of a spell of duty with the Chindits.

Taxi Sergeant

I had been in India for two years, when at Dum Dum, I contracted M.T malaria and after recovery, was sent on 'Convalescent Leave' to Darjeeling for three weeks, wandering about the foothills regaining strength. On my return to RAF Dum Dum, I was informed that I had been posted to 'Special Forces Headquarters, RAF Gwalior', effective from 5th February 1944. So, pack your kit, collect your railway warrant and report to Signals Officer, Fg./Off. Goodsell. There was no other information forthcoming so the event was rife with speculation, conjuring up many types of operations, clandestine and otherwise.

After a couple of days in the train and a dusty journey by road I arrived at my destination. I was then informed that I was originally posted to take over the N.C.O. i/c Telecoms appointment to work with the RAF Wireless Operators who were behind enemy lines in remote parts of

Burma, attached to the Army on Chindit operations.
However, because of the greater than expected 'casualty rate' through sickness and infirmity I was now to join 16th Infantry Brigade, Column 21, under Col. B.E. Ferguson, subsequently Brigadier and Lord Ballantrae. The move was immediate, with no further training. So down to the Quartermaster's store to be kitted out. Full pack (webbing), jungle green outfit, bush hat (Australian type), boots, studded, spare socks, vests, underpants, water bottle with well fitting wet cork, small pack with knife, fork, spoon, tin mug, mess tin, tooth brush, razor, soap and mepacrine tablets (anti malarial) and water purifying tablets (Chlorine).

That lot together with seven days supply of 'K' rations, a .303 rifle with twenty rounds of ammunition, two seven second hand grenades to destroy the radio equipment if necessary, and a jungle knife. The whole lot weighed 70lbs. You also had to take your turn on the Bren. gun. One ground sheet, one blanket wrapped round the main pack completed the list. No ranks to be worn and you were expected to help with any tasks besides your own.

I was then transported to Sylhet where I boarded a Dakota aircraft and flown into Aberdeen Airstrip where both 21 and 22 columns of the Second Battalion of the Queen's Regiment were getting ready for operations behind the enemy lines down towards Indawgyi Lake. Having made contact with the members responsible for the communications for the column, off we go on our first jungle march.

Was it tough? Blistered shoulders and blistered heels, I was unaccustomed to this routine. Two hours walking non-stop, fifteen minutes rest if you were lucky, because I had to help to unload the mules and then reload them.

I was not suitably trained for this type of exercise. The M.O. sprinkled sulphonamide powders on the blisters after cutting away the wrinkled upper surface skin. The hardship, grin and bear it. I remember the added responsibility of communication with base for supply drops and aircraft support when in difficulty, much more than when I was flying. Failure represented disaster. After a couple of weeks, I was appraised of the impending operation concerning the attack on the airfield at Indawgyi Lake and that some 'forced route marching' was necessary. Our speed of progress was greatly dependant upon the pack-mules pace with their loads, thus we trudged along jungle paths, sweating profusely, and sometimes having to clear the overgrown tracks with our 'pangas'. Then it came - the first real obstacle to be overcome was the crossing of the railway, river and road at night.

Sgt. Brown, Tiffy Harris (muleteer) and myself, set about checking the loads on the mules, using blankets to muffle the sounds from the creaking mules pack, then adjusting our own 70lbs packs for secure and tight fitting. At 21.30 hours, a slight breeze had sprung up and the clouds were scudding across the moon, causing constant changes in light and shadow. Nerves were jingling, because a similar crossing on the previous expedition, had nearly ended in disaster and with several casualties. At last the railway came into sight and I was told to get across as quickly as possible with 'Taxi' leading the other two mules and Sgt. Brown behind. I had just crossed the railway when 'Taxi' decided to amble, sniffing at some bamboo shoots and I was passed by the other mules in our section. Cursing and swearing under my breath (total silence was in order), I tried to catch up but 'Taxi' continued at a steady gait. The same performance recurred crossing the river, fortunately shallow before the monsoon rains, and the road.

Another couple of miles into the thicker jungle to the selected bivouac area and we were able to unload the mules. The manoeuvre was completed without incident, but I had to set up the radio equipment and transmit four messages back to base at Sylhet.

Some ten minutes elapsed before I could pick up Headquarters call-sign through the static, return the Tx to the Rx frequency and get the messages off. After acknowledging receipt, I was told to close down and open up again in the early morning for the replies. I then opened my 'K' ration pack, ate some cold spam and dried biscuits and a drink of water from the water bottle. Fires were not allowed, so no brew up. I then packed up the radio equipment ready for the morning hike. (We never stopped in a bivouac area for any length of time). I then made sure that 'Taxi' had been watered and fed and then got my head down for a couple of hours.

This was the general pattern throughout my sojourn with the Chindits. After a few more weeks trudging along jungle trails with 'Taxi' in tow, we eventually returned to Aberdeen Airstrip from where we were flown to Imphal with the mules.

The first actions were to get rid of our jungle clothing, bathe in hot water with Lifebouy soap and re-clothe in fresh Army Issue K.D. Bush hats were retained as souvenirs and the Chindit badge was press studded to the right arm.

The Catering Officer (?) had arranged a hot meal of bacon, eggs, beans, tinned tomatoes, sausages, and fried bread with strong sweet tea to wash it down.

The resultant mixture was in most cases spewed up shortly

afterwards because our digestive systems could not cope after living off the American 'K' rations. It was necessary to have our beards shaved off and our hair trimmed, before proceeding to Bangalore for two weeks convalescence, re-kitting in appropriate uniform, inoculated after a medical inspection and to receive our back pay before proceeding on a well earned leave.

I had said my farewells to the chaps in our platoon and to 'Taxi', who was being sent back to the foothills of Northern India to live out his life in comparative comfort.

At least that was what I was told and I hoped it was true.

Canonbie — Bill Clapperton.

Warrant officer Matthew Cochrane, D. F. M.
(Wireless Operator/Air Gunner)

Matthew Cochrane was born on 22nd February 1921, at Cairnmill, Thornhill, Dumfriesshire. He was educated at Lockerbie Secondary School and the De Bear Commercial College, Dumfries.

After leaving college he became an assistant farmer, but volunteered for air crew duties in the RAF at the age of twenty, enlisting in Glasgow on 20th March 1941.

After enlistment and medical examination for aircrew duties, Matthew was sent to the Signals Recruit Centre at Blackpool and from there to Signal Training School at Jurby, I.O.M., he completed his signals and gunnery training at Madely and the Air Gunnery School at Barrow-in Furness where he qualified for his Sergeants Stripes.

Below he gives an account of his further progress through Operational Training where he joined his first crew who were Australians, and with whom he joined his first squadron No.446 at Leconfield in Yorkshire; the last squadron to operate in Wellingtons before being re-equipped with Halifax bombers.

In all Matthew trained and operated in eleven different types of aircraft. He completed his war service in Transport Command, being finally demobilised from RAF Oakington, near Cambridge on 13th June 1946. Resuming civilian employment as an agricultural sales representative; Matthew is married and they have one son. His hobbies are curling, walking, and restoring antique clocks.

Wartime Reminiscence.

There are always certain incidents that stay in the minds of servicemen, some funny, some serious and some unbelievable.

My first experience in the air was at A.O.S. Jurby in the Isle of Man. About ten raw newly trained wireless operators were detailed to fly with navigators who were also under training. We were at the time awaiting a refresher course. We were expected to accompany the u/t navigators during their cross-country exercises, just in case their navigational skills were not sufficient to get them back to base. I might add that it was a case of the blind leading the blind for the u/t wireless operators were as green as they were, and in many cases - more so.

The radio sets were antiques from the 1930 era, and also there was a dire shortage of experienced radio mechanics to service these antiques;

the 'gen' men of radio mechanics were no doubt servicing the equipment of operational Bomber Command squadrons at that time.

Most of the equipment on training stations, including the aircraft, was war-weary and this occasionally led to dire consequences, such as ditching in the Irish Sea. Eventually the wireless and gunnery refresher courses arrived which entailed flying in Defiants, and firing at targets towed by, I think, the Hawker Henley, and some of the target towing pilots would have been much safer in the Battle of Britain.

On completion of our gunnery course we wireless operators were promoted to Sergeant, which was a great step forward, and we were dispatched to 27 O.T.U. Lichfield, where we were to crew up with a group of Australians. This is how I met my first crew.

After various lectures, drills and cross-country exercises, we as a crew, were detailed to show our competence by delivering a load of propaganda leaflets to Lille in Northern France. While we were over there we were chased by an ME 109. However, the cloud was our refuge and after some deliberation between the pilot and navigator we then tangled with the barrage balloons we reckoned were guarding the approaches to Southampton. I might add that the balloons were more frightening than the German fighter. We eventually landed at the first convenient airfield, which turned out to be Harwell in Oxfordshire. The result of this episode was that the navigator was removed from our crew. This left us three, pilot, wireless operator and tail gunner.

The Skipper and myself were allocated the task of screening new crews for three months, until one of our training crews was involved in a mid-air collision in which their pilot was killed, the result of this was that we were allocated the navigator and bomb aimer whose lives had been saved by parachute.

During our spell as screened instructors I had to accompany the duty pilot on air test flights etc., and on one occasion the duty pilot, a big jolly Australian called Pete Hallet, cornered me to do an air test with him. Pete had the reputation of being a bit of a barnstormer and instead of taxiing aircraft round the perimeter he more or less flew them to the dispersal. We were in a Wellington, and Pete threw the 'plane around doing things that any normal pilot would not do. We were about 10,000 feet when he said to me "Now Jock I'll show you something that you have never seen before." I replied "No Pete, let's have none of the funny tricks". He then switched off the port engine and feathered the prop, and as it slowly windmilled to a stop, the bold Pete put his hand out of the window and calmly shook hands with the prop - all very impressive.

I was sorry to learn sometime later that he and his crew had paid the supreme sacrifice while he was on his second tour. He was well liked and very popular.

Next stage in our career we were posted to 466 Australian Squadron at Leconfield. This was to be the last Wellington Squadron on operations, and after several mine laying operations and one or two bombing operations we were converted to Halifaxes.

During our stay at Leconfield with 466 Squadron the story got around that an old lady in Beverley wrote to the Station Commander asking him to stop his aircrews changing gear over her house as they were coming in to land. I will not vouch for the truth of this story but it sounds possible.

On one operation, heading for Stuttgart on a moonless night, but a very starry one, when suddenly our pilot, Flying Officer 'Bluey' Osmond, came on the intercom to the gunners and said "How about a shot at an ME 110?", and sure enough, about 200 feet above and in front of us was an ME 110 flying along and minding his own business.

The gunners were very enthusiastic and it was decided that instead of backing off, as one would normally have done, they, would, and I quote "Give the b------ a fright". The Skipper advanced his speed,; we were ahead of the ME 110, but still below by about 200 feet, and when both gunners agreed that he was a sitting duck they opened fire. He dived down behind us with smoke pouring from his port engine, but we did not see him hit the ground or catch fire. After bombing Stuttgart and returning to base we were credited with a probable kill.

After thirteen operations at Leconfield our pilot, "Bluey" Osmond, gathered us together and informed us that we had volunteered to go on Path Finder Force. We, the crew, told him that it was only silly b------s that volunteered to PFF, and he replied that the description suited us , and so we joined No.35 Squadron at Graveley in Huntingdonshire, where we converted on to Lancasters.

One of the tasks for certain PFF crews was that of Master Bomber, or Deputy Master Bomber, and this entailed circling the target during the entire attack while advising the main bomber force which target indicators to aim at. Normally, Pathfinder crews carried a half load of markers and half load of bombs - on the first run-in the markers were dropped, followed by a second run to drop the HE's.

We completed two tours with Flt/Lt. Osmond, DFC., but the Flight Engineer and the Mid-Upper Gunner had still about thirteen operations to complete their tour, and Bluey Osmond volunteered to see these two chaps through, and on his 91st operation, they were shot down by a night fighter with upward firing guns. All the crew, except the Mid-Upper Gunner, escaped by parachute, but he had been killed in the attack. Bluey and the remainder of his crew had a spell in a P.O.W. camp.

At the finish of my bombing tours, I asked to be sent to Transport Command. It was not quite so nerve wracking as the Bomber Force, and one had the advantage of seeing the world at tax-payers expense.

Stationed at Stoney Cross in the New Forest area with No.242 Squadron and flying converted Stirlings, we flew troops and aircraft spares to India via Tripoli, Egypt, Palestine and Iraq, landing at Karachi and then on to Calcutta, Palam, Allahabad and Poona. Occasionally we landed at Malta and Sardinia. We did one trip to the Azores Islands and landed at Lagens, which at that time was an American base. These American had never seen a Stirling and they were very impressed. We stayed at Lagens for two days, and the Yanks treated us like Royalty.

I had a very high regard for the American flyers - they had what one would describe as a really tough time during their daylight raids over Europe and whilst some used to treat these boys as trigger happy they often had good reason to be.

On a flight from Karachi to Madras we landed at Poona for re-fuelling, and having a few hours to kill before take-off the crew decided to visit the town of Poona. On return to the airfield we were greeted with the news that our aircraft had been damaged by a whirlwind which had picked up a smaller aircraft and thrown it up against the Stirling, causing damage to the extent that we were obliged to stay at Poona for three weeks awaiting spares to repair the Stirling.

During our stay in Poona the Japanese war ceased, and our crew were invited to the celebrations laid on by our Air Force hosts and others. A great time was had by all.

Later on our return to the U.K. we were converted to York transport aircraft and they were much more comfortable than the Stirlings, both for the crew and the passengers.

I was finally de-mobbed at Uxbridge after 5½years in the RAF, fitted out with a civvy suit and travel vouchers and thrust into the wide world to face the facts of life.

It was with mixed feelings that I left the Royal Air Force, however, they did not need me any longer, so ended a time of my life which I have never regretted, but I was one of the lucky ones.

Lockerbie M. Cochrane

Flight Lieutenant George Purslow, D.F.C.
(Wireless Operator/Air Gunner)

George Purslow (Lockerbie) was a WOP/AG with 63, 52 and 12 Squadrons. His hobbies are golf, fishing and gardening. He is a retired headmaster. Among his many operations he sends this episode which is entitled....

A Bridge too High
A Survivor's Story.

The retired headmaster was puzzled as he looked through the glass of his living room window....spread over the grassy surface of the hill away to his right, and overlooking his town, were many white objects. "What could they be?" he asked himself. The date was 22nd December 1988; the town was Lockerbie, a name now known throughout the world, for all the most wrong and tragic reasons.

The puzzled viewer was George Purslow, a well known member of our Branch, for on that fateful day he realised that the white objects he was viewing were shrouds. They were covering the corpses of the victims of one of the most infamous acts of terrorism in aviation history - the cold blooded manic destruction of the Jumbo Jet of Pan-Am Airlines bearing the Flight Tag 103, bound for the U.S.A. It had been cruelly blasted out of the sky by a terrorist's bomb on the night of 21st December, wreaking death and destruction, not only to the plane's crew and passengers, but also to equally innocent residents of this wee Scottish Borders town. By this bloody act terrorists screamed to the world, "We just don't care, we seek revenge."

George raised his eyes to the hill's skyline, silhouetted there he could see men carrying stretchers upon which lay gruesome burdens. A macabre spectacle, forever etched on his mind.

Then a kaleidoscopic picture from the past swirled in his brain - reaching back 47 years, when he was involved in a WWII landing, very unintentional, a crash to be exact. He survived, unlike three of his fellow companions in that Mark II Wellington Bomber, all those years ago. Young people, just like so many in that Flight 103 Jumbo.

George tells the story, it is very graphic, because he tells it quietly, and with disarming modesty.

A native of Innerleithen, near Peebles, he left his work in a local mill and volunteered for the RAF. This was in 1938 and he was accepted for training as a WOP/AG. Came the war he found himself with No.12 Sqdn, on duty in France, flying Fairy Battles, slow, cumbersome aircraft, which were very much at the mercy of the Luftwaffe fighters. George, quite understandably, recalls with pride that two fliers with his Squadron, F/O Garland and Sgt. 'Dolly' Gray were the RAF's first V.C.'s of the war.

George survived his combat activities in France with the Advanced Air Strike Force, and was flown back to the U.K. He says he has a most unusual entry in his log nook. It reads "Previous log book lost during the evacuation from France, 1940." His first log book had been with his kit, with ground crew, and was never recovered.

In his flying career he had come up through the ranks - LAC....to Flight Lieutenant. He had returned to the U.K. as an LAC, after nine months serving in France, and eventually converted to Wellingtons, still as a WOP/AG.

It was on an operation out of Binbrook in Lincolnshire, to Cologne on the night of the 16th August 1941, and when over that city his aircraft 'N' Nellie hit trouble. The port engine was out of action by enemy fire, and the Canadian Pilot, Norman McVeigh, succeeded in nursing his damaged aircraft away from Germany and the Low Countries, and out and over the North Sea. And it was over the drink that George hit his Morse Key and started sending those dramatic three 'dits' , three 'dahs' and another three 'dits'. The S.O.S. had been received O.K. and a course was plotted for a 'drome near to Briston, in Norfolk. All the time the pilot was struggling to maintain height but it appeared to becoming a losing battle, the Wimpey slowly dropped lower and lower....George recalls how they flew just above roof top height over Norwich, slicing through telephone wires and power cables, and trying to avoid church steeples, and still the plane was losing height. The skipper spotted a railway line and began following it, the semi-masked signal lights were faintly visible and searchlights were swinging and pointing to their landing destination. But they were destined never to make it, in spite of being so close.

'N' Nellie struck a low railway bridge, "We just didn't have the strength to get over it." George recalls. "What none of us knew was that we still had our 2000lb bomb aboard - it had hung up due to an electrical fault. "If it hadn't been for that I think we could have made it".

In the crash three members of the crew were killed, Second Pilot, observer and Front Gunner. George suffered severe concussion and a leg injury, he still suffers to this day from a thrombotic condition as a result, but with a wry grimace, says it only occasionally keeps him off the golf course. His Canadian Pilot had both legs broken, and he and George spent many months in hospital. The other survivor was the Rear Gunner, but he was severely burned.

A former LAC, Ken Stacey, from Falmouth, spent two years trying to trace the survivors, and he succeeded. The three men came together in September 1987, meeting again for the first time for 45 years.

Norman McVeigh, the Pilot , journeyed from his Canadian home in Vancouver. - "It was a very emotional meeting", says George.

Our picture shows George, with his skipper, on the bridge into which their Wellington crashed on that night so long ago. George is pointing to the area where the damaged plane, and the unexploded bomb, ended up in the field on his left.

The airmen killed aboard 'N' Nellie are commemorated by a plaque in Briston Parish Church, placed there by villagers to honour their memories.

George completed 50 operations during his flying tours, latterly in Lancasters, and after a post war career in teaching he retired from his position of Headmaster at Eaglesfield School, Dumfriesshire.

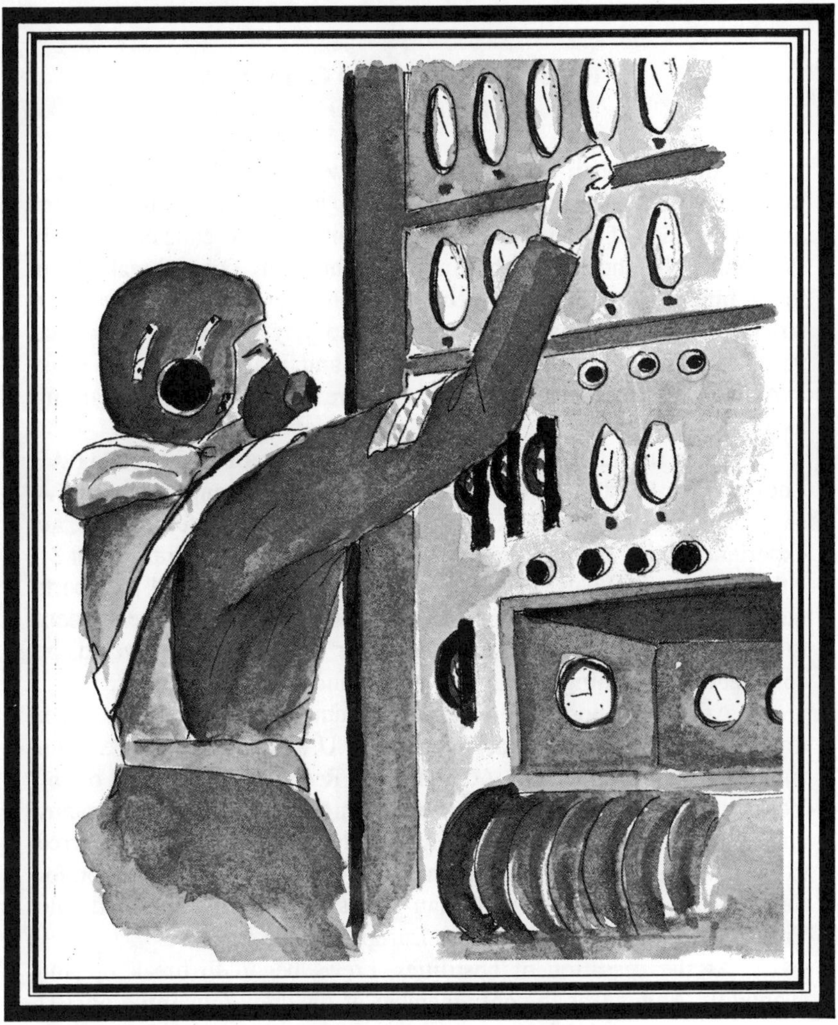

The Engineers' Boost

Flight Sergeant Angus Cobban. (Flight Engineer)

Angus Cobban was born in Glasgow in August 1911 before his family, for health reasons, moved away from industry to the Fort William area at the head of Loch Linnhe. Angus completed his education at Fort William High School before becoming a technician. The outbreak of war found him employed in armaments as a gun fitter and as such was in a strictly reserved occupation. Determined to play a more active role he volunteered for aircrew duties in the R.A.F. and finally managed to enlist at A.C.R.C. London in February 1944, where he was selected for training as a flight engineer.

From Initial Training at Newquay in Cornwall he moved to RAF Locking near Weston-Super-Mare, where training on engines began. A short visit to the E.F.T.S. at Kidlington, Oxford allowed a few hours of air experience flying before joining the School of Technical Training at St. Athan in South Wales. Angus found both the training and the sports facilities at St. Athan very much to his taste, until an unfortunate accident in the gymnasium put him in hospital for six weeks. Recovered, he completed his training gaining his brevet and sergeant's stripes.

Angus was posted into Bomber Command and joined a crew for training on Halifax bombers at No.1658 H.C.U. at Riccal near York. After training his crew joined No.166 Squadron, R.A.A.F., at Driffield on the Yorkshire Wolds from where they flew one night operation over Germany and two daylight raids after which his purely RAF crew were transferred to No.102 Squadron at Pocklington, south-east of York. The reason for this move was that the Australian crews were being absorbed into Transport Command as the war in Europe drew to its close.

At the cessation of hostilities, crews began to break up and eventually Angus was the only member of his crew remaining on 102 Squadron. As a stand-by crew member he flew on several flights over Germany when ground crew and others were allowed on the flights to see the effects of the bombing offensive. During that period he had one narrow escape; intending to fly as flight engineer on an air-test flight the composition of the crew was changed at the last minute and Angus did not fly. Regrettably the aircraft crashed and most of the crew were killed.

In September 1945 Angus was posted to RAF Ibsley in Hampshire where experiments were being carried out in the technique of recovering gliders by air-pick-up from the ground. Wartime experience showed that gliders were the most practical means of air transporting troops into action in sufficient concentration to be effective. The 'pick-up' technique was designed to rescue both troops and glider from capture by the enemy once their objective was achieved - perhaps behind the enemy lines.

Dakota aircraft fitted with a hydraulic arm and winch were used in these experiments. Angus flew as 'winch man', a critical role since to bring the glider from stationary to flying speed could only be achieved by careful application of the winch brake. The grounded glider had a nylon tow-rope attached which was suspended in a loop between two eighteen-foot poles; the pilot of the Dakota had to fly low at full power and capture the loop with the hook of the aircraft's tow-rope at the end of the hydraulic arm - a manoeuvre also calling for skill and judgement. For training purposes, when at a safe height, the pilot of the glider would release the tow in preparation for landing again at Ibsley. The rope was then wound in by the Winch man in the Dakota.

After the course at Ibsley, Angus was sent home on embarkation leave before being flown out to Singapore in November 1945. The route out involved numerous stages and the passengers were quite relieved to arrive finally at their destination. Once in the Far East Angus served on both No.48 and 215 Squadrons flying Dakotas on transport operations. He flew on numerous sorties delivering stores to many places including a long flight to Hong Kong in January 1946. Two assignments are remembered with interest. Firstly a long flight taking Lady Mountbatten and senior female staff officers to visit hospitals in Sumatra and Java. Before reaching Djakarta in Java, the aircraft developed engine trouble but they landed safely. All next day Angus and their corporal engine fitter worked on their aircraft, transferring spares from another Dakota grounded on the airfield, and they were able to continue their journey on the following day. Having finally brought their party safely back to Singapore they were warmly thanked by Lady Mountbatten for all the work they had done on the flight. A second flight Angus remembers was to Medan in Sumatra to pick up a Senior Japanese officer who was to appear before the War Trials Commission in Singapore. He was driven under escort to the aircraft in a big car and got a great send-off from his fellow officers.

Angus left his squadron at the end of May 1946 and in June joined a ship for the U.K., arriving at Southampton on 14th July. Demobilised shortly afterwards he looks back on his period with the R.A.F. with some nostalgia for an experience he enjoyed. Had he not already been a married man with a young son he might well have elected to remain in the Service.

Flight Sergeant Eric Till
(Flight Engineer)

Born in Annan, Dumfriesshire in 1923, Eric Till was the son of a Regimental Sergeant Major in a Cavalry Regiment. His boyhood followed the established pattern common to all service families and at the age of two and a half years they moved to India, first to Rawalpindi and then to Peshawar on the North-West Frontier. Here young Eric enjoyed life with much to interest a child going on around him; soldiers and farriers constantly busy with horses, troopers exercising, gymkhanas, polo and cricket matches, imbuing in Eric a love of sport which he still retains. As a birthday gift he was given a donkey with which he had many hours of fun apart from its ingrained habit of putting him off over its head each time they returned to the stable court-yard. Fortunately children fall light and injury to pride was the only result.

Reaching school age he started school at the very strict garrison school which he attended for about a year before his family were posted to Egypt. Eric well remembers the passage through the Suez Canal, the heat, and the dust and the smells of the Canal Zone. Staying for a year near Alexandria. Eric was able to visit the Sphinx and the Pyramids a number of times before they returned to England, to Aldershot, where his father was soon to be discharged from the army after twenty-two years service.

Returning to Scotland the family stayed in Eastriggs for two years before settling in Gretna where Eric attended the township school. Happily for him the school was highly oriented to sports and Eric not only enjoyed football but got into his favourite game, cricket. The family later moved back to Annan and Eric completed his education at Annan Academy, where he again played in the school's cricket and football teams. He remembers hitting a glorious six straight through the window of the English classroom! Much of his time away from school was spent on the golf course or performing as a drummer in the local pipe band.

On leaving school Eric entered engineering as an apprentice fitter in 1938. The early years of the war found him serving in the Home Guard and training in the A.T.C. When old enough to serve he volunteered to enter the Royal Navy to serve on motor torpedo boats. A period of nine months silence followed which he eventually broke by re-visiting the Naval Centre in Dumfries to ask why he had not been called for service. He was told that he was in a reserved occupation since his firm were training Army fitters in their workshops. Disappointed but undaunted he promptly crossed the road and volunteered for aircrew duties in the RoyalAir Force.

Whilst awaiting the results of this latter application he took the precaution of brushing up on maths with the help of a retired maths teacher. When the time came for him to be assessed in Edinburgh as to his suitability for flying duties he was completely successful. In due time Eric was enlisted at A.C.R.C.A in London and selected for training as a Flight Engineer. After going through the usual mill for kitting up, inoculations and so forth his intake was sent to RAF Cirencester for air experience flying in Oxfords and Ansons to assess their suitability for further training - not everyone can perform well in the air.

Initial Training at No.8 I.T.W. Newquay followed during the winter of 1943/44; very cold with even the inshore sea frozen, Eric has vivid memories of his flight having the 'honour' (their Corporal's word) of helping to launch the life boat on 'calls out' in bitter conditions. Physical training on the golf course was also a daunting experience.

Eric spent the following three months at RAF Locking near Weston-Super-Mare for technical training - flight theory, engines, electrics, hydraulics, more maths, aircraft recognition and first-aid. Having passed the course Eric then moved to the School of Engineering at St. Athan in South Wales for "Type Technical Training", in his case Halifax bombers. Four months of intense study and hard work followed until every detail of the aircraft had been mastered; two days of final exams followed, then, finally, the passing out parade when the Flight Engineer's Brevet and Sergeant's Stripes were awarded.

Going home from St. Athan on seven days well earned leave, an incident occurred on Cardiff Railway Station which sticks in Eric's mind. Walking along the platform with two other newly promoted N.C.O.'s from Scotland they heard a Service Policeman call out 'Sergeants'. It took another three or four steps before it dawned on them that the S.P. was addressing THEM.

After leave Eric was posted to No.1665 H.C.U. at Tilstock in Shropshire to join a crew. Once again the 'waiting game' came into play and Eric found himself helping to section a Rolls Royce Merlin engine to be used in the training school which was being established at Tilstock. After a few weeks Eric finally joined the crew which was to stay together throughout their first squadron tour. At Tilstock, flying Halifaxes the crew settled in well to working together in the air. The period was not without incident and Eric recalls three burst tyres on landings and one occasion when the undercarriage collapsed and the aircraft was a write off. On another occasion, when flying with a different crew as second engineer there was again an undercarriage failure and Eric got badly flung about. Feeling sticky fluid running down his leg he imagined that he must have injured his leg, however when stripping off his flying suit he discovered to his relief that the source of the fluid was two well-flattened oranges. He had to endure a good deal of laughter from the rest of the crew.

After H.C.U. the crew spent two weeks at RAF Matching in Essex where they learned the technique of glider towing before joining No. 298 Squadron at Tarrant Rushton in Dorset. Tarrant Rushton was a No.38 Group station; a Group with special responsibility for army co-operation and transport. Squadron training continued, dropping paratroops, supplies, jeeps and towing gliders. The gliders were Horsas and Hamilcars, the latter capable of carrying light tanks.

(A vivid account of mass take-offs of towed gliders is given elsewhere in this volume by Donald Whyte, rear gunner in Eric Till's crew. Ed.)

Eric's crew were quickly involved in 'Special operations', dropping supplies and equipment to underground resistance fighters. Their first sortie was to Holland where the dropping zone could be identified as a field beside a small wood - very precise navigation needed. On arrival over the D.Z. they received no response to their coded signal and stood off to the south for about 30 minutes. Returning to the D.Z. they again evoked no response so had no alternative but to return to Tarrant Rushton with their load still aboard. They later learned that due to enemy activity in the area the resistance fighters had been unable to reach the zone.

Similar operations continued until V.E. Day, supplies etc. being dropped to most occupied countries. For the five days immediately following V.E. Day the Squadron was actively engaged in ferrying the airborne division of the K.O.S.B. to Norway after which trips were flown to Brussels to repatriate freed prisoners of war. Eric then went on leave for a week.

On returning to Tarrant Rushton Eric joined a fresh crew flying Halifaxes Mk.VII. On the 18th July 1945 they took off for India for operations against the Japanese. They staged through Castle Benito, North Africa, Lydda in Palestine and Shaibah in 'The Gulf', arriving at Mauripur, Karachi, on 21st July. After a stay of only four days at Karachi they moved to their main base, RAF Raipur, in the Central Provinces of India. Eric aptly describes Raiphur as being 'out in the middle of nowhere' and remembers that the beer supply was very poor except when augmented from flights to other stations.

Squadron training continued from Raiphur which enabled Eric's crew to visit many other RAF stations in India. He lists, among others, Peshawar, Rawalpindi, Dum Dum, Lucknow and Allahabad.

V.J. Day was celebrated in style with not a few sore heads as a result. One week later Eric took off to fly over 'The hump' into China, landing at Kumning - the first Halifax to do so. The return flight was made carrying eight prisoners of war now released from Japanese hands. In all, Eric made five trips to Kumning, the later trips to ferry in stores of food and fuel. On the last occasion it had been the intention to fly on from Kumning to Chung-King in the Province of Szechwan, but the flight had to be aborted due to bad weather and a failed engine.

Returning to Raiphur they were moved to a forward base at Meiktila in Burma from where they were employed dropping rice to the hill people of Burma. (Again, Donald Whyte has supplied details of this task. Ed.)

The next event of interest was to take part in a test flight to Australia, but which was called off after Eric's crew had flown the first leg to Colombo, in then, Ceylon. Their next move was to the more pleasing climes of Baroda where they spent a happy four months before being returned to the U.K. in a York aircraft staging at Habbanyia in Iraq and Luqa in Malta, where they had a great time visiting Valletta. Eric had been posted to join No.47 squadron at Fairford in Gloucestershire, but found on arrival that the expected new Hermes aircraft had not yet arrived. A short wait was filled in flying sporadically as a relief crew member until his demobilisation.

On his return to civilian life Eric initially returned to his previous employment, compensating for the lack of further flying by speeding around on a B.S.A. motor cycle. Marrying in 1949 he moved to Thornhill, employed in the retail milk business. Whilst at Thornhill he joined the Royal Observer Corps which enabled him to retain contact with the RAF. After two years he moved to Lochmaben and took employment at the in embryo Nuclear Power Station at Chapelcross near Annan, which was being constructed on the site of a disused wartime airfield and from which he remembers seeing Lysanders, Hurricanes and Wellingtons flying. Eric found his new employment a challenge and through being in 'on the ground floor' plenty of opportunities for promotion. He took full advantage and remained at Chapelcross for the next thirty years.

Eric has maintained a wide variety of interests. For twenty-three years he had very happy times with No.1153 Squadron (Dumfries), Air Training Corps, of which he was Squadron Commander on retiring from the A.T.C. in 1973. He still retains a connection through the Civilian Committee. A keen caravanner he is a member of the Committee of the Scottish Caravan Club Centre for Dumfries and Galloway. He has spent time as the Vice-Chairman of the Lochmaben Community Council and is a member of the Chapelcross Fellowship for the retired workpeople. Last, but by no means least he is an active member of the Aircrew Association, acting as Supply Officer to our local branch.

Eric looks back on his service in the Royal Air Force as a very happy and worthwhile experience; the time spent abroad a satisfying period enabling him to see and visit many places which might otherwise be only names in an atlas. He feels that the service training and discipline have been a great help in his subsequent civilian life. His interest and nostalgia are amply demonstrated by his being a member of the R.A.F.V.R. (T Branch) for twenty-three years.

By using their caravan on numerous trips stretching from Inverness to Cornwall, Eric and his wife succeeded in renewing contact with all his first crews members. A reunion was arranged forty-seven years after leaving H.C.U. and they all met again at Tilstock in Shropshire. An enjoyable time was had by all and the ladies played the game, giving the men plenty of time to visit their old haunts.

Flt.Lt. Reginald Eastoe, R.A.F.
(Flight Engineer)

For the following account of Reg. Eastoe's career in the Royal Air Force we are indebted to his widow, Mrs. Barbarba Eastoe, resident in Dowding House, Moffat in Dumfriesshire.

Reg was born at Barton on Humber on 13 December 1912 and educated in Scunthorpe, Lincolnshire. Leaving Cole Street Grammar School in 1928 he obtained employment in the offices of Appleby Frodingham steel works. A bachelor of mature years he volunteered for air crew duties in the RAF early in 1943. Being in a reserved occupation he was a volunteer in every sense of the word. After enlistment he went through the usual mill of A.C.R.C. and I.T.W. before training as a Flight Engineer at No.4 School of Technical Training at St. Athan in South Wales. From thence he went to No.1652 Heavy Conversion Unit at Marston Moor in Yorkshire, to train on Halifax bombers. Barbara reveals that Reg was very reticent about his wartime experiences but since his death in December 1990 she has pieced together a vivid account of his tour of operations.

Barbara does outstanding work in fund raising for the A.C.A. and Service charities; we are honoured to have her as an associate member of our Branch. Let her now take up Reg's story from H.C.U. in her own words.

A New Lease of Life

"Here he met up with the "boys" who would eventually form a crew and fortunately they all remained together for most of the "ops" that were to follow. The boys all averaged 19 years of age but Reg was ten years their senior. They looked on him as a father figure and always relied on his advice. This was confirmed by one of the "boys" whom Reg had been out of touch with for forty five years and met again in 1990. This "boy" who was by then a retired man told me "Reg was a life saver to all of us, in times of stress he kept our courage high, and helped us immensely".

In early August 1944 they all went to their first operational base Pocklington, Yorkshire, No. 102 (Ceylon) Squadron, flying Halifax bombers.

Looking at Reg's log book I note that on the 15th August 1944 the aircraft on a raid over Eindhoven was damaged by flak. Two days later the target was Sterkrade but when they reached the Dutch coast the port outer engine was on fire and they had to return to base. It must have been an unlucky period for the crew because one week later on a raid on Brest they made two bombing runs because of cloud. There was severe damage to the aircraft and it also mentioned that they had to orbit the target for five minutes.

After this there were other minor mishaps including on the twelfth of September on a raid on Munster marshalling yards, the entire bomb load was hung up and had to be jettisoned into the sea. On the fourteenth of October operations took them to Duisburg and they had to be diverted to North Creak, where I believe they had a great time with the Americans. Fortunately Reg got safely home to base and then made his way to Scunthorpe with all the members of the crew, because he would be leaving his bachelor status on the eighteenth of October, 1944, the date we were to be married and the wireless operator, an Australian was to be Reg's best man. The remainder of the crew were guests. After a lovely wartime wedding, we went to Torquay for our honeymoon.

Reg returned to Pocklington at the beginning of November, and the crew continued with their tour of operations. These were more or less without incident until 26th of December when the target was St. Vith. the fuselage bomb load was hung up and after seven runs on the target they were able to release all of the bombs manually.

Nothing really significant happened after this until the 5th of January 1945 target Hanover. Here the aircraft was attacked by a JU88 but the attack was successfully evaded and then on the 16th January, although a ME 109 was sighted, there was no attack. The last raid on the 22nd January was on Gelsenkirchen without incident.

Reg decided to stay on in the RAF when the war ended, and was posted to 66 MU Cuckney, Notts. 40 Group, and then from there to Initial Training, Equipment Branch, Bicester, after which he returned to Cuckney.

In July 1946 our daughter Gillian was born and when she was three months old Reg was posted with the British Commonwealth Occupation Force (BCAIRD) to Iwakuni, Japan. I was due to join him in nine months time along with the baby. However everything happened to him in Japan.

1. The Officers' Mess and sleeping quarters caught fire and was burnt to the ground during the early hours of the morning. He and the rest of the officers lost everything they possessed apart from their sleeping gear which they escaped in. Two of Reg's comrades perished the fire.

2. They had an earthquake and here I am able to tell you of Reg's

experience, from the letter which he sent home, and I quote:

"I was already awake when the tremors first commenced, I assumed the reason being, that a slight initial tremor had startled me into wakefulness. The first sensations were as if a rough breeze was beginning to blow, then in a very few seconds, the earth began to quiver, and there was a rumbling sound, and there were successive tremors, slight at first, but growing in intensity, with the continuous accompanying dull rumbling, not unlike distant thunder getting nearer and nearer.

The Mess building which is constructed solely of timber was by this time shaking, as if by concussions caused by bombing. I was startled into a state of feverish activity, as I knew that it could not be anything else but an earthquake. I scrambled out of bed and hastily slipped on my dressing gown and slippers, and rushed out into the corridor. Probably 30 seconds had elapsed, no more, but the whole building was rocking and swaying, and the tremors were at their utmost violence. I rushed downstairs, my first thought being to get away from the building, which I thought could not possibly remain intact any longer. Consistent with the rumbling noise and movement of the building there were electrical flashes of vivid brilliance and colouring, caused by the disruption and severing of electrical cables from the Grid systems and Power Stations, of which there are quite a number in this part of Japan. Our own electric supply had been cut off at the mains in the initial stages of the tremors, thus we all scrambled about in the darkness. My room is on the upper floor of the Mess, which has the two floors - ground floor and upper floor.

On arriving outside, the undulating movement of the ground could be plainly discerned and the building I had just vacated was rocking back and forth as if being shaken by some mighty hand.

Before I decided to leave the building, I found myself in somewhat of a dilemma, for, although the building was moving alarmingly it was difficult to know whether one was safer in the building, which, though swaying and creaking noisily, was still holding together, or outside, where there was a terrific dull rumbling din and noise.

Another point to consider was, being one of the first into the corridor, would I cause a wholesale panic by rushing downstairs, as the Mess housed 200 Officers. The tremors lasted for about 3 ½ minutes altogether by which time everyone was outside in open space, shivering in night attire.

It is interesting to relate that everyone acted with commendable self control, there was no signs of panic. The Station Fire Brigade acted quickly and were in a state of preparedness had there been an outbreak of fire.

I am quite convinced that had the building been constructed of brick or masonry. it would have resulted in a major disaster here, because undoubtedly it must have collapsed like a pack of cards and we therefore owe our safety to the wooden building, the main means of construction throughout Japan.

The after effects were ones of amusing and graphic discussions of the experience, and the disruption of the electrical and central heating, thus giving us visions of a cold weekend.''

3. Reg's work took him into Hiroshima, and after being in Japan eight months he developed cancer. After undergoing an operation he was flown home for Radiation treatment at Westminster Hospital, London, so of course my trip to Japan was not to be.

Reg continued his work in the RAF and during the next years he was at Church Lawford, Rugby, then Great Ashfield as Bomb Storage Site Officer. This was followed by a posting to a Satellite Site at Attleborough, Norfolk. He was responsible for Bomb storage and clearance of Bomb dumps on obsolete RAF stations.

In 1949 Reg was posted as Commanding Officer to 59 MU Rhoose, Glam. S. Wales. No.42 Group, Bombs Servicing Unit, and here is a copy of a letter from Air Commodore C. W. Gore, OBE, thanking him for his work there, and I quote:

"My dear Eastoe,

I am taking this opportunity of thanking you, your Officers and all personnel on your Unit for the good work you have put in during 1949 and for the loyal support which you have accorded me.

42 Group has a big task to perform often under difficult and trying conditions, but I am confident that in 1950 we will make even greater headway, and I am proud to know that I can always rely on your support.

I wish you all a very Happy Christmas and the best of Good Luck, Good Health and Prosperity in the New Year.

Your sincerely,

C.W. Gore."

Reg's next posting was to RAF Surface Movements, Isle of Dogs, dealing with shipments of Bombs and Explosives. However in 1950 secondary cancer broke out and after an operation at King Edward VII

Sanatorium, Midhurst, Sussex, it necessitated early retirement and Reg's RAF life was over in 1952.

It was difficult finding work because of Reg's medical problems, but he eventually obtained the job he wanted which was on the Admin. side of Babcock and Wilcox Engineers.

Reg became disabled in the 1960's and after using crutches for a number of years he was confined to a wheelchair. He was always cheerful despite a lot of pain but he always regretted having to leave the RAF.

Reg loved his life in the RAF and the comradeship, so you can imagine how delighted we both were when in October 1988 we were given the opportunity to come and live at Dowding House, for what was to be his last years of life. Here he had the comradeship of other ex-RAF men and when after a little while he joined the A.C.A. at Dumfries it made his life complete.

In a way it was a NEW LEASE OF LIFE hence my title, but this ended with his death on the 17th December 1990."

Moffat — Barbara Eastoe.

Flying Officer George Johnson.
(Flight Engineer)

George Johnson was born in Edinburgh in July 1922. His family later moved to Orkney and George was educated at Kirkwall Grammar School. He volunteered for aircrew duties, but before being enrolled at A.C.R.C. London in May 1943, he had held a variety of jobs, including those of Plate Layer and Tunnel Miner.

Selected for training as a flight engineer he completed his initial training at RAF Torquay before being posted to the School of Engineering at St. Athan in South Wales, where he qualified in April 1944.

As his own story tells, George found himself in a Canadian crew and he completed his active service with No.424 (Tiger) Squadron as part of No.6 (R.C.A.F.) Group, Bomber Command. From his wartime contemporaries he learned of the 'Cranwell Revolt' of which he gives a brief description. Although his knowledge of the event is second-hand, his account is authenticated by a recent review in a Canadian newspaper of the story of No.6 Group by Spencer Dunmore and William Carter, published in Canada and titled "Reap the Whirlwind". (Now available in Britain by "Crecy" Books).

Since demobilisation in 1947, George has followed a variety of occupations including those of Chief Industrial Radiologist and Quality Control Manager. In his own words he has been a 'rolling stone'.

Married and in retirement, he and his wife recently moved from Annan to Galashiels in the Borders, his wife's town of origin. They have no family; George's hobbies are photography and bowls.

Virgin Airman

No. 6 Group (RCAF), Bomber Command. The Cranwell Revolt.

In late 1942, the first Canadian volunteer aircrew arrived at Cranwell to form the nucleus of No.6 Group, Bomber Command. Although this new Group would, predominately, be staffed by Canadians, it was to be administered by the RAF and its personnel subject to RAF discipline and command. Accordingly, RAF non-coms were drafted in to break in these colonials using time-honoured methods - lots of square bashing, route marches, etc. Unfortunately, the colonials did not take kindly to these proposed activities. Drills, route-marches? Hell, they had volunteered for flying duties and not marching. They ignored the orders at the first attempt to take them on a route march, broke up into groups and drifted away.

The RAF, determined that they should toe the line, posted in an RAF Flight Sergeant and a covey of drill Corporals to the base. At the first parade one of the Corporals, betraying an unfortunate lack of judgement, laid hands on a grinning Canadian who he thought was laughing at him, only to be floored by a single punch.

The Canadians then returned to their barracks, removed all the furniture and burned the lot. So began the Cranwell Revolt, which was to have far-reaching results, the first of which was the arrival of an RAF Air Vice Marshall whose remit was to quell the rebellion and discipline the mutineers. Two of these mutineers had, however, been selected by their compatriots to go AWOL to London and they returned with an emissary from the Canadian High Commissioner, Vincent Massey.

Shortly afterwards, in conjunction with the political machinations of the Canadian Prime Minister MacKenzie King, the Air Ministry agreed that No.6 Group would become No.6 (RCAF) Group, and that the Canadians would command the Group and be responsible for its organisation and development. In return the Canadian Government would be financially responsible for all the expenses of its operation.

From this inauspicious beginning the Group swiftly grew until it commanded fifteen Squadrons, all based in Yorkshire, where they are still remembered with affection and respect.

In April 1944, when I qualified as a Flight Engineer, I learned with some surprise and not a little apprehension, that I was being seconded to No.6 Group to fly with these wild colonial boys. Any apprehension I may have felt was soon dissipated when I arrived at the "crewing-up" centre at Topcliffe. They felt no ill-will against RAF personnel - rather the reverse - as their resentment had been directed against what they called "chair-borne wallahs".

Canada trained all her aircrew with the exception of Flight Engineers who had to be obtained from the RAF. Crews requiring a Flight Engineer, plus a slightly larger number of Flight Engineers, were posted into these centres where, for a period of ten days, they could mix together and get to know each other with a view to mutually agreeing the crew make-up.

Fortunately for me and two other Scots in the intake the Canadians still believed the myth that Scots made the best Engineers and, consequently, we were in great demand, being wined and dined by these rich Canadians who had rates of pay four times that of RAF personnel.

Incidentally, the RCAF asked the Air Ministry if they could pay the same rates of pay to the RAF personnel, but this request was turned down, unfortunately.

The crew which I eventually joined had all re-mustered from Wimpeys and had flown over enemy territory while I had never even been airborne.

1666 Heavy Conversion Unit

More Dangerous than Ops...

The least said about this game of Russian Roulette which masqueraded as a Heavy Conversion Course, the better. Flying Halifax I's and II's which were, more or less unserviceable veteran rejects from the front-line Squadrons, powered by clapped-out R.R. Merlins which had a predilection to overheat and burst into flames - sometimes one after the other - was, in my opinion and that of others who survived, more dangerous than Ops.

The casualty statistics of 6 Group. in common with the rest of Bomber Command, make grisly reading. Of every hundred aircrew, 26 survived, 6 were taken prisoner and the remainder perished. One wonders how many of the latter were, needlessly, lost during training at H.C.U.'s. The almost inexhaustible supply of keen young volunteer aircrew made the policy of reserving the new heavy bombers for the front-line Squadrons a practicable proposition but, morally it was indefensible.

No. 424 (TIGER) Squadron

Gardening in France.

On our arrival on 30th May 1944, at Skipton-on-Swale - a satellite of Leeming Bar - we were allocated a brand new Halifax III for type familiarisation and 'circuits and bumps'. Only those with experience of flying in clapped-out Halifax I's and II's at H.C.U. will know the sheer exhilaration we felt as we hurtled down the runway under the thrust of four 1,675 hp. Bristol Hercules Mark XVI engines to soar upwards at over 1,000ft. per min. on cruising boost and not take-off power. We could scarce forbear to cheer.

On 6th June, shortly after the D-Day landing we, along with six other crews from 424 an 433 Squadrons, were called to Briefing. The Briefing Officer, looking more than usually serious, opened his Briefing by saying "You have all been selected specially for this extremely important Operation'' In the short pause that followed we looked at each other in utter bewilderment. We knew we were one of the best crews in Bomber Command, but how did he know? Here we were, a rookie crew, being considered good enough to be mixing with the creme de la creme of 424 and 433 Squadrons. As the briefing progressed we begun to wish that we weren't held in such high regard.

Intelligence reports had indicated that there was to be an attempted break out by the U-boats at present in the submarine pens in Lorient Harbour - there were rich pickings for them to be had in the English Channel where large fleets of supply vessels were engaged in ferrying in supplies for the Allied invasion force.

In an attempt to prevent this we were going ''gardening'' - mine-laying - in the long narrow inlet leading to Lorient Harbour. Each aircraft would be carrying four mines - a mixture of contact, magnetic and acoustic to make mine-sweeping more difficult and dangerous - which, because of their size, would mean that the bomb doors could only be partially closed.

The Briefing Officer then outlined, one by one, all the snags facing us:

(a) There would be a full moon over the target with no haze or cloud cover - not so much a bomber's moon, more a night fighter's moon. (b) We would be the only aircraft flying over France, the only blips moving over the screens of the German early- warning radar stations. There would be no spoof raids or Training Command feints to draw off the night fighters, so they could give us their undivided attention. (c) Because the bomb doors could only be partially closed we must not exceed 140 knots indicated air speed or take any violent evasive action if attacked. To do so would result in the bomb doors being ripped off by the slipstream. (d) We would be within the operational orbit of five night fighter 'dromes. (e) There would be no RAF night fighter cover.

To ensure accurate positioning and adequate dispersal of the mines, each aircraft was allocated different ''Gee'' co-ordinates on which to bomb, When he finished the briefing he said ''Good Luck''. I felt he should have also added ''and Good-bye''.

When we took-off, any secret hopes we may have had that the Met Report was wrong, were dissipated. It was a crisp clear night without cloud cover or haze and the brilliant moon made the runway lights seem almost superfluous.

And so it continued until we were, at low level, approaching the mouth of the inlet. Then disaster struck - the ''Gee'' set failed! Fortunately the navigator and the bomb-aimer had made plans to cover just such a contingency. They had plotted the position of the "Gee" co-ordinates on their maps along with identifiable landmarks on the shores of the inlet adjacent to the release points. The H2S radar had been switched on to assist in the map-reading. the shores of the inlet would show clearly on the screen and the silver ribbon of the inlet in the bright moonlight would make the identification of the release points fairly simple.

Up ahead there was considerable light ack-ack activity particularly over Lorient itself as the defences were alerted to our approach but, as yet, there was no sign of the expected night fighters. As hoped, the visibility was so good that the outline of the coasts were clearly discerned. We were now at our most vulnerable to fighter attack, clearly silhouetted against the bright waters, bomb doors open, flying straight and level, unable to take any evasive action. the seconds ticked by slowly until we heard the welcome "Mines away" and "Bomb doors closed" and we were banking steeply to starboard through the tracer and "flaming onions".

The return flight was as uneventful as the outward flight had been. After landing, we taxied to flight dispersal and I carried out my post-flight checks before dropping through the rear hatch to join the others. To my mortification and the gleeful laughter of the crew, my knees buckled and I collapsed in a heap. With hindsight I feel that this reaction to the night's events was quite appropriate - after all, hadn't I just lost my virginity?

The de-briefing officers expressed some astonishment that all seven crews had returned safely. Their theory to explain the non appearance of the night fighters was that the Controller had assumed that we were merely a spoof attack designed to persuade him to commit his aircraft prematurely before the expected arrival of the main bomber force. What they found baffling was his failure to dispatch two or three night fighters to deal with seven bombers in ideal attacking conditions. With enemies as stupid as these who needs friends?

Then our pride was dealt a severe blow - far from being "specially selected for the operation we were merely a "clerical error". Only crews with at least eighteen successful operations to their credit should have been picked, but someone had included us by mistake. We were just another rookie crew.

The following day we received another jolt to our pride when we were informed that we weren't going to be credited with the operation as we had not sown our mines using "Gee" co-ordinates. A favourite "cranfordism" of mine is "I cannot spell correctly since I lost my teeth" and, evidently, it was felt we could not sow mines correctly without our "Gee". On appeal we were, grudgingly, awarded three operational points to go towards the 120 required to completed our tour of operations.

Epilogue

At the time we never did find out if the break out of the U-Boats had taken place and, if so, with what result. 44 years later while I was browsing through Annan Public Library, I came across a book by a German submarine ace whose name escape me now. Idly leafing through the pages I found that the last chapter was devoted to Lorient. Reading on I found that the attempted break out had, indeed, taken place shortly after our operation. One U-Boat successfully negotiated the mine-field only to be detected and sunk by a patrolling British frigate as it emerged into open waters. the rest were so badly damaged in the mine-field that no more attempts were made.

Even after the passage of so many years I experienced a glow of satisfaction at the thought that at least one of the operations in which I had played a small part had been such an unqualified success. Ironically, it was also the only operation in which no blood was shed on either side.

Galashiels — G. Johnson

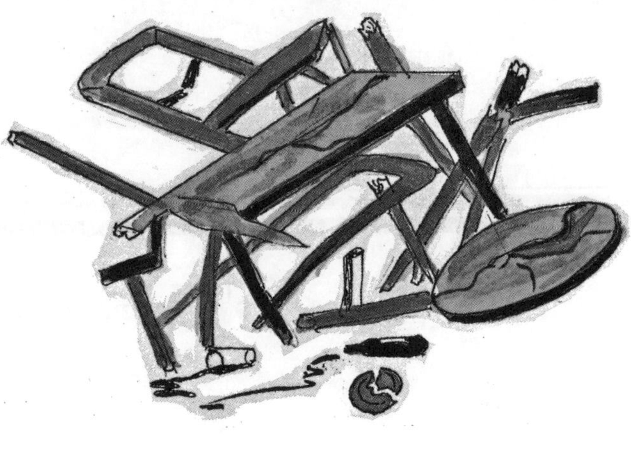

The Navigators' Narratives

Squadron Leader Jack Francis David Jarmy, D.F.C., R.A.F. (Rtd). (Navigator)

Jack Jarmy was born at Romford in Essex on 26th April, 1922 and educated at Ilfracombe Grammar School. Prior to joining the Royal Air Force, he was employed in the family business at Purbrook in Hampshire. Whilst still only eighteen years of age he volunteered for aircrew duties in the RAF and was attested at RAF Uxbridge on 17th April 1941 - ten days before his nineteenth birthday.

After the usual mill of A.C.R.C. in London, Jack reached No.9 I.T.W. at Stratford-upon-Avon where his aircrew training commenced. From thence he went on for ab initio flying training at the E.F.T.S. at Clyffe Pypard in Wiltshire, from where he went forward for pilot training in North America.

Successfully completing primary flying training on Stearman PT 17 biplanes at Carlstrom Field, Arcadia, Florida; he was moved to Gunter Field, Montgomery, Alabama, for basic training on Vultee BT 13 monoplanes. There, to use his own words, he succumbed to the system and was posted back to Canada and selected for further training as a navigator. He finally graduated as a Pilot Officer Navigator in November 1942 at No.7 A.O.S. Portage La Prairie, near Winnipeg.

Returning to Britain on S.S. Queen Elizabeth, Jack went forward to complete two operational tours in Bomber Command.

On the cessation of hostilities in Europe, Jack elected to remain in the Service and was awarded a permanent commission in 1948. He completed a further flying tour with No.511 Squadron at Lyneham in Transport Command, flying Hastings aircraft before taking a course in maritime operations at Kinloss. From thence he entered Coastal Command and completed a further flying tour on Shackletons with No.240 Squadron from Ballykelly in Northern Ireland. Remaining in Coastal Command he became involved as a staff officer in both training and planning in the developing techniques of anti-submarine warfare.

Turning next to the administrative role he served as adjutant and later, on promotion, as Senior Secretarial Officer in numerous stations both in the U.K. and Middle East, including a staff tour in the Operations Centre, Near East Headquarters. Finally turning to the Supply Branch, Jack became Officer Commanding Supply at the Helicopter Flying School at Ternhill in Shropshire.

Jack completed a full and varied career in the Royal Air Force with a tour at No.14 Maintenance Unit, Carlisle, retiring from the active list on

26th April 1977. Now retired he and his wife live at Gatehouse of Fleet in Kirkcudbrightshire. They have four adult sons. Jack is a keen angler and lists his other hobbies as golf, country pursuits and home brewing.

Wartime Experiences.

Following initial pilot training in the U.K. and the Arnold Scheme in the U.S.A. where I flew a 100 hours, I succumbed to the system and returned to Canada, finally graduating as a Pilot Officer Navigator in November 1942.

Operational training followed on the Wellington lC in April 1943, where the navigator improved his muscles by winding the under-carriage up and down with 120 turns. My pilot was a New Zealander, Sgt. Alan Mayfield and the Bomb-aimer a Scot, Jock Somerville. Apart from a crash landing on take-off when an engine on the Wellington failed, we progressed well and moved to Waterbeach to convert on to the Stirling I.

July saw us joining No.75 (N.Z.) Sqn. at Mepal, near Ely, to fly the Stirling III, the Squadron having recently moved from Newmarket where they flew Wellingtons. Our first initiation to operations followed within a week, when we indulged in 'Gardening', the code name for laying 'vegetables' (sea mines) near the Friesians.

Our first bombing operation, 3rd August, nearly ended in disaster, for as we approached the enemy coastline at 13,500 feet, all four engines cut. Hands reached for the parachutes as the aircraft commenced a steep descent, however in what seemed a lifetime, and a loss of 4,000ft, the engines spluttered back to life, whilst our engineer apologised for pushing the cocks the wrong way. He never made that mistake again! We staggered back to maximum altitude and attacked Hamburg, which was one of the most successful raids we participated in, the fire could be seen when we were 100 miles to the west, returning across the North Sea.

A few nights later a further 'Gardening' operation was flown, this time off the coast of Bordeaux. Returning across France at 1,000ft in bright moonlight, our bomb-aimer sighted a train, which we circled, dived to a low level and attacked with front and rear Brownings; finally the engine exploded. We were subsequently warned at de-briefing not to repeat this performance, since the Germans had recently introduced Flak trains, which would provide a deadly reception for heavy bombers at low level. Nevertheless, this little diversion into fighter tactics left us quite elated.

Routine attacks on the major cities in Germany continued every few days during the next few months. Turin provided a welcome rest from

German opposition, with little enemy action and sighting of Mont Blanc in the moonlight.

A daylight fighter affiliation exercise (Bullseye) caused a few tense moments when an over zealous Typhoon came too close and clipped our starboard wing-tip as we corkscrewed to confuse him. Its pilot baled out successfully as his aircraft spun out of control. Our aircraft was made of more 'Stirling' stuff and only received slight damage.

Towards the end of August Peenemunde was attacked from about 8000ft. As we approached the PFF markers I fortunately stepped into the astrodome, and on looking up, a Lancaster with its bomb doors open, was less than a 100 feet above us. I shouted "Turn hard port" and as we moved a stick of H.E's dropped past our starboard wing-tip. Obviously the Lancaster bomb-aimer, focusing on the target indicators ahead had not seen us just below him.

Nuremberg provided another close shave, we landed at Ford on the South East coast after 8 hours flight time with the fuel gauges showing zero, and as we taxied in two engines cut due to lack of fuel. The aircraft had sustained considerable flak damage, so after a few hours sleep, we journeyed, in flying kit, complete with parachutes, sextant etc. by train back to Cambridgeshire.

Berlin, Mannheim, Frankfurt and other heavily defended targets followed, and each night comrades failed to return. All Stirlings suffered heavy losses at this time and '75' became known as the 'Chop Squadron' in 3 Group, because our losses were particularly heavy, frequently in excess of 10%. We were just unlucky, for in no way were the crews to blame and morale remained high, though I confess we were somewhat fatalistic.

In mid- December, with several more operations to fly before our tour of 30 operations was reached, we attended the daily 'Morning Prayer Meeting' to learn with astonishment that 3 Group Headquarters had ordained that our crew and one other had completed our tours, the first on 75 Sqn to do so since our arrival - a most acceptable Christmas present!

Within the month, Stirlings were no longer used on raids on main targets because of the heavy losses they were sustaining.

I found New Zealanders excellent comrades and highly efficient airmen. We shared frequent tense moments when flying together, every crew member depended on each other and a great spirit of companionship existed at all times. Their popularity was enhanced by the sharing of their frequent food parcels, which included delicacies such as tinned oysters and rich fruit cake, unheard of luxuries during wartime Britain.

A year followed instructing at No.3 Lancaster Finishing School at

RAF Feltwell on Lancasters, then re-crewing and posting to 218 (Gold Coast) Sqn. at RAF Chedburgh in January 1945 for my second tour of operations.

My new skipper was Flt.Lt Guinane, an ex-flying instructor on his first tour, but our two gunners, who were aged 28 (and considered senile) were also on their second tours and very experienced. We participated in the attack on Dresden and nearly came to grief. After several night fighter attacks in the target area I climbed into the astrodome about ten minutes after bombing to check the stars to find Polaris on my port side instead of starboard, we were heading for the Russian front!! Our H2S was unserviceable and the D.R. compass was damaged. Recovering composure we navigated back to base using gyro, P12 compass and astro compass checks when available, to land 9 hours 25 minutes after take-off, our longest sortie.

After qualifying as a GH Radar Marker crew, we participated in many daylight raids to support the army, attacked Berlin amongst other targets at night in April.

I completed my second tour on the 24th April, two days before my birthday.

A few days later the war in Europe was over.

Gatehouse of Fleet — Jack Jarmy

Flying Officer K Anderson D.F.C (Navigator)

Ken Anderson was born in Liverpool in 1918 and was educated at Anfield Road School there. On leaving school he obtained employment in a Cotton Broker's office.

In July 1939 he joined the Liverpool City Police and two years later - when the Police were allowed to join the Armed Forces he volunteered for flying duties with the R.A.F. He was called up in October 1941 and went to Padgate with two other members of the Force, Frank Preece and Dick Penman. The three of them stayed together through their ITW, EFTS in South Africa, AFU in Llandwrog, finally parting when crewing up in Lossiemouth.

Ken represented Liverpool Schoolboys in athletics, sprints, and after his RAF career continued his running, winning the Police Championships for seven successive years; the Lancashire and Northern Counties Championships. He represented Lancashire, the Northern Counties, AAA, England and Great Britain and was a member of the Great Britain Olympic Team in 1948. Ken also represented the National Police Team in Stockholm in 1950. During his running career he did his training with the Liverpool Football Club.

He retired from the Police in 1956 and opened a Detective Agency in Edinburgh and Glasgow - retiring in 1983 to live in Springholm. He is married with one daughter.

He lists his hobbies as bread making, photography (darkroom), reading and the Big Band Sound.

Every Little Helps

Hitler's personal war against me started in August 1940 when the Luftwaffe commenced their many attacks on Liverpool, where I was serving as a young policeman at the time. On the first raid one of the bombs dropped just behind my home. I didn't like that.

When the bombs dropped the nearest police officer took charge of the incident as it was called, organising the required services, ARP, ambulances, Fire Brigade and Home Guard. I was serving in the dock area and such a job was my lot on many occasions. Besides organising I had to get stuck in and clear rubble from bombed buildings and homes, in an effort to get out the injured, and in many cases, the dead. It was a harrowing experience.

Police at that time was a reserved occupation, but a year later the Home Office relented and allowed us to join the Armed Forces. I joined the RAF in July 1941.

After completing I.T.W. (Initial Training Wing) course at St. Andrews in Scotland, I was posted to the Transit Camp in Blackpool to await overseas air crew services under the Empire Training Scheme. Eventually, on board the "Stirling Castle", at Liverpool of all places, we set sail in convoy for South Africa; but not directly, for we docked in Brazil - first at Bahia, then Rio de Janeiro, before re-crossing the Atlantic to disembark at Durban.

At Durban we were welcomed by Perla Siedle Gibson, an International concert star, dressed in white, who was known as the Lady in White. All convoys which stopped, or passed through Durban would see this lady standing alone on the North Quay, with outstretched arms, singing "Land of Hope and Glory" and many more familiar tunes, She never missed a convoy from April 1940 to August 1945.

On to 47 E.F.T.S. Queenstown, to take the Observer Course, day flying from there, with the navigation and bombing course, and night flying from Aliwal North, then to Port Alfred for the gunnery course. We played hard but had to work hard as two failures in any subjects meant 'kaput'. Eventually passing out, returned solo to the UK. on board the "Ile de France".

Posted to 20 O.T.U. at Lossiemouth to crew up in the traditional RAF ritual of 'walk about'. It worked well and everyone seemed satisfied. Indeed it was for me, for I finished my tour with those in whom I put my trust, as they did with me. Then on to H.C.U. at Marston Moor, where at one time the C.O. was Group Captain Leonard Cheshire, V.C. We converted on to Halifaxes before being posted to 158 Squadron at Lissett, where the reason for joining would begin.

In the early days of the war navigation was a little haphazard due to lack of navigational aids, but by the time I arrived on the Squadron two further navigational aids were to add to the Distant Reading Compass which was already fitted in the aircraft. I considered the D.R.C and the new "Gee" and "H2S" equipment were most important in keeping an aircraft on track and also to assist in target finding.

The D.R.C. had a Master Unit placed near the tail of the aircraft as far as possible away from magnetic interference from engines etc., its readings were transmitted through two repeaters, one for the pilot and one for the navigator. The D.R.C. had two advantages over the ordinary magnetic compass which suffered from acceleration and deceleration errors on E and W headings and sluggishness due to other ferrous metals in the pilot's cockpit.

"Gee" involved a system of a Master Transmitting Station with two slaves stations, and the time difference between the radio signals to the aircraft from the Master Station and slave stations determined where the aircraft was at that particular time. Where the lines crossed on a lattice type chart showed that position.

"H2S" consisted of a rotating radar scanner situated below the fuselage which produced echoes of the ground over which the aircraft was flying and they gave an image on a cathode-ray tube. Where the contrast was sharp between land and water, i.e., coastlines, lakes, rivers and canals the image was clearly defined.

My personal war started on the 10th may 1944 with a trip to the marshalling yards at Lens. There was some apprehension when crossing the enemy coast at Dunkirk where there was some light flak, and I thought we had been hit as a fire started under my seat, if this is the first one what are the rest to be like, I thought, but relief, for what had caused the fire was a short circuit in the electrics.

Further raids on marshalling yards and railways followed before my first encounter with the Krauts. This was at the end of May when Field Marshal Montgomery sought help from Bomber Command to remove a Panzer division which was delaying his progress at Bourg-Leopold. We duly obliged and so precise was the bombing the target was frequently obscured by smoke and dust. Although there was interference from night fighters, the attack was a great success and Monty was pleased to be on his way.

Soon after this we went to Sterkrade in the Ruhr to put some nasties on the Fischer Tropsch Synthetic Oil Plant. Although there were some fighters about we were never engaged. On landing back at Lissett, I was silently pleased with this operation, for it was my first into Germany and I had taken some revenge for what had been done to Liverpool.

My next two trips were to 'V' weapon sites and by damaging them we were delaying further attacks on London and the South East.

On returning from a trip to Stuttgart we were homing on a "Gee" line when just south of Newark our Flight Engineer decided to inform us that we had only fifteen minutes fuel left so we diverted to Syerston, at that time a Lancaster Finishing School, which was a little to port. We decided that we wanted an explanation from our Flight Engineer and he told us that he had fallen asleep. We landed at Syerston 7 hours 45 minutes after take-off.

After being de-briefed by whom we considered a very inexperienced Intelligence Officer, he asked us "What happens now?". Taffy, our rear gunner, who liked his food was quick off the mark with his reply, "A flying breakfast - steak, egg and chips." We got it!!! After re-fuelling we returned to Lissett for a proper de-briefing and another breakfast, but no steak.

In early August ten of the Squadron were briefed to bomb the 'V' weapon site at L'Hey. We, together with PFF got there early, so we all circled the target - it was a daylight -and true to tradition of PFF, they delayed lighting up until the allotted time when they would put their markers down. While this circling was going on we got hit by flak and were losing oil from one of the engines and at the conclusion of the raid everybody belted back home except us. We thought this very naughty of them, leaving us to fend for ourselves.

Later in the month we went to Duisburg on a daylight raid with 1,012 other aircraft. The Squadrons bombing time was 0909 to 0911 hours and in those two minutes over the target ten of the Squadron aircraft were hit by heavy flak at 18,000 feet, and we were one of them but we all got safely back to base. Later that night 1,008 Bomber Command aircraft again bombed Duisburg, and I understand that they could map read from the coast due to the smoke we had caused earlier.

There was a disappointing end to my tour of operations for on the 23rd October we were briefed to attack Essen and our Squadron was to lead the Command. Our aircraft was to lead the Squadron. My pilot, Tommy Coles and I were F/O's and we were to lead the Main Force of 1,055 aircraft of Bomber Command to Essen. It was, as I read somewhere, asking a midshipman to be in charge of the Fleet, but that would never happen in the Navy.

However, the detail was scrubbed for a few hours due to weather, but before it was on again our crew had been informed that we had been screened and our tour was over. I would have liked to have done that trip, but maybe it was for the best, for us at least.

Having finished my tour it was back to Lossiemouth as an Instructor, and after a spell there I was posted to 132 O.T.U. Coastal Command at East Fortune as a Navigation Instructor.

Although there were pupils, all I can remember is that the staff consisted of Administration and Flying Control. I was surprised to find that there were no aircraft except an Oxford, which no one seemed to know anything about. The only flying personnel on the station was a tour expired pilot and myself.

He and I had sleeping out passes in Edinburgh so we decided to have more than a look at the Oxford. We did all the checks, inside and out, very thoroughly may I add. There was fuel in it, so we gave it an air test and as all seemed well we set course for Turnhouse. We asked the maintenance staff there to give it a service and fill her up, which they did. We returned to East Fortune the following morning and on arrival there no questions were asked, so accordingly the two of us used 'HN 410' as a means of transport to and from our work while at East Fortune. I wonder what happened to that aircraft after we left.

I enjoyed my career in the RAF and especially Squadron life, which was casual, while at the same time there was a self inflicted discipline while flying. With anti-aircraft fire and fighters having a go at you, flying through the box barrages of flak, and heart in the mouth time, when , after dropping your bombs you kept straight and level to get a photograph of where your bombs fell. I am not afraid to tell I was frightened to hell and bloody scared at times.

It is said that as you progressed through a tour you got more experienced, maybe, but to survive you had to be very lucky and I was one of these.

My two Police colleagues who joined with me were not so fortunate, as one was shot down on his twelfth trip and became a P.O.W, while the other was shot down and killed on his first op. As I said, I was lucky.

I do not regret my service life for I joined as a boy and came out a man, and I am sure it shaped my future.

Springholm K.Anderson.

Flight Lieutenant Jack Bisbey
(Navigator).

A native of Wolverhampton, Jack Bisbey was born on 4 September 1921. At the age of sixteen he joined the RAF as an Aircraft Apprentice, enlisting at Halton on 24th August 1938, and was sent for training in the Group 1 trade of Wireless Mechanic and Operator to No.1 Electrical and Wireless School at Cranwell. Qualifying in November 1940 as an Aircraftman 2nd class, he was posted to the Middle East to join the Desert Air Force.

After the final, allied victory in North Africa, Jack, now a Corporal, moved to Sicily and Italy where he continued front line duty with a Forward Fighter Control Unit throughout the Italian campaign.

Returning to the UK. at the end of 1944, Jack was employed on maintenance duties and whilst at Kemble, in Wiltshire, he made his third bid to re-muster to air crew duties. Passing through ab initio flying training at Grading School, he was advised that, because of the surplus of pilots available at the end of the war, further training as a pilot would be indefinitely delayed, however, training as a navigator was immediately available. This he accepted, gaining his brevet and being commissioned at No.3 A.N.S., RAF Thornhill in Southern Rhodesia, in 1948.

On his return to the UK. Jack was posted into Bomber Command and having passed through operational training at No.230 O.T.U. at Scampton in Lincolnshire he joined No.617 Squadron at Binbrook on the Lincolnshire Wolds, flying (appropriately enough) Lincoln bombers. Whilst with 617 squadron in September 1949 Jack took part in certain special operations to detect fall-out from a suspected detonation of the first Russian atomic bomb.

Further service on Lincoln squadrons continued with No.57 Squadron at RAF Helmswell in Lincolnshire. In May 1951, No.57 was one of the squadrons selected for conversion to the American Superfortresses (Boeing B.29). Conversion to these long range bombers was carried out at RAF Marham in Norfolk, after which No.57 were based at Coningsby in South Lincolnshire. In May 1952, from that base, No.57 Squadron conducted provocation flights over the Iron Curtain to test the Russian defence response.

After operating B.29's for two years, No.57 Squadron was reconstituted as a Jet Canberra Squadron. Jack passed through the Jet Conversion course at No.231 O.C.U. at Bassingbourne, Cambridgeshire, in May 1953 before rejoining the squadron at Coningsby; shortly afterwards he was transferred to No.21 Squadron at Scampton, near Lincoln, where he completed his tour on Canberras. During that period almost all Bomber Command squadrons were reconstituted as Canberra squadrons, the force having a primary role as a striking arm in the forces of Western European Union, the nucleus from which the N.A.T.O. forces in Europe later emerged.

Jack continued to serve in Bomber Command until July 1960. In December 1954 he qualified as an instructor at the Bomber Command Bombing School at RAF Lindholm in Yorkshire, before taking up the post of Wing Weapons Officer at Marham. In the autumn of 1956 he attended the 'V' Bomber Conversion Course at RAF Gaydon in Warwickshire, converting onto the Vickers Valiant, the aircraft with which the Marham squadrons were then being re-equipped. In November that year he went with the Valiant force to Malta for operations against the Egyptian Air Force during the attempt to re-possess the Suez Canal as an international water-way. Despite the air and ground forces operations having to be called off prematurely due to international pressures against Britain and France, the air offensive at least achieved its main objective, as Nasser's newly acquired jet forces took refuge at bases in Saudi Arabia. In Malta, Jack acted as one of two Operations Officers controlling the operations of the Valiant squadrons.

In July 1960 Jack entered the Air Traffic Control Branch, qualifying at RAF Shawbury in September that year. He subsequently served in that capacity at various stations until retiring from the active list in September 1964. After retirement he continued A.T.C. duties as a civilian. Now retired he lives at Gatehouse -of-Fleet. Below he gives an account of his service with the Desert Air Force as a young man, which he modestly described as 'exciting'.

Service in the Desert

Following my Apprenticeship at Cranwell I was posted to the Middle East to join the Desert Air Force, leaving Liverpool on the SS Strathnaver in the middle of November 1940. We sailed via the Cape to Suez calling en route at Freetown, Sierra Leone, and Durban, arriving in South Africa at about the same time as the well remembered Australian Army contingent were making their presence felt in Cape Town. Fortunately for us the South Africans did not allow that to affect the marvellous welcome we received in Durban. We reached Suez on 28th December

1940.

I joined 274 Squadron operating in support of Wavell's 30,000 in the Western Desert for the first 6 months of 1941 and then moved on to Headquarters 211 Group Desert Air Force. I had found my role - the next three and a half years were to be spent on Army liaison duties as an NCO with No.1 Forward Fighter Control Unit, a Detachment from the Group. The only breaks in that period in N. Africa were two brief visits to Alexandria and the occasional sortie in an old Bristol Bombay doing Cas. Evac. with the New Zealand Army. But Forward Fighter Control was exciting work involving close contact with the front line for visual and radar direction of fighter bomber attacks against enemy strong points.

In early summer of 1942 Rommel launched his big push against the Eighth Army and advanced from Cyrenaica to El Alamein during which I and a small group of about fifteen others successfully evaded the enemy net closing in on Tobruk by driving through the perimeter during the hours of darkness and heading south into the desert as fast as we could go. Fortunately there was a brilliant tropical moon and by travelling at night and hiding up during the day we eventually rejoined our own lines four days later.

Operations with the FFCU continued throughout the rest of the desert war. Following the battle of El Alemein in October 1942 came the almost continuous advance to Tunis, a distance of almost two thousand miles, where we joined up with the 1st Army moving in from Algeria, thus ending the North African war on 12th May 1943. From there we flew back to Alexandria to prepare for and take part in the invasions of Sicily and Italy. I returned to the United Kingdom from northern Italy via Naples and Algiers just after Christmas 1944.

Gatehouse of Fleet J. Bisbey

Flight Sergeant Hugh Crawford.
(Navigator)

Hugh Crawford was born on 15th May 1921 at Craigton Farm House, south-east of Castle Douglas. After Primary School in Castle Douglas he progressed to Preparatory School at Warriston, Moffat for three years. From thence, between 1935 and 1938, he was a pupil of Strathallan Public School at Forgan Denny in Perthshire.

After leaving school he attended Agricultural College in Glasgow with a view to pursuing a career in farming. In 1940 he volunteered for aircrew duties in the Royal Air Force, his only means of entry to the armed forces since farming was a reserved occupation in wartime.

Now retired he and his wife Wendy live in Castle Douglas. They have an adult family of two daughters and one son. Kirsty, the eldest has the degree of Msc. in Statistics, Fiona has BN in Nursing and Cameron, the youngest, a Bsc. in Civil Engineering. There are five grandchildren.

Hugh's service commenced at the RAF Reception Centre at Paignton, in Devon; in April 1941, moving on for I.T.W. training at Newquay in Cornwall. Hugh crossed the Atlantic on the S.S.Stratheden to complete air crew training in North America. From No.31 P.D.Unit at Moncton, New Brunswick, he was sent to Lakeland in Florida for primary flying training as a pilot, flying Stearman PT 17 biplanes. Hugh went solo in under nine hours and by 29th October 1941 had completed thirty hours of solo flying. He then moved to Gunter Field, Montgomery, Alabama, for basic training on Vultee BT-13A monoplanes. Although he flew solo after only nine hours training he had the misfortune to have further pilot training discontinued, a frustrating experience termed "Washed Out". He was returned to the P.D.Unit at Moncton where he spent Christmas 1941. Here he claims a record, quote:

"I had placed my name with the Y.M.C.A. for hospitality. In three days I ate five complete turkey dinners, plum pudding etc., mid-day, evening, mid-day, evening and mid-day; and not a drop to drink!".

Re-mustered as a navigator he was posted to No.7 A.O.S Navigation School at Portage-la-Prairie near Winnipeg, Manitoba, where he qualified as an air navigator on 11th September 1942.

Back in the U.K. Hugh passed through A.F.U. training at Wigtown in Galloway, and on 8th January 1943 commenced operational training as a crew member at No.29 O.T.U. North Luffenham and Bruntingthorpe, flying in Wellington bombers. Late in August 1943 his crew moved to No.1660 Heavy Conversion Unit at Swinderby where

they flew Manchesters and Lancasters before being posted to No.57 Squadron at East Kirkby in Lincolnshire on 12th September 1943. The Squadron was equipped with Lancasters Mk.5 and on these aircraft Hugh went to war in earnest.

Hugh's tour of operations was cut short by medical problems and having been 'grounded' he retrained as an airfield controller, a job which at least kept him in association with aeroplanes.

Following his demobilisation in 1946, Hugh re-commenced farming at Craigley, near Castle Douglas, an occupation he continued for the next thirty years. Additionally, Hugh holds a diploma from the Gemmological Association of Great Britain and a 'Sponsers' mark from the Edinburgh Assay Office for silver. His hobby is facetting gem stones and mounting them in Sterling Sliver.

A First Operation.
(Which was almost his last)

This was the night their rear gunner was awarded the Immediate Conspicuous Gallantry Medal, having been recommended for the Victoria Cross.

Hugh was a navigator with 57 Squadron at East Kirkby and on the 18th October 1943 at 17.20 hours took off in Lancaster "Y" Yoke for Hanover. Sgt. Mike Cowham was the rear gunner.

On leaving the target the bomb doors had just been closed when they were attacked by two ME 109's from about 100 feet with cannon and machine gun fire. Cowham engaged them, but lost his left eye with a splinter. He did not tell the crew of his injuries. Over the intercom they could hear him singing. He said afterwards that it was only painful for about twenty minutes. Most of his turret was shattered and broken and the cold air made his wound numb - they were at 22,000 feet and the outside air temperature was -60°f. The port inner engine was on fire and had stopped.

Approaching the Dutch coast some twenty-five minutes later they were attacked by an ME 110 which Cowham engaged and succeeded in driving off. At the Dutch coast another ME 110 attacked and this was also engaged by Cowham who again succeeded in driving off the attack. In each attack the defence of the aircraft was co-ordinated by Cowham who, with only one eye operational and in pain, directed the pilot into barrel

Plate 1 Aircraft Apprentice James Farish, early 1936.

Plate 2 Hawker Audax aircraft of No.20 Sqd.. at Miranshah, N W Frontier Territory, 1938

Plate 3 Part of the Khyber Pass; not favourable territory for forced landings! (James Farish)

Plate 4 An armed Buccaneer as flown in the Gulf War of 1991 (Steve Tait)

Plate 5 Commander Dan Brooks, Royal Observer Corps, posed beside the "sharp end" of a Liberator.

Plates 6 & 7 Flight Lieutenant Reginald Eastoe, before and after serving in Hiroshima, Japan

Plate 8 Jack Jarmy and his crew, with "Edith" who had 84 bombing raids to her credit

Plate 9 The end of Submarine U1060, off the Norwegian coast, 4th November 1944 (John Wray)

Plate 10 John Waugh with other escapees and members of the French Resistance, after liberation by American troops.

Plate 11 "Wings up at last", Jack Geekie with his faithful Harvard at Feltwell.

Plate 12 Flight Lieutenant George Purslow with his Captain, Wing Commander McVeigh at the bridge which was too high

Plate 13 Ju 88 shot down in the Western Desert, June 1942. (Jack Bisbey)

Plate 14 Winston Churchill visits troops at Amiriya, Western Desert, August 1942 (Jack Bisbey)

corkscrews, the evasive manoeuvre. In these last attacks they lost the starboard outer engine as a bullet had nicked the glycol radiator and the engine seized; the port outer engine was also damaged and started to misfire. By this time they were well south of track and heading 'roughly' for England.

Hugh used the Air Position Indicator and the forecast wind for a quick course after each attack. Excessive use of 'window' avoided further fighter attacks. Slowly losing height "Mayday" was called and they got an instant response, searchlights coming on up and down the East Coast pointing to balloons and airfields and after a flight of 5 hours and 15 minutes they landed at Coltishall in Norfolk.

The Station Commander and the Intelligence Officer both put Mike Cowham up for a V.C but this was not to be. Hugh is firmly of the opinion that it is not what you do but more of who sees it. At that time their pilot was a Flight Sergeant.

Shortly after arriving back at East Kirkby, with the rest of the crew, in Hugh's car (courtesy of Aircrew Recreational Petrol Coupons) they visited the RAF Hospital at Ely to find Mike Cowham in one bed and the Mid-Upper Gunner, Frank Fox, who had a bullet through his foot, in the next bed. Sgt. Cowham had been notified of his award by then. He was eventually sent to the Plastic Surgery at East Grinstead, but unfortunately Hugh lost touch with him.

Hugh did a total of four operations before being medically grounded, and one night, he having been grounded with a cold, the crew took off on a operation with a spare navigator and failed to return!..Hugh blesses his luck. See also in "In Action With The Enemy - The Holders of C.G.M. (Flying)" by Alan W. Cooper - 1986.

Experiences in the Far East

After being grounded Hugh was sent to Flying Control School at RAF Watchfield and became an Air Traffic Controller. From East Fortune and Silloth he went to India, then to Burma where he joined No.92 Mobile Flying Control Unit at Hmawbi.

During 1944 the airstrip at Hmawbi, a satellite of Mingladon the main Rangoon airport, was operated by No.92 Mobile Flying Control Unit, consisting of fourteen flying control 'bods' living in tents in the jungle and protected by an army 'box'. The single runway was constructed of Laterite, a by product of tin mining. Control equipment was limited; Very pistols and Aldis lamps plus a single Jeep with VHF and an army 64 radio set in the rear. The tented camp situated about 2½ miles away was approached by a so called road badly chewed up by tank tracks.

Two weeks before the summer monsoon there was sheet lightning but no thunder, then the rain started; the heaviest recorded was 2.65 inches in one hour, the strip being flat was unable to drain and very often was covered by up to seven inches of water. The humidity resembled a Turkish bath. Grass grew abundantly - a fact soon noticed by the local herd of buffaloes and their herdsman.

Aeroplanes and buffaloes do not mix well and orders were given to clear the strip. Charging with a Jeep, blowing horns and waving arms proved ineffective - the 'buffs' just moved elsewhere. It was then realised that Very cartridges were composed of sodium which when mixed with water causes a violent reaction. Firing Single Star Reds downwards into water among the buffalo's legs had an instant response. The ball of sodium fizzled about rapidly and noisily in all directions; the herdsman was last seen running for his life towards the jungle, closely followed by his herd. Word apparently got around in buffalo circles and the controllers had no more trouble from them.

Living conditions in the jungle at Hmawbi were understandably, primitive. During the monsoon everything felt damp; shoes placed under beds quickly grew long whiskers. Bed legs had to stand in tins filled with paraffin to prevent ravages by termites causing a sudden collapse in the middle of the night. Despite liberal use of chloride of lime flies congregated in clouds at the latrine trench which could be distinctly off-putting. On a brighter note a simple shower was ingeniously constructed from parts salvaged from a crashed Liberator aircraft nearby; the impetus for the water being supplied from a manually operated short stroke hydraulic pump.

Despite, the difficulties of life in the jungle V.E. Night was celebrated in style at Hmawbi. The spirit ration had arrived that day consisting of one bottle of gin, half a bottle of whiskey, six bottles of Canadian Black Horse beer, and from somewhere, two bottles of Navy Rum, 200 over proof. It was said to be the month's ration but it was all the Unit ever saw!

The Unit's 'Army Box' had a Company of Ghurkas on one side. The Jemadar and the Subadar Major were invited to help in the celebration. Drinks were consumed from issue pint mugs. The capacity of the Ghurkas was astounding; mixing rum, gin, and beer and holding out for more with large grins on their faces - "their stomachs must have been lined with tin" says Hugh.

Hugh moved from Burma in a large convoy of ships for the re-invasion of Singapore. The convoy was held at sea until the second atomic bomb was dropped on Japan. At Singapore Hugh was a controller at Kallang airfield when it was made operational as were the airfields at Seletar and Changi on Singapore Island. Hugh remained at Kallang controlling aircraft of many different types for five months. He records that on the apron at Kallang, in front of the Control Tower, stood a York aircraft, allocated for the personal use of the Supreme Commander S.E.A. Lord Louis Mountbatten.

Hugh also records that the sight of the British Prisoners of War being brought out on stretchers "With the largest diameter of their legs their knees joints" was a harrowing experience.

In March 1946, Hugh was demobilised and came home by sea on S.S. Andes passing through the Suez Canal on route.

Flying Officer Robert Combe (Observer).

Bob Combe was born in Inverurie, Grampian, in 1912. After completing his formal education he trained in accountancy and was employed in the accountancy department of the Co-operative Society in Aberdeen. He also taught book-keeping at evening continuation classes. In the spring of 1940 he volunteered for aircrew duties in the Royal Air Force. Below he gives an amusing account of the trials and tribulations, he and his fellows underwent both in the U.K. and in North America, in their endeavours to qualify in their allocated aircrew roles. Despite the lack of oil in the wheels of the training scheme in those early days, he and his fellows qualified and in due course, went to war in earnest. After passing through advanced flying training at Wigtown in Scotland, and operational training at Turnberry, south of Ayr, Bob was posted to the Middle East where he became first an observer on No.47 Squadron - torpedo dropping from Beauforts; transferring to No.203 Reconnaissance Squadron based in Malta in March 1943.

After more than a year of operational flying, Bob became a navigation instructor at No.75 O.T.U. in Egypt. A year later in January 1945, Bob had returned to Britain and took an administration course at RAF Credenhill, leading to a post as assistant adjutant at RAF Wickenby in Lincolnshire. Bob's wartime service ended in January 1946 when he was demobilised.

Involvement in Defence activities by no means ended at that stage. Returning to accountancy in civil life he progressed up the ladder gaining both experience and qualifications enroute until in 1956 he was seconded to the Civil Service in the U.K. Treasury, Organisation and Methods Division, qualifying as an O & M Examiner. In 1957, he moved to Supreme Headquarters Allied Powers Europe, as an examiner, serving both in France and Belgium. In 1961, he became a Management Analyst in the Chief O&M Branch, where his duties included reviews and surveys of all subordinate H.Q's in Nato countries from Oslo in Norway to Izmir in Turkey.

A frustrated service pilot, Bob took up gliding in 1961 and subsequently qualified as an International Instructor following a course at RAF Bicester. Retiring from S.H.A.P.E. in Belgium in 1974 he then took up sailing and bought a small bilge keel yacht.

A Tale of Self Promotion

In thinking about my story in the bizarre category I found that I had to go back to the beginning of my time in the RAF. I volunteered for air crew in the spring of 1940 but was not called for Medical and Selection Board until September 1940. It was clear from the start that the aircrew volunteers far outnumbered the capacity to train them. This was illustrated by the fact that after being accepted for aircrew the choice was given to go home and wait for call or join immediately and do ground duties such as guards etc. until vacancies for training were available. I elected to go home and wait as did most of the others with me.

The call up came six months later in March 1941 when I went to No.1 Receiving Wing at Torquay. Inevitably in a rapidly expanding training programme new places and procedures were being brought to use. Our billet, The Babbacombe Hotel, was newly requisitioned and the first instruction our group received was to wash the place. I am not sure if the former proprietors would have appreciated the cleaning technique some bright spark proposed. Water was poured on the stair at the top of the hotel and lining the stairway, armed with brooms, the squad swept the cascade until it went out at the front door.

Inoculations were a part of these first few days. Normally these were given in each arm and because it made the arms sore to move, then next day was free of duties. Some doctor had the bright idea that giving inoculations in the chest would avoid the sore arms. Unfortunately he forgot that the chest muscles move at every breath. That night there were a lot of men sitting around looking very miserable and trying not to breathe.

On completion of our two weeks initial training we were posted to No.11 ITW Scarborough. Two flights of forty men were billeted in the Prince of Wales Hotel, once again newly requisitioned. The first night guard and fire picquet duties were assigned. In carrying out the patrol of the hotel the fire picquet discovered the kitchen with eggs, bacon and frying pan laid out for next mornings breakfast. A late night meal for those on duty did not seem unreasonable. The very next day workmen arrived to install a metal grid so that the kitchen could be seen but no access for illicit meals.

The ITW course was scheduled to last eight weeks but drifted on for thirteen weeks the additional five being largely used for filling sandbags and making air raid shelter pens on the paths leading to the beach. At last the news of our next posting was given. The top thirty on the course would be going to the United States and the remainder to Canada. The USA were not in the war so the group would be going as civilians and in due course we were issued with Fifty shilling Tailors grey flannel suits and shoes. To complete our kit we also got ''Bombay Bowlers'' the flat topped topee and khaki drill.

The group scheduled for the USA were given a special briefing by an Air Commodore of Training Command. We were told that we must look upon ourselves as ambassadors of Britain and behave accordingly. We would be trained by the US Navy and on successfully completing the course about a third would be commissioned and the rest made sergeants.

In due course loaded with kit we arrived at Liverpool to embark on a troopship. Not a cruise liner but a converted meat cargo boat about to do its first trip carrying troops. Teething troubles for a new venture are normal but from the word go this was an unmitigated disaster. The hold had been fitted up with tables seating ten men and ten hammocks had to be slung over each table. With the hammocks in place there was solid line of bodies, alternating head to toe like sardines in a tin. The feeding arrangements were that each table sent off four men to collect the food. At the main meal there was one each for meat, veg, pudding and the fourth with a kettle for hot water to make tea with the dry rations we had been provided. The man with the kettle had to queue up on the deck where there was a steam of boiler which boiled sufficient water for 16 kettles every ten minutes. The queue for all food could be 100 men long, resulting in the food arriving at the table in different permutations at every meal. Sometimes the pudding came first then the meat followed by the tea and the veg last.

While the feeding arrangements, were, to put it mildly inefficient, the ablutions were diabolical. Two huts had been erected on the aft deck, one as latrines and the other for hot water showers. With calm seas this might have been satisfactory but with a raging storm, which started as soon as we reached the Atlantic proper, the conditions in the latrines as the ship rolled were disgusting. The problem with the showers was that as the ship rolled there would be no water one minute then either a rush of cold water or scalding hot.

For the first few days when the storm was at its worst there was no respite for those that were sea sick. Hammocks had to be stowed every morning and everyone up on the deck to sit around on hatches or if lucky in a sheltered place. Apart from boat drills, duties, such as look-out or guarding stores were allocated. At this time no buttons were polished, they took on a green hue that matched the unshaven faces of the sea sick men. I suspect that the officer in charge was "Hors de Combat" for these early days but surfaced about the fifth day to order all to parade at the next boat drill, shaved and with polished buttons and buckles. This rather nightmarish journey lasted fourteen days before docking at Halifax, Nova Scotia.

The transformation from troopship to troop train was unbelievable. The carriage seats converted into beds and the meals served in the dining car compared favourably with a four star hotel. After two nights we arrived at Toronto and came under the care of the RCAF. Their organisation worked like a well oiled machine. Unlike our experience so far of the RAF, where waiting was standard for any issue of kit or processing here they selected the number of men they could handle in a given time and the rest were free to explore Toronto. We were supplied with visas for the USA complete with thumb prints and wearing our civilian suits sent off by train for the US Naval Air Station, Pensacola, Florida.

We may have been dressed as civilians but many American citizen seeing us falling-in at the railway station at Pensacola in three ranks, dressing by the right and marching off to the bus would have to be very naive to think we were civilians.

Once again we were the guinea pigs as the first RAF contingent to arrive at the Naval Base. We were billeted in similar rooms to those of the US cadets and at first messed along with them. Then they found out that we were aircrew cadets and not Officer Cadets so we were switched to the enlisted men's mess. Instead of meals being served we now queued with the sailors to receive the food in sectioned trays. This did not last too long and as more RAF men arrived a mess was made available for the RAF. We were a very democratic group perhaps a bit older than the pilot trainees, being mostly in our late twenties and included school teachers, lawyers accountants and bankers. When we had difficulties we would have a meeting and brief our spokesman to bring them to the attention of the RAF Admin. Officer. Florida in summer can be very hot, over 100 degrees in the shade at mid-day and very humid. Our khaki drill being tunic and trousers was totally unsuitable. The trousers were designed for use with braces and cut to be snug under the arm pits! After our complaint we were quickly kitted out with the US Navy "Suntans", trouser and shirts which made us look as respectable as our US classmates.

The course was planned for the first part to be classroom training and on successful completion we would start flying. The classroom work took two months and the flying part, navigation and gunnery one month. All our course passed with very good marks, generally better we were told than our US classmates. This was understandable, while we could concentrate on navigation, morse and meteorology, they were all trainee pilots and failure for them to make the grade in flying meant being off the course, no second chances.

Rumour had it that it was planned that we would ultimately crew up with the RAF pilots and wireless operators being trained elsewhere and fly back to the U.K. Clearly the difference in the training time scale made this a non-starter. Our group having finished the course were now an embarrassment, we had to be moved to make way for others. We were told that we would not be getting our brevet and promotion which was a disappointment to us and to the RAF Admin. Officer as well as to our US instructors. The RAF Admin. Officer told us he would raise it with the powers that be but nothing was heard of it. We were sent off to the US Naval Air Station, Norfolk Virginia.

In theory we were attached to an Atlantic Patrol Squadron for further training, in fact, in two months we each got about two flights of two hours as supernumeraries which meant four of us acted as extra look-outs. Then came Pearl Harbour. Our Patrol Squadron took off for the Pacific and we were again an embarrassment to our hosts who now had a war on their hands. While the RAF were making up their minds what to do with us we made the most of our free time. A dollar a day does not give much scope but we hitch-hiked to New York, Washington and other East Coast towns, this was made easier because we were now in uniform. At the end of December we were on the move back to Canada for return to the U.K.

We took a very poor view of the way things had turned out. The briefing we had about being ambassadors and that we would be promoted on successful completion of the course had come to nothing. We also heard that our Scarborough friends who went to Canada had now been promoted. Our spokesman raised the question with the RCAF Commander at Moncton but he said it was outside his jurisdiction. That we could understand but we also knew that aircrew cadets who returned to the U.K. from Canada still as LACs were those that had failed the course. We were also concerned with being the dogs-bodies on a troopship if it was going to be like the one on which we came to Canada.

So a unanimous decision was made we would promote ourselves to sergeants and put up Observer badges. The stripes and badges were sewn on our tunics but no stripes on our greatcoats. We paraded as LACs until we got on the train. Once on the train everybody got busy sewing stripes on to their greatcoat. At this point the officer in charge of the contingent for the troopship came into the carriage. His immediate exclamation was "What the hell was this? A sewing bee." We explained the whys and wherefores of our decision which he accepted, as his concern was to ensure everyone got on to the troopship.

Our fears of another badly converted cargo boat and a repeat of our outward journey were unfounded, this time it was the Stratheden a 48,000 ton cruise liner. We were still in hammocks but the messing and washing facilities were good. There were so many aircrew sergeants on board, mostly RCAF, that a lounge on "B" Deck was allocated as a sergeants recreation room. The convoy consisted of four large liners with two escort vessels so that the crossing, despite the January Atlantic gales was very fast. We docked at Greenock and in the blackout got on board a train, very different from the ones we had experienced in Canada. After an interminable night of stops and starts we were given biscuits and drinks. The Canadians were given meat pies but not the Brits, we told them that now that they were in rationed Britain the food was normal and that we accepted that we had to make sacrifices for our allies. They began to wonder what they had let themselves in for. We later found out that because of an air-raid our train had been diverted and missed a rendezvous with a kitchen coach, hence the lack of food.

We arrived in Bournemouth in the blackout, shepherded on to trucks, taken for a meal and billeted in an unheated house furnished only with beds. On parade the next day it appeared that there were 30 missing LACs and 30 extra sergeants. We were paid as sergeants and very soon off on leave. On return we were all posted to No. 1 AFU Wigtown, Scotland to be indoctrinated into RAF procedures and to do more gunnery and bombing.

A few days after our arrival we were mustered in the briefing room and the Wing Commander in charge of training addressed us. He read out the signal he had received from the Air Ministry:- "The erroneously promoted sergeants could retain their stripes and observer badges but while on the course would be considered as LACs and paid as such."

It has always surprised me that to my knowledge no one was ever questioned as to how we came to be sergeants.

Tail Piece.

During my time in the RAF I have only come across one other case of self promotion, this was in Egypt in 1944. A sergeant pilot had managed to install himself in an aircrew hostel for NCOs. He decided that on his evening outings he would do better as an officer. He had been expecting to be commissioned and in anticipation had bought an officers forage cap, so all he required were rings for his shirt epaulets. This he did and made himself a Wing Commander. Unfortunately he got drunk on one of his outings and became a bit obstreperous to a real Wing Commander who called out the Provost Marshal and the masquerade was discovered. I only knew about the case because I was present at the Court Martial where the sergeant was reduced to aircraftsman.

Kippford — Bob Combe.

Sergeant Desmond Athol.
(Navigator)

Desmond Athol, born in Birkenhead in 1929, was educated at the Birkenhead Institute, before entering the offices of the Borough Treasurer. He was not long in deciding that an office was not his true metier and he volunteered for aircrew duties in the Royal Air Force.

He enrolled at North Weald and was selected for training as a navigator which he completed successfully, qualifying as a 'Navigator 3' at RAF Topcliffe in Yorkshire, in the autumn of 1949.

The rather quaint title of his professional grade came from an ill-fated experiment in the RAF aimed at setting air crew grades apart from long serving NCO's of the ground trades and, to some degree, placing the aircrew apart from administrative responsibilities. Needless to say, young ground tradesmen and the like were baffled as to the true status of the air crew and had little idea how to address them! Happily, the experiment was short lived and it was not too long before Desmond could put up his three stripes in the time honoured way.

Below Desmond gives a colourful account of his training and subsequent service with two squadrons of No.3 Group, Bomber Command, and his subsequent introduction to the advanced mathematics required for the Specialist "N" course at RAF Shawbury. Sadly, there his promising career had to end.

After leaving the RAF Desmond embraced a career in financial services which he pursued successfully to retirement. He, with his wife and two children, now lives in Kirkbean, a pretty village close to the Solway Coast - and not too far from the testing eighteen hole golf course on the coast at Southerness. This last is of vital importance for, though Desmond may well have other hobbies, golf is his ruling passion.

A Promising Career Cut Short.

At the age of seventeen and nearly two years in the Borough Treasurer's office, I just knew there had to be more to life than being in an office from 9am to 5pm five days a week for fifty weeks in the year. I decided to opt out. Where to go? I know - I've always fancied flying, I'll join the Royal Air Force - simple as that! No problem, just relief to get out and about.

After passing the Crew Selection Boards at RAF North Weald, I was selected for training as a navigator, I then received a Railway Warrant and orders to report to RAF Wilmslow in Cheshire for initial training, in other words 'square bashing'! It was at Wilmslow that I met Corporal Marlow. Corporal Marlow was something special - his introduction to me and my fellow cadets was brief, viz., "I'm Corporal Marlow and I'm a bastard. What am I?" In my innocence I replied "you are Corporal Marlow and you are a right bastard". This solitary reply of mine was the direct cause of my first introduction to 'Spud Peeling and Tin Room'!! With the benefit of hindsight I know I was right, Corporal Marlow was a "Right Bastard".

After a few weeks the good news came - 'Report to No.1 Air Navigation School at RAF Topcliffe in Yorkshire', to join No.9 All Through Course. It was sometime before I understood why it was termed an 'All Through Course' - of the twenty on the course only seven of us qualified!! The rest were 'all through' and re-mustered to 'A.C. plonks'!! That was tough.

I've just remembered how tough it was initially. During my first week at Topcliffe I was on crash crew duties together with others of my course; unfortunately, a Wellington stalled on take-off resulting in a fatal crash just outside the camp gates - what a mess and a most horrible experience.

Immediately after that duty all of us were put into a Wellington and given a pre-familiarisation flight - a very twitchy business indeed.

Despite a rough start to the course, life at Topcliffe was most enjoyable, probably the best time of my short service career. Good fun, plenty of sport, particularly Rugby when I was a forward in Pete Yarranton's team. Pete is now President of the English Rugby Football Union.

Topcliffe was a happy Station and I enjoyed my flying experience in Ansons (winding the undercarriage up and down) and in Wellingtons. Navigation itself I found absolutely fascinating and a terrific challenge. To plot by Dead Reckoning and to hit your turning points on time was always a thrill no matter how many times you did it. Perhaps my greatest personal satisfaction came from a long cross country flight over Germany when virtually all the electrics failed - no H2S, no Gee, initially no radio, 10/10 cloud and no sun. there we were with no aids whatever and me a 'sprog navigator'! However I navigated purely by D.R. and kept giving the 'Skipper' courses to fly etc. I recall that after about 6 or 7 hours I indicated that we should be over the Leeds/Manchester area in which case we should turn to port and keep going for an estimated time then be -

hopefully - over the Irish Sea. Once over water, and if the cloud cover broke, we could come down and fix our position more accurately. As luck would have it, and within only a few minutes of my E.T.A. for over the sea, the cloud did break and there we were over Liverpool and the Mersey. Being a lad from Birkenhead I knew exactly where we were and I was absolutely 'chuffed' when the Skipper said "You'll do son, if you can navigate for the time you have without any help, you'll do for me". Great - I knew I would complete the course now - nothing would stop me.

Finally, the great day came - Passing Out Parade, Brevet and Booze up, before saying good-bye to good friends and buddies of the past two years. Then ten days leave before reporting to RAF Swinderby in Lincolnshire to join a crew.

From Ansons and Wellingtons to yet more Wellingtons but the pilots were very different; all of those we were to crew with had just qualified, having trained principally on single engine Harvards! A very wary young navigator looked carefully around and, lo and behold, there among all these young guys was an older Flight Lieutenant with ribbons up to boot! Obviously he had served in the war and at one-time had been seriously burned. He's for me I thought, bags of experience and thus I crewed with Flt.Lt. Eric Cook, a great guy and one I was most happy to fly with. I like to think we made a good team with our Gee homings bringing us over the airfield every time and my blind approaches using 'Rebecca' working out perfectly every time.

Regrettably, when we finished operational training Eric and I were separated - I never understood why as we had worked so well together. It wasn't until 30 years later that I met Eric again - he was playing the fruit machine at my golf club; I found out that he was also a member. After the initial shock of recognition I queried how he had fared in the service "How far did you get?" said I, "Wing Co., Groupie?" "No" said Eric "Air-Vice Marshal"! "Well" said I "I knew I could pick the good pilots". Eric had obviously been destined for higher things way back at Swinderby. A great guy who unfortunately is no longer with us.

The next posting from Swinderby was Scampton for conversion onto Lincolns, nothing very exciting but a most interesting time particularly acquiring skills with H2S. Eventually posted to my first squadron, No.149 Squadron at Mildenhall. A squadron with a good war history and Pilot Officer Middleton, V.C. who, incidentally, is buried in Mildenhall cemetery. This was a great time and another great skipper Jerry Moore. Cross country exercises lasting anything from 12 to 15 hours were commonplace so you had to be on the ball all the time.

Mildenhall was to play an interesting part in my life some 35 years later when I renewed acquaintance with the Bell and other local hostelries as assistant manager with an Assurance Company!!

Those days on 149 Squadron were great, bags of flying, great hospitality and no B29's!! But all good things come to an end and one day we were told the Americans were taking over Mildenhall and we were moving out. Some of my pals went to Marham and the luxury of B29's; the more skilled of us (?) went to 214 Federated Malay States Squadron at Upwood. As a matter of interest I was the navigator of the last Lincoln to leave Mildenhall - a sad day. Still, Upwood wasn't far away and we could still go to parties at the Nurse's Home at Brampton - about which I have nothing to put into print, but they were some parties!!!

Incidentally, No.35 Squadron were at Upwood at the same time and the C.O. was Squadron Leader Dowding, son of the great Lord Dowding. Whilst my stay at Upwood was relatively brief it was highlighted by two events; the first being the visit of the Maharajah of Johore who had presented the Squadron silver, and the second having bought my first car for £5 (a 1929 bastardised Austin) fitted with an automatic starter by Freddy Ebbs the crew Engineer and a 'swede basher' from King's Lynn. I passed my test in Peterborough in Freddy's 1939 Chrysler - Al Capone model!

Whether the squadron wanted to get rid of me or they thought I might make a decent navigator sometime, I don't know, but I found myself on the way to Shawbury to join a specialist little 'N' course. This was some course involving polar navigation and using "three dimensional spherical trigonometry". I loved that phrase. Unfortunately, I was not destined to complete the course due to a flying accident which put me in RAF Halton for six months. Leaving hospital I had no choice but to leave the service, a great heartbreak, from A1G1 to A4G7 in five years. I finished a few months at No.1 ANS Thorney Island as an instructor but with no long-term prospects, I finally ended up at Innsworth and demobilisation.

Kirkbean Des. Athol.

Flight Lieutenant E.G. Faulder, M.A., J.P. (Navigator / Bomb-aimer)

Born at Longtown in Cumbria in April 1922, Ted Faulder was educated at Carlisle Grammar School. Leaving school at the age of 17 he immediately volunteered for aircrew duties in the Royal Air Force. Since the RAF did not normally accept volunteers before the age of 18 years a slight 'fudge' had to be taken with his birthdate and he was sent to Cardington for enlistment. The path to the 'aircrew brevet' was often thorny and Ted had his full share of frustrations before he finally qualified as a navigator and bomb-aimer in Canada and gained a commission.

Service in Bomber Command followed and Ted flew in many different roles in the Stirlings of No.199 Squadron. After a very full year with his squadron he was sent for training in Ground Controlled Approach procedures and finally ended his wartime service as Senior Operations Officer at No.103 Staging Post at Istres near Marseilles, in the rank of acting Squadron Leader. Following a year in this appointment Ted returned to the U.K. for demobilisation in February 1946.

On his return to civilian life Ted was accepted as a student by Queens' College, Cambridge, where he read agriculture gaining his degree, later raised to M.A. He has since been engaged in farming near Longtown and has served as a District Councillor for the past twenty-seven years. Twenty-four years ago he was appointed a Justice of Peace, an office which he still holds.

His private interests follow those of his father who was a keen student of local and family history, and, like many farmers, shooting.

From Young Volunteer to Senior Operations Officer.

As a youngster I had been fired with an enthusiasm for flying, ever since the age of 12 spending the huge sum of five shillings (in present day money - 25 pence) on a flight at an air circus in an ancient bi-plane, which was covered on the outside with adverts for Typhoo tea. From that moment I resolved to join the RAF.

When the war started I suddenly found that they would not accept anyone below the age of 18 years - or so I was told by the recruiting sergeant at Carlisle, and was told to return the following day when I was a year older, thus according to record, my date of birth was 16th April 1921.

I was given a travel warrant and arrived at Cardington at about

11pm on the night of 7th December 1939. We were attested the following day and remained at Cardington for about a week. I remember being impressed by the huge hangars which had been built for airships and were then being used for balloons and the training of balloon operators. I also remember the loud reports which used to go off at regular intervals at the gas works which produced the hydrogen.

From Cardington we were sent to Catfoss in East Yorkshire, for recruit training. Catfoss was very cold and exposed, particularly in the middle of the night on guard at a gunpost with the wind blowing straight across the North Sea from the Ural Mountains.

In January I was posted to Duxford on general duties while waiting for a Wireless Operators course. These general duties consisted of shovelling snow, working in the coal yard and assisting at the Station Sick Quarters during a 'flu epidemic'.

I got to Yatesbury in early April on my Wireless Operator's course. At first everything went well for I found the technical side easy but finally got scrubbed from the course because I could not increase my Morse speed beyond twelve words a minute.

I recall while there, being called out one Sunday morning and spending the whole day, until 10.30pm, erecting tents for men arriving from Dunkirk. I also remember being put on Paratroop guard, our job being to repel an expected invasion of German Paratroops. For this purpose we were armed - each man being issued with a pick-axe shaft.

Having failed the Wireless Operator's course I hoped to become an Air Gunner and was told to apply at my next station. Unfortunately, I was sent to a Radar Station in 60 Group and my application for aircrew did not seem to meet with any response. I spent a year on this station in Berwickshire. There I took part in my first military funeral when we buried a German who was washed up in Coldingham Bay.

I was posted to Islay, also in 60 Group, and my break came when on the way my old motor bike gave up the ghost on the Great North Road. I was picked up by a Group Captain who was Senior Air Staff Officer of a Group in Flying Training Command, and with his help I was finally accepted for flying training after being before a Board in Edinburgh. Even so, there was an interval of a few months before I was posted to A.C.R.C. at St. John's Wood in London, and once again had to get used to the same discipline which I had as a recruit a couple of years earlier.

From there I was posted to the Initial Training Wing at St. Andrews and most of my intake were re-mustering airmen from L.A.C. to Senior N.C.O.'s and one Warrant Officer. All of us wanted to be pilots but we learned during the course that the requirement for pilots was being reduced and most of us would not achieve that aim.

After I.T.W. I was posted to the E.F.T.S. at Scone, near Perth, and did about twelve hours on Tiger Moths and then learnt that I was to be a bomb-aimer.

I went to Heaton Park, Manchester, to await passage to Canada. We moved to Hastings, were bombed out of there, sent to Harrogate and then back to Heaton Park, and finally, off to Canada.

In Canada I went to Paulson, Manitoba, for bombing and gunnery training. It was about 40° below most of the time and we did our air to air firing in a Bolingbroke, the Canadian version of the Blenheim Mk.IV. Finally, I was sent to Winnipeg for navigation training, and eventually came the great day when we graduated and awarded our brevet and Sergeant's Stripes.

We were sent to Moncton for passage back to the U.K. and there I learnt that on my final results I had been granted a commission.

At Harrogate I got myself kitted out with an Officer's uniform and then I was posted to No.10 Advanced Flying Unit at Dumfries. We did a little bombing and gunnery there, most of the firing over the Solway and there was a bombing target on Racks Moss.

From Dumfries I went to No.11 Operational Training Unit at Westcott where I met my crew, or at least five of them, and we got used to working together in a Wellington IC. From Westcott we moved to No.1657 Heavy Conversion Unit at Stradishall, in Suffolk where we were joined by a mid-upper gunner and flight engineer, and we had to get used to flying in Stirlings.

On the 1st October 1943 we were posted to No.199 Squadron at Lakenheath, in Suffolk. The first month we did a few mine laying trips and I saw my first flak from German Flak Ships. In November we continued with a couple of trips to Mannheim and Leverkusen, but the weather was really appalling. After that there was a lull as Stirlings were taken off German targets.

In January, 1944, our Skipper went into hospital for an operation and our crew was taken over by the Squadron Commander, Wing Commander Bray, later Chief of Air Staff, Danish Air Force.

Bray had spent all his previous Service career in India, flying Hawker Hinds on the North West frontier, and whilst he was a first class pilot when airborne his take-offs and landings in a Stirling were enjoyable only to those with a thirst for adventure. We did some bombing of 'V' weapon sites in Northern France and then went on to supply dropping to the French Resistance, mainly in Southern France. This was carried out at low level in moonlight. In March we had an operation in Northern France at low level and we were severely shot up by flak. We were lucky to get back as the aircraft had a cannon shell through the main spar. The colours of the day in the Wireless Operator's desk were set off and we had a fire inside the aircraft. The Wireless Operator, Flt/Sgt. Donaldson was both wounded and badly burnt. We managed to put out the fire and Donaldson was awarded the C.G.M.

In April the Squadron was withdrawn from operational flying and on 1st May 1944, we moved to North Creake in Norfolk, which was in 100 Group. There the aircraft were fitted with special equipment for our new role in Bomber Support and we were given an extra Wireless Operator to operate it. The rest of my time with the squadron was spent on this role which consisted of misleading enemy defences. In all I spent just over a year with 199 Squadron.

According to Bomber Command Diaries, No.199 Squadron flew the greatest variety of operations in Bomber Command. I can say that I flew on every type and even filled in as Acting Adjutant on one occasion.

Later I was sent on a Ground Control Approach Course at Honily and eventually became Senior Operations Officer at Istres, near Marseilles. I was there for about a year before demobbed in February 1946.

Longtown E.G. Faulder

Flight Lieutenant John Wray.
(Navigator)

Born in Bridlington, Yorkshire, on 22nd January 1922, John Wray was educated as a boarder at the Royal Masonic College (Public School) in Hertfordshire. In 1940, at the age of 18, he volunteered for aircrew duties in the Royal Air Force, but was not called for enlistment as a Cadet until April 1941. In the interim he worked as an Agricultural Student, an occupation which, if he had so chosen, he could have pursued throughout the period of hostilities. He had chosen differently and was selected for training as a navigator. After initial training at No.8 I.T.W. Newquay in Cornwall he was troop-shipped to Canada arriving at the Air Navigation School at Malton, Toronto, in November 1941.

John qualified as a navigator on the 13th April 1942, and was commissioned as a Pilot Officer. In that capacity he returned to the U.K. in convoy, but in rather greater comfort than his outward journey. Below he tells his own story of maritime operations in Coastal Command.

After his wartime service with the RAF and secondment to B.O.A.C., John entered Manchester University to read English in which he gained his Bachelor of Arts Degree. He entered the teaching profession and for the last twenty years before retirement was Headmaster of a large High School having upwards of 2,000 pupils. Now, retired, he and his wife live in Dumfries; they have a grown-up family of a son and two daughters.

Maritime operations.

I was called up in April 1941, and began the usual training preliminaries, before being troop-shipped to Halifax, Nova Scotia, and thence by train to Toronto where I was posted to the Air Navigation School in Malton. For someone who had only recently left school Canada was impressive. Not only was it a vast and beautiful country, but the Canadians themselves couldn't have been more hospitable. We adjusted quickly to the size of the country, for example on arrival in Toronto we were given a days leave - what to do? ''Go see Niagara'' suggested fellow Canadians - ''but it is the best part of two hundred miles and we've only got a 24 hours pass''. ''No problem, you hitch along the Queen Elizabeth highway''. We did, Niagara was breathtaking, and in those days unpolluted.

Training over I returned to the U.K. not on a troop-ship this time but as a sprog P.O., one of six passengers on a cargo liner in convoy. There were a couple of U-boat alarms on the way back, but we didn't take them too seriously. I was not to know that, much later, I would actively be involved with U-boats.

As many ex-aircrew will remember we found ourselves soon after arrival in the U.K. at the Royal Hotel in Bournemouth awaiting posting. One morning we were paraded on the forecourt, and the assembled group divided into two, the dividing line separated my friend and I. His 'half' were posted to Bomber Command, whilst I was posted to a torpedo training O.T.U. That arbitrary dividing line was to determine our fate from then on.

No.50 O.T.U. for torpedo training was at Turnberry, south of Ayr in Scotland. We spent our time dropping dummy torpedoes from 50 feet at targets on the sea. We were flying Beauforts and even to me at that time Beauforts didn't seem the ideal torpedo aircraft though better, I suppose, than the Swordfish of the Fleet Air Arm.

Our posting came through; I and my crew were to join No.39 Squadron in Malta. Thanks to the success of Operation Torch and the tremendous advances made by the Eighth Army, we were able to fly ourselves out to Cairo. Taking-off from Portreath in Cornwall on 16th February 1943, we flew to Gibraltar, a flight of seven hours duration. On the 18th we moved to Blida in Algeria, then by stages, avoiding Tunisia, we made our way through Libya to land finally at Cairo on 26th February. In all, our journey took some 24 hours flying time to complete. Shortly after our arrival we moved to RAF Shallufa in the Canal Zone for a Special Torpedo Training Course, practising in the Gulf of Suez. Our posting to 39 Squadron was delayed and I finished up in charge of flying control at Suez.

Then out of the blue came a call for a volunteer crew to test out a new aircraft in the U.K. We jumped at the chance and we were sent to Cairo from where we were flown home as first class passengers by T.W.A. John Steinbeck, who was a war correspondent at the time, was one of the passengers.

We arrived at Prestwick, and reported in, explained who we were, and why we were there, only to be met with quizzical looks. It was suggested we go on leave and we would be contacted when they had sorted it out. Surprisingly no word came and after some three months I phoned. I cannot remember to whom or where, and was then assigned to No.502 Halifax Squadron at Holmsley South, near Bournemouth. (If I hadn't phoned would I still be on leave?).

No.502 (City of Belfast) Squadron was an anti-shipping, anti-U-boat squadron operating over the Atlantic and the French coast. The squadron moved to St. David's in South Wales and then to Stornoway, Isle of Lewis, where we were to operate not only off the French coast, but also off the Norwegian coast and on to the Kattegat and Skagerrak. Obviously our flying was different to that of the lads of Bomber Command, we operated either alone or in twos and threes, and on special missions, both by day and night, I completed a tour with 502.

My crew had sighted and attacked a number of U-boats in the Atlantic, North and South, and we had one confirmed kill off the Norwegian coast.

On one occasion a U-boat had been sighted travelling on the surface towards Narvik and three of our Halifaxes were sent to locate and attack it . As it was in an area close to where the German battleships were berthed and was heavily defended by fighters, we were to set out at night over the North Atlantic at 50 feet to avoid radar detection. Our E.T.A. at the target was to be first light. We were to climb, search and attack if the target was located. All went well with us, as day broke we climbed. It was a beautiful clear day and the Norwegian coast looked superb in the morning light. Then we saw the U-boat heading N.W. as had been reported. Expecting fighters at any moment we went in low, straddled the U-boat with depth charges and headed home smartly at 50 feet.

Our kill was confirmed within hours or our return. What of the other two crews? They returned reporting much low cloud over the target area and being unable to see returned to base. Those two aircraft had a couple of very shrewd navigators on board!

On another occasion we were sent to attack a U-boat which had been reported to be returning to the U-boat pens at St. Nazaire. Between the Isles D'Oleron and De Re we picked up a contact, dropped flares and bombed on the second run. We straddled the target and the rear gunner said it broke in two. All hell had been going on the whole time, flak, search-lights, tracers and we headed home very much worse for wear. Within 24 hours the sinking was confirmed, it was not a U-boat, but a German A.A. naval vessel. The excessive flak was explained. After that attacking the shipping in the Kattegat was a more relaxing experience. We often flew near to the Swedish coast and seeing the lights of a country at peace gave us a glimpse of normality.

I was sent at the end of this tour to "Spec.N" Navigation School at Shawbury, and on completion of the course was posted back to my squadron as Squadron Navigation Officer, and then, by the end of the

European war, Station Navigation Officer. During those last few days before V.E. Day it was obvious the end was near, our sorties encountered no opposition, and a 48 hour party began. The hangover I had proved not to be a hangover at all, but appendicitis, so I was in dock when the members of the squadron were landing at Norwegian and Danish aerodromes and taking the surrender of the local garrisons.

When we were all awaiting developments which might have sent us to the Far East, I was accepted by B.O.A.C. and was one of many who helped get our civil airline on its feet again. Then B.O.A.C. split in two, the European line became B.E.A. I was on the Middle East and Central African runs, all in DC3's. After ops it was all very laid back, for example, depart Hurn airport, land Lisbon, a change crew took over whilst we had a days rest. Then Lisbon to Accra, hand over to another crew and have four days off in a 'rest house'. Then to Khartoum and Cairo and a week off at that end and then back again. Finally I decided that this was not for me, too much poker and bridge, and after 18 months called it a day. I decided to mend the break and enter University.

It is almost fifty years ago to the day when war began for me. Leaving aside the morality of war, its futility and its waste, what are my abiding memories of those years? How young we all were (the sharp end of all wars are fought by the 18 to 24 age group) and how quickly we grew up and discovered things in ourselves which we might never have found out. Once, when I was in the mess at Staff Navigation College, I was having difficulty packing for postage a couple of bottles of Sherry obtained on a 'training' flight to Gibraltar, and a voice behind me said, "Let me help, before I joined up I worked behind the counter in the Co-op". He was a very young, highly decorated, Wing Commander. If there had been no war would he still be behind that counter? I remember the tensions of ops, and comrades with the twitch, and post-op booze ups. I remember that I was proud to be in the service in which rank merely defined the job one did but otherwise had little significance, and to have served on squadrons manned by aircrew from the whole of the English speaking world.

Dumfries J. Wray.

Flying Officer James Fyfe, M.A. (Navigator)

James Fyfe was born on 23rd May, 1925, in Clackmannan and completed his education at Dollar Academy. As soon as he was of appropriate age he volunteered for flying duties in the RAF. Placed on deferred service he was sent to the University of St. Andrews, spending six months studying on an Arts Course and completed all initial air crew training with the University Air Squadron.

Finally called to A.C.R.C. in London for enlistment he was able to by-pass further initial training and proceeded to RAF Desford in Leicestershire for ab-initio flying training on a grading course.

As a result of his grading he was re-mustered for training as a navigator. By this stage of the war the overseas training schemes had developed a back-log and waits en route to further training became inevitable. As a result James was sent to complete a combat training course with the RAF Regiment before enduring a long wait at the transit camp at Heaton Park in Manchester. Finally, overseas to Canada where he qualified as a navigator at Malton, near Toronto, Ontario, and was awarded a commission.

With the cessation of hostilities in both Europe and the Far East, a great many aircrew were made redundant from further flying duties, James among them. However, his having already made headway in advanced studies in both French and German, James was eminently suited as a volunteer for the RAF Missing Research and Enquiries Service in Europe. Below he tells of harrowing experience in this role in Germany. (His story also forms part of his book "The Great Ingratitude" published by G.C. Books of Wigtown in July 1993).

After demobilisation in October, 1946, James re-entered St. Andrews University where he gained an M.A. (Hons.) degree in Modern Languages. This he has put to good use since as the author of many published text books. Now living in Dumfries, he has a son who is a solicitor and a married daughter who is a school teacher.

In Some Quiet Corner

When the war ended in Europe in May 1945, it was estimated that of the 46,268 members of Bomber Command who were killed in action or posted missing or died while prisoners of war, the fate of some 20,000 was not known. A considerable number had no doubt been claimed by the waters of the North Sea or simply disappeared without trace.

Many had been buried by the Germans and, if identified, had a cross bearing their name and date of death over their grave; if unidentified, there were only three stark words on the cross to tell the world that here lay an "Unbekannter Englischer Flieger" (Unknown British Airman). It was the task of the RAF Missing Research and Enquiry Service, formed shortly after the cessation of hostilities, to comb the Continent, but mainly Germany, since that was where most of the 'Missing' were, in an effort to find and possibly identify the bodies of all those who had been laid to rest in those unmarked graves and to have the wooden crosses suitably inscribed with name, rank, number and date of death. In successful cases next of kin would be immediately informed so they may derive some comfort from knowing that son, husband or brother was lying in a named and tended grave in Cologne or Osnabruck, and not just somewhere on the long line between Munich or Berlin and the North European Coast.

Later on all bodies of RAF personnel were collected from umpteen resting places all over Germany and reburied in certain large British Military Cemeteries, which are now looked after by the Commonwealth War Graves Commission, these being situated in Berlin, Reichswald, Rheinburg and Bad Tolz, and there are smaller ones in Soltau and Oldenburg.

When Japan surrendered in August 1945, nearly all aircrew in the U.K. became redundant, some of them - particularly if they had a knowledge of German - were asked whether they would like to go to Germany as members of MRES. Volunteers reported to Gatwick, where they were taught to drive a car if they could not already do so, provided with a corporal driver, a Humber 4 x 4 and some items of specialised equipment. My own unit went first of all to Headquarters in Hamburg, then to Iserlohn (near Dortmund), where we became No.4 Unit, RAF, Missing Research and Enquiry Service, and were given very comfortable accommodation in a former Nazi official's mansion on the outskirts of the town. Driving through the devastated cities of the Ruhr Valley confirmed our fears that we couldn't have been allocated a more difficult area in the whole of Europe in which to carry out our investigations. "Happy Valley" had claimed a high proportion of the total number of bombers lost and we knew that they had fallen into its town and outlying areas with such frequency that the surviving German policemen and officials would in many cases be unable to produce all essential records because these had been destroyed by fire, and would be incapable of remembering any particular aircraft out of several on any particular night. It was a much easier task for units covering countries such as Norway or Switzerland , when a crashed RAF bomber was not a common occurrence and could therefore be recalled with a fair amount of accuracy, even if not documented.

Each of us was offered the services of an interpreter, usually a fraulein not long out of high school, but whose English was normally very good.

Every missing aircraft known or suspected to have crashed in the area was dealt with individually by the Air Ministry on a separate sheet, which gave all essential details; its type and number, the target, the date of the raid, time of take-off, the names and ranks of each member if its crew and, in some cases, its last known position. It was always a more simple matter to learn where the aircraft had crashed, if it had come down in open country - in our case between the Ruhr and the Dutch border - whereas it was often an exacting and even insuperable exercise trying to trace the occupants of a bomber which had ploughed into a large town such as Essen or Cologne on a night when a score of others had done the same thing.

One can imagine that on the morning following a large scale bombardment the German authorities were more concerned with a whole multitude of tasks they considered more pressing than the burial of the remains of the 'terror flyers' who had caused the havoc and the carnage which surrounded them. In such circumstances dead aircrew were invariably disposed of unceremoniously after much more vital work had been done, and it sometimes happened that hungry town dwellers were somewhat peeved when told that their well tended vegetable patch was to be dug up because there were probably RAF bodies beneath it. To an urban population long hardened to all the horrors of heavy raids the loss of their potatoes or their cabbages was a matter of far greater concern than the fact the bodies of human beings lay nurturing their soil.

Each grave had to be exhumed and the remains searched for any items which would help towards identification - for some unaccountable reason discs had usually been removed by the Germans and not used for identification purposes. Rings and watches (if still present) were sent back to Air Ministry, who had them examined in turn by the next of kin of the missing crew members. If something was definitely recognised as having belonged to a certain sergeant, and there had been three men of this rank in the crew, only one of them could be identified; but if the personal effects of two sergeants were recognised, then you knew who the third was as well, or, if six members of the crew were identified (which was very rare) the seventh also became known. Airmen from the same aircraft were normally interred alongside each other, but very seldom did you have a complete crew. Various items found in the pockets were often invaluable in achieving success - letters being the main one, but bus or train tickets and unusual mascots did often help. But before a new cross was erected by the Germans bearing the man's name, rank, number and date of death, there had to be not the slightest doubt concerning his identity.

When some Burgermeisters or police were interrogated they were found to be rather reticent and even devious, and it was often suspected in such cases that airmen had been murdered by bomb crazed civilians or the SS. Although one or two Germans were in fact tried and executed by the British Authorities for such crimes, it was exceedingly difficult to obtain information leading to an arrest; those questioned could so easily deny all knowledge of a certain crew's existence, and if we had no idea of what had happened to their aircraft there was very little that could be done about it.

In cases where cemeteries were hit by HE bombs, with the result that British and German dead were intermingled to such an extent that the authorities had no idea who was who, all the remains were put together in a communal grave. There were also profitless digs in open ground where RAF personnel were reported to have been buried, but time and circumstances had often dulled the memories of those who had participated in the disposal of the bodies...sometimes those were just thrown together, coffinless, into a hastily dug hole.

Trying to find the last resting place of an individual bomber crew was a painstaking and harrowing business for MRES personnel, many of whom had themselves been operational. It placed much stress and strain upon them, but there was the occasional intriguing case such as that of a Norwegian officer pilot of a rocket firing Typhoon who, it was stated on the Air Ministry sheet, had definitely been seen alive and well by his former ground staff when a POW camp was liberated. Yet the Germans had reported him killed very late in the war, and buried in a village cemetery near Osnabruck. The Research Officer who interviewed the local Burgermeister noticed that the latter became slightly taken aback when told the grave was to be exhumed; accordingly he pumped the official with a barrage of questions and the hesitant and unconvincing replies he received served only to bolster his initial impression. In order to prevent any further hanky-panky, the RAF Officer was by now fairly certain all was not right, he said he would go to the cemetery without delay and wait the arrival of the diggers, whom he expected to be there within the next half hour.

They duly appeared and he stood to one side as they got down to work. When the coffin - and he was surprised there was one at such a late stage in the war - was opened, he could not subdue a gasp of astonishment as he gazed down upon a perfect human skeleton - quite improbable considering the short time lapse - and apparently wearing only an unzipped RAF Irving flying jacket. He got down into the grave and found, clearly printed in indelible ink on a tag at the back of the collar, the Norwegian's name, rank, and number, exactly the same as was inscribed on his cross and in the Air Ministry particulars; not a single item of underwear, no trousers, no socks, nothing else; as far as could be seen, not a single bone had been broken in the entire body, making it blatantly obvious that this man had not met his end thundering into the ground in a Typhoon.

The Officer made his report, emphasising his strong suspicions about the surreptitious nature of the whole matter, and the Unit CO was informed in due course that a Home Office Pathologist would be sent to investigate. Whether he eventually arrived or not I do not know as most of us were demobilised soon afterwards.

We wondered if the Norwegian pilot had been working for enemy intelligence and reported by the grateful Germans as killed so that he might escape punishment. If the ground staff had been right in their identification - and they were adamant that they had no doubts whatsoever - the man could easily have lost himself in the waves of wandering humanity which were part and parcel of the immediate post-war scene all over Europe, but on the other hand why should the Germans, who were not exactly without their worries in the Spring of 1945, have bothered to go to such pains when everything around them was collapsing. Then again it was difficult to accept that any Germans, notorious as they were for lack of subtlety in their thinking, would have resorted to a ploy so unbelievably amateurish that it wouldn't have duped a five years old; and finally, was it likely that a young Norwegian pilot, who had escaped his country in a small boat to reach the U.K., would have been in league with the enemy? Unless, of course, he had been sent to Britain for that very purpose.

Such cases, however, were extremely rare, and the one just described quite exceptional. Usually the work entailed the same old slog day after day. Travelling amidst the never ending rubble and pitiable inhabitants. Some of us became rather depressed, not only with ghoulish task, but with the odds against achieving satisfying results.

Yet, we did derive much consolation from the fact, thanks to our endeavours a number of families did learn where loved ones had been put to rest and were later able to visit their graves.

Dumfries James Fyfe.

Warrant Officer Rowland Maddocks. (Navigator)

A Lancashire man, Rowland Maddocks was born in Bolton on 2nd April 1915. After leaving Bolton Secondary School he attended both the Bolton School of Art and the Manchester School of Art, and became a lithographic artist in 1934 - an occupation he followed until joining the Royal Air Force. Rowland volunteered for aircrew duties in the RAF on Monday the 4th of September 1939, the day following the declaration of war. He trained as a navigator and between 1940 and 1941 was employed as an instructor at No.5 and 54 O.T.U.'s in Fighter Command, teaching map reading and other navigational techniques to both day and night fighter pilots. During that period he flew in Defiants, Blenheims and Beaufighters.

In March 1942 Rowland was transferred to Bomber Command and completed a full tour of operations on Halifax bombers with Nos.12 and 103 Squadrons. About this period he is totally reticent. However he did take part in one further night operation which, for five of his crew, was the final disaster. Rowland evaded capture initially but was betrayed into enemy hands. Below he gives a splendidly eloquent account of his treatment as a prisoner of war and final release to freedom, in which personal initiative played a great part.

Demobilised in December 1945 Rowland returned to his pre-war profession and formed a Design Company in Edinburgh. He finally retired in June 1979. Now, sadly, a widower, he lives in the Royal Air Force Residential Home, Dowding House, in Moffat, Dumfriesshire.

Never Volunteer (and if you don't believe me, read on..)

This story begins on Tuesday 20th October, 1942
Location:- RAF Elsham Wolds, North Lincolnshire. Squadron:- 103.

Three events happened that day, not world shattering as such but would have a far more reaching effect than I could have imagined at the time.

(1) I had finished my tour of Operations. (2) I was posted to OTU Sutton Bridge, Lincolnshire, under Wg.Cdr. 'Sailor' Malan. Having been with him previously at 54 OTU in late 1940 I was very pleased. (3) Unless there was a major operation before the weekend the Squadron was to stand

down for conversion from Halifaxes to Lancasters.

Wg.Cdr. Malan arranged to collect me on the following Monday, October 26th, so I asked my wife to come down from Edinburgh for the weekend.

On Saturday morning , the 24th, an Operation was announced for that night. As it was going to be the last trip for the Squadron Halifaxes I was gently invited to go as Bomb-aimer, an offer I couldn't refuse. A second Pilot, on his first trip to gain experience, made up our crew of eight. Although we were not to know it at the time, the offensive was starting at El Alamein. Our target was Milan, I suppose to let the Italians at home know there was a war on.

The most difficult task for me, after dragging my wife all the way down from Edinburgh, was to break the news that owing to unforeseen circumstances I would not see her until Sunday morning. I leave her reaction to your imagination.

We took off at 6.30pm with a full bomb load, extra fuel and a flight plan to touch down on our return at Ford on the Sussex Coast to refuel for the journey back to our base (Note that name). We crossed the channel, passed to the north of Paris and began the long haul south. Climbing steadily to cross the Alps we were jumped by a ME.110 fighter at 20,000ft., east of Paris. The aircraft was a flaming torch within seconds and only three of us in the lower front managed to bale out, Bert (Dizzy) Spiller, Geoff Woolerton and myself. The other five crew members died in the wreckage and are buried in the tiny cemetery of Nant-le-Grande in the Meuse Department.

Bemused and bloody wet, I found myself sitting in the middle of a muddy field. After a few minutes I assessed my position. It was 9pm, Saturday night, I had five Craven 'A' cigarettes, a packet of Horlicks tablets, a few Francs and seven and six in loose change. At home a new wife and a pending commission, now finished. I wondered why I had opened my big mouth on the previous day but there was no way of calling the whole thing off. At least I was alive and unhurt. I could see no lights or habitations so I crept into some trees at the edges of the field, wrapped myself in the parachute and tried to sleep.

Came the dawn and the sound of a church bell in the distance. It was 8am. I buried the chute in the wood and wandered cautiously around expecting a German behind every bush. I came to a road and with a stroke of luck found a milestone, or should it be a kilometre stone, Toul 40klms. The Intelligence Service of the RAF, with commendable foresight, had supplied a handkerchief map of France which soon gave me an approximate position. Making for the Swiss border on 'Shank's Pony' had never really been one of my ambitions but it had to be attempted. A distance of 120 miles at 10miles a night could see me yodelling within a fortnight if I could find or steal some grub.

The road went due east towards Germany, no thank you, so that night I moved south across the fields. By dawn I had maybe done six miles with pretty rough going and, with no sign of a decent road, it was time to lay up for the day. That evening I found a road to the south which looked promising and made progress easier. I crept through a couple of small villages but feeling that the crash site was still a bit close I kept very quiet and cautious. If it became necessary to leave the road because of traffic or a village too large for comfort progress became a nightmare of ditches, fences, streams and worst of all, half the cowshit of Northern France. I was also feeling the pangs of hunger. A turnip from a field provided little in the way of nourishment but at least it was something to chew on.

Twice in one night I tried to make contact at houses where I saw a chink of light but in both cases the doors were closed on me. I spoke to a woman on the edge of one village but she took to her heels and ran. Even in 1942 they seemed to be afraid of tall dark strangers. Must have been the impeccable accent. By now I thought I had done 20 miles, as the crow flies, and spent a whole sunny day overlooking a canal with plenty of barges on the move. However judging by their size they were heading for the Moselle or the Rhine. It was better to leave well alone.

That night I cheered up when I came across a railway line heading South. I followed it for hours before I realised the rails were rusty. Shortly before daybreak on the fourth day, back on the road, I was unable to avoid a gendarme going to work on his bike. His advice to get off the road and into the trees, although well intentioned, seemed rather pointless if he had noticed the state I was in, unshaven and muck up to my knees. When I mentioned food, "J'ai faim, avez du pain", he pondered for a moment then led me to a small tumble-down cottage at the edge of the village. The woman in the house gave me a very welcome breakfast of egg, mushrooms and bread. I expressed my gratitude as best I could but alas, there was a heavy price to pay. I couldn't followed their conversation but I soon found out she intended to claim the 10,000 francs, offered by the Germans for Allied Aircrew. The gendarme, who I believe to this day would have put me back in the trees, compromised as he was, had no alternative but to arrest me. Incidentally, the penalty for aiding airmen was summary execution for a man and concentration camp for a woman. When I went back in the sixties I was told she collected the reward but on liberation in

1944 the Resistance cut off her hair and paraded her through the village. She died in 1956.

After spending the night in the local cell I was collected next morning by a Wermacht Officer and guard and taken to Army H.Q. at Bar-le-Duc. Under German Military practice each Service looks after it's own, so I was handed over to the Luftwaffe at an airfield near St. Dizier. The pilot who shot us down came to see me. He was very correct and polite, commiserating with words to be repeated so often to so many "For you the war is over".

On to Germany and the Interrogation Centre at Dulag Luft, Frankfurt-on-Main. Two weeks in solitary gave one all the time in the world not to fill in the bogus 'Red Cross' form. "What is your religious denomination?" "Where are you from? Where were you going? What was your bomb load?" With hindsight the solitary confinement and some of the stupid questions were designed just to put one firmly at the bottom of the Third Reich pecking order. After a three day rail journey in cattle trucks, visiting most of the network's sidings, we arrived at Stalag Luft 3 on the Baltic Coast, some 30 miles east of Rostock.

Much has been written and documented about life in the camps so I'll only touch briefly on the first year. We were well treated by the 'Goons'. Six of us to a room, cooking facilities, showers, plenty of Red Cross food parcels and good recreational activities. Once settled we messed the Germans around as best we could. We dug tunnels, very easy to dig in the sandy soil but easier to find. If the Security Guards became suspicious in came a heavy steamroller to cover every inch of the compound putting paid to our excavations. It was all good fun and kept everybody busy. There was a romantic novel in the camp library which most people read about a British P.O.W. in the first world war who escaped and was befriended and hidden by a German prostitute till the end of the war. We had a chap Miller who got away but was brought back after a week or so complaining bitterly about wandering around Germany unable to find a prostitute. The guards were mainly old sweats and took everything in good part. In June I got my first letter from my wife. She heard my name in February on the Lord Haw Haw programme. Up till then she only knew I was listed missing by the Air Ministry.

In July we got the "Blitz" on Hamburg. The prevailing wind carried the smoke for over a hundred miles and blotted out the sun for days. With intensive raids on Lubeck, Rostock, Peenemunde and Berlin, attitudes began to change and the phrase 'Terror Flieger' entered the German vocabulary.

October 1943 saw us on the move again. We were trundled to a new camp, Hydekrug, on the Lithuanian border in the usual wagons, (8 Cheveaux or 40 hommes). The previous winter had been cold by our standards, sometimes 20-30 degrees below, but this place was getting uncomfortably close to the North Pole for our liking, and neither was the camp comparable to our last home. Around this time the first of the Americans arrived from the Fortresses and their numbers steadily increased. Winter dragged on making a bleak landscape even bleaker. The snow finally gave way to a Spring of slush and more slush. Summer finally came and with it the best news yet, 'D' Day. The first real hopeful sign that we would not be here for ever. The excitement of the Normandy Invasion had hardly died away when the rumble of faraway guns signalled the approach of the Russian Northern Front. It was now July and the fact that over 2,000 British and USA aircrew could soon be liberated was not lost on our captors.

We were on the move again. Most were sent westward by rail but about 700 British were to go by sea from the port of Memel, 40 miles away. When we arrived at the mile long dockside we saw a beautiful Liner painted overall in Arctic Blue but, needless to say it was not for us. Just ahead was the S.S. Insterburg, a 1500 ton collier with a smokestack a la John Masefield. We were loaded aboard 300 in the front hold with me and another 499 in the rear hellhole, the only exits being two vertical steel ladders reaching 40 feet up to battened down hatches. We set sail. The vibrations and rumblings suggested the Insterburg was first cousin to Brunel's "Great Eastern". In batches of ten, about every ten hours, we climbed the ladders to the scuppers for the luxury of a breath of fresh air etc. etc. Down below again the creaking and leaking rivets plus half an inch of steel plate between us, the Baltic, Russian submarines, mines and aircraft raised ones doubts again about the wisdom of joining up in '39. However, after a three day "cruise" we arrived unscathed at the naval base of Swinemunde. For all the world like miners coming off backshift we emerged from the depths and were met at the bottom of the gangway by a squad of army and civilian blacksmiths. We were crudely riveted and manacled in pairs with a 15 inch length of chain and escorted to the familiar wagons. As if the gods were not completely satisfied the U.S. Air Force put on a daylight raid on the docks. Oil drums set on fire to create a smoke screen made the conditions very unpleasant. If the Reader, assuming he or she is still with us, would like a little more, the heavy cruisers Prince Eugen and Liepzig lying alongside no more than fifty yards away, opened up with their big guns. My previous experience with firearms had been with the .303 calibre so I was quite impressed.

24 hours later we arrived at the Polish Border. At a small wayside halt we were met by a new company of guards. These were young Kriegsmariners who, with fixed bayonets looked menacing enough without one of our clots deciding to air his German, asked if they had no ships left to sail in. There seemed to be an unusually large number of Dobermans and Alsatians around as we formed up in columns of 200 and set off at ten minute intervals along a dirt road between pine trees. With a noon temperature in the mid eighties, fully dressed and laden with our few belongings the dogs were released and the sailors began prodding with their bayonets. Within seconds, hustled along faster and faster, we were in full flight. It is terribly disconcerting to be singled out by a slavering Doberman; I would willing have given two weeks back pay for a large bone to throw to that animal. Luckily he took a fancy to a slower moving body just as my partner, some six inches shorter than myself, took off like a 1944 Seb Coe. We both survived unhurt, at least physically . There had been much talk about the recent murder of RAF Officers and with 'Friend Hitler' in a foul mood, a mass grave round the next corner was never far from our thoughts. Many collapsed, brought into camp in a very distressed condition and few of us escaped without a painful jab, dog bite or bruise. Harry Richards and I, having developed a close affinity during this time, meet every year. He lives in the Welsh Valleys and I shouldn't wonder if he kicks hell out of some poor unsuspecting Corgi when no one is looking.

Stalag Luft 6, Gross Tyschow, welcomed us in style with a bodyguard flanking both sides of the entrance clubbing with rifle butts. The hassle of the last few days was said to be in retaliation for similar treatment meted out to German POW's in Canada. No foundation for this claim was ever substantiated after the war. In RAF Prisoner of War folklore our journey has become known as the infamous "Run up the Road".

The camp itself was in an unfinished state. We spent the next two months in small sheds about 12ft x 5ft high at the apex. They held about eight bodies but we could never quite agree with the Germans what to call them. They said chalets so we compromised and called them dog kennels. Food was in short supply, the Red Cross Parcels having dried up, presumably because of the chaos and military demands on the transport system. We existed on bread, awful potatoes, soup and occasional meat which turned the soup into stew.

Apart from the attempt on Hitler's life, bringing with it a rash of Nazi salutes morning, noon and night, there was little of note as the Allies made slow progress. The German Offensive in the Ardennes put the wind up us somewhat because of the song and dance propaganda the Germans made of it. However within a month everything was back to square one.

With the Americans and British now massing on the Rhine, the Russians having taken Warsaw and sweeping across Poland it was decided to move us again. On February 6th we began a forced march to the west covering about 20miles a day depending on the 'hotel' accommodation. We slept in barns, woods and once or twice in the open with temperatures well below freezing. Straggling along the roads of Northern Germany we were caught up with thousands of refugees fleeing from the Russians. We were given a small but regular bread ration and we had a Field Kitchen which supplied hot soup. Nevertheless, many of our numbers fell by the wayside and were picked up. The more serious cases were transported to central areas. After a month on the road the horse pulling our kitchen dropped dead so we had him for supper. The guards rustled up another one which happily lasted until the end. Dysentery became a serious problem and we were grateful to the USA publishing industry for the supply of paperbacks which had recently become available. After crossing the Elbe we finally arrived at Stalag 11B, Fallingbostel, on Luneburg Heath in early April. We had walked 600 kilometres. The camp was overcrowded with every nationality but at least we thought we could sit it out until the end.

This was not to be the case and with the British less than 50 miles away the King's men of the RAF were marched again towards the Elbe. After a day this yo-yo existence became less and less appealing. Having noticed a marked reduction in the number of guards a disappearing act by some of us seemed feasible. That night four of us, G. R.Gregory, Dave White, Fred Simpson and myself left the group and made it back to the camp. It was a shambles and most of the guards had deserted. Some Army POWs, including some Paras. taken at Arnhem helped us greatly by sharing what food they had but it was not a very attractive place to be. However a couple of days later half a dozen tanks of Seventh Armoured pulled up at our front door, said Hello! and carried ON. At last we were free, or so we thought.

The ill and injured were to be evacuated to the U.K. first and the remainder would have to stay put for some weeks. Once again we decided to make our own arrangements and went on the move again. We walked down into the small town of Fallingbostel and got a lift on a large transporter, with an escort. They were taking a load of steel mesh further north to be used as temporary runways. We got off at Soltau, some 12 miles on, and found ourselves in the middle of a small scale battle. In the town square there was a field dressing station treating wounded of both sides.

Although there was only small arms and sniper fire we were now confirmed pacifists and beat a hasty retreat. In a quiet part of the town we noticed a car in a driveway and decided to liberate it. A fattish civilian got overexcited when we pushed the car onto the road but , not understanding the language, we chose to ignore him. After pushing for some time without success a REME Unit, newly arrived in a garden opposite, listened to our tale of woe about the car, an Opel, then set about it. Within an hour we were on our way with a new battery, a full tank, 'K' rations and three Enfield rifles. These were in case we encountered "Werewolves", German fanatics who still expected to win the war. At the beginning of the long march I had purloined a Road Atlas of Germany from an unattended guardroom and this now came in very useful to plan our way south. It is still a prized possession.

On our way we tried our luck at a small farmhouse to get eggs. The woman gave us two and told us she was very worried about her husband who was a prisoner of war in Normandy. We promised to have a word with Mr Churchill when we got back. Inspired as this answer was it failed to produced any more eggs. As we drove on we could see an aerial armada of Fortresses going east. We also passed small areas of white crosses, evidence of some short battle only a day or so passed. We reached Neinburg on the river Weser in the afternoon. Once again a REME Unit entertained us. A grenade thrown into the river provided supper and with plenty of local booze we had a night to remember. A Dutchman attached to the Unit as an interpreter advised us to take the car to his father, a doctor, in Eindhoven and we would collect 4,000 Guilders. Maybe we could get some reward after all. The following morning we hardly recognised the car. It had been serviced and camouflaged and roundels on the wings. We got a great send off and it was, Eindhoven here we come.

Good progress was made without incident so by mid morning we had got round Osnabruck and reached the Dortmund-Ems Canal. then disaster struck! While crossing a Bailey Bridge we were stopped by a Military Policeman whose mother had never known wedlock. Despite our explanations and protests we were divested of our car, bottles and rifles and taken to a Displaced Persons Camp. A really charming place where Typhus, Typhoid and Dysentery were freely available without prescription. We were well and truly in it up to our necks. The Camp was run by an elderly British Army Captain and a dozen soldiers. Under different circumstances he would have got our sympathy but in no uncertain terms we made our position clear that we had no intention of staying in his rat infected old mill. Sensing he might have a mutiny of sorts on his hands he said there was an airfield some five miles away and even provided transport for us to go and check it out.

Although the field had runways, it was very heavily cratered. Apparently deserted, we had almost given up hope but saw of all things a Manchester Bomber revving up in a blast bay. The pilot, an American with no crew, was engaged in flying medical supplied forward and was now on his way back to Brussels. On hearing our story he said "Jump in boys and make yourselves comfortable". Lucky us!, a British pilot may have asked for identification, leave passes or form so and so. With a scratch crew of six, we had just picked up two New Zealand soldiers from the rat camp. We took off and arrived in Brussels 20 minutes later. Following him into a Marquee full of WAAFs, lipsticks and typewriters he was given his next destination. "Where are we going?" I asked. "I'll have to check the map, it's a place called Ford" he replied. "Don't bother" I said, "I know where it is". The Germans were still throwing up some flak from isolated pockets on the Belgian Coast but we landed safely at Ford about 7.30pm. I had made my landing back home to the right place but almost exactly two and a half years late. It was April 23rd.

We had taken less than 36 hours to travel from a battle zone in the middle of Germany. What more could we ask? We found out later that our poor companions on the Elbe were still marching. After crossing the river once more, they were attacked by our own rocket firing aircraft, being mistaken for an enemy column. They lost many dead and injured but were finally set free and flown back home at the end of the month. Meantime we left Ford the following morning, first to London and then on to Cosford for a medical and delousing. I was pronounced fit but had lost three stones in weight. We were given three weeks compassionate leave and I happily celebrated VE day in Edinburgh.

After the war Gregory, White and myself kept in touch but were unable to trace Simpson. Then four years ago I was given his address in Middlesborough. On our way home from Northampton to Edinburgh I decided to call on him. After briefing my wife and guessing that he was unlikely to recognise me on a cold and frosty morning forty-three years on, I rang the bell. His wife opened the door and confirmed a Mr. Fred Simpson lived there. She invited us in and called him from the bathroom. Still the same old Simmy. "Good morning" he said, obviously not recognising me, "What can I do for you?". "Well, Mr Simpson, I have just travelled up from the south because I heard you were interested in a 1935 Opel Saloon". "Who told you that?, what a laugh, I hate the Germans". "I am sorry about that, but I had it on good authority that you once had a quarter share in an Opel''. ''Definitely got the wrong bloke, mister, I've always had Fords''. Unable to keep a straight face after that gem I had to say, ''Well, Fred, all I can say is that you have a poor memory, I'm Lofty Maddocks''. There was a silence of a tomb then an explosion of mild expletives. We had found our survivor and a new 'Re-union member'.

We still have one nagging question that will not go away. What did that Military Policeman on the Dortmund-Ems Canal do with that BEAUTIFUL OPEL?

(I hope he got drunk on our bottles of booze and fell into the canal!)

Moffat R. Maddocks.

Flt.Lt Stevie Tait (Bucanneer Navigator) 208 Sqn, RAF Lossiemouth.

The Gulf War Jan-Mar 1991

I was born on the 5th of August 1961 in Dumfries. My family lived in the village of Penpont, 15 miles north of Dumfries, but moved to the town itself in 1972. My secondary education was completed at Dumfries High School and Dumfries Academy. At the age of 17, I left school and joined the merchant navy with the P & O Shipping Company as a deck officer cadet. Due to the decline of the British merchant navy, I was made redundant in 1982.

RAF officer training was completed at RAF Cranwell in the summer of 1983, and after this I was posted to RAF Finningley in South Yorkshire to start my navigator training. I was then posted to Buccaneers in March 1985, and arrived at Lossiemouth in June 1985 via 4 months flying the Hawk aircraft at RAF Chivenor in North Devon. Buccaneer training was initially on 237 OCU, a 6 month conversion course. I was married to Diana in September 1985 in Trowbridge, Wiltshire. On completion of my OCU course I was posted to 208 Sqn in Jan 1986, and after becoming a Qualified Weapons Instructor, an Electronic Warfare Officer and after attending the AAFCE Tactical Leadership programme I was once again back on 237 OCU this time as an Instructor. This was in September 1990 and the Invasion of Kuwait had taken place that summer, so tension was already beginning to mount.

In the Autumn of 1990, a work-up of several crews, including myself and my front seater Flt.Lt Ian (Beks) Baston, had taken place but by Christmas the Maritime Buccaneer Wing had been told that there would be no requirement for the ageing 30 years old Buccaneer to go to the Gulf. During our first week back at work in January 1991 the Air Officer Commanding No.18 Group (the Buccaneers Group) visited RAF Lossiemouth and told the aircrew present that the Buccaneers would definitely not be required. That was on a Tuesday afternoon, and on that Friday evening at 7 o'clock, I was among the 3 initial crews that took off from Lossiemouth in a Hercules bound for Muharraq on the island of Bahrain.

During those hectic couple of days at Lossie many jobs had to be done, including some modifications to our grand old aircraft. At one of the press conferences in London prior to our departure, the then Defence

Secretary Tom King was asked why a 30 years old geriatric bomber was being sent to what was a "high tech war". His answer was "to increase the accuracy of the precision bombing."

The Buccaneers had been deployed to support the Tornados, who by now had reverted to a medium level bombing campaign. We were to act as laser designators for laser guided bombs carried by the Tornados. After 3 training sorties, to look at this new type of attack, the Buccaneer was deployed in anger in the war. The initial targets tasked were bridges in Iraq, the re-supply routes of Saddam's army. Success rate was excellent. Bridges were followed by selected buildings on airfields and the runways themselves. Later in the campaign the Buccaneers carried their own bombs for targets of opportunity in addition to designating for the Tornados. The attack package was vast with Electronic, Fighter and Tanker support.

Beks and myself flew 16 missions the last being at the end of February. We were then placed on standby before returning to a glorious welcome at Lossiemouth in the middle of March. The Buccaneer had shown its flexibility to adapt to new demands and new theatres of operation, the grand old bomber had acquitted herself marvellously with not one mission lost through unservicabilities. Every member of the Buccaneer detachment (nicknamed the Sky Pirates) was proud to have flown this terrific old aircraft.

Coming up to date, 237 OCU folded in September 1991 and I returned to 208 to form the Buccaneer Training Flight (BTF). The BTF trained new Buccaneer pilots until the middle of March 1993. I am posted to Tornados in May of this year to eventually go on to 617 Sqdn at the end of 1993 and return to Lossie with 617 in April 1994. As I leave the Buccaneer after almost 8 years, I will have in the region of 1700 hours on the Buccaneer.

My wife, myself and our two children, Fraser (six) and Jennifer (three) live just outside Lossie in the village of Lhanbryde. My hobbies include golf, gardening and I have recently qualified as a football referee.

Lossiemouth

Stevie Tait.

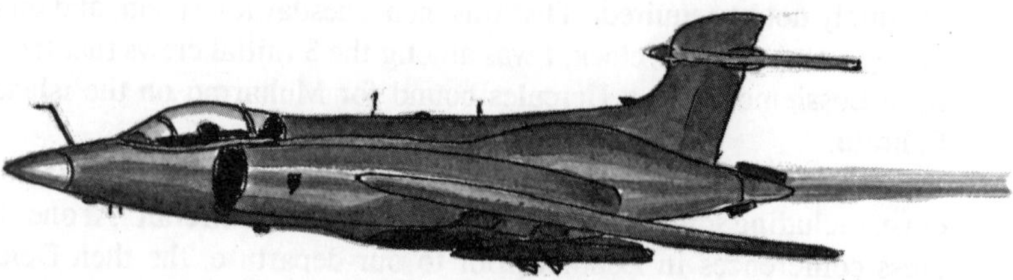

The Pilots' Perorations

Squadron Leader Peter J.S. Boggis, D.F.C., R.A.F. (Rtd.) (Pilot)

Peter Boggis enjoyed a full career in the Royal Air Force, serving with distinction as a pilot in Bomber command. Born in Barnstaple, Devon in September 1918 he attended Bloxham School in Banbury and was granted a short service commission in the RAF in August 1939; which was later raised to a permanent commission in the General Duties Branch.

During a span of twenty-eight years Peter flew no less than seventeen different types of aircraft including a range of heavy bombers, Wellingtons, Stirlings, Halifaxes, Lancasters, Lincolns, Mosquitoes and Varsities. He had the privilege of being the pilot chosen to fly the Stirling aircraft presented to Bomber Command by Lady McRobert carrying the slogan "McRobert's Reply". Lady McRobert also gave four Hurricane fighters to the RAF; these gifts commemorated her three sons all killed in the air, two whilst on wartime operations.

On retirement from the active list in October 1967, Peter became a Welfare Officer with Wiltshire County Council. Now retired and living with his wife Kay, in Kirkbean on the Solway Coast, they have one daughter qualified in Medicine and specialising as a radiologist. Peter lists his hobbies as stamp collecting and golf, and is a keen supporter of athletics and rugby. He is also deputy chairman of our Branch of the A.C.A Below he gives two accounts of wartime experiences.

Naval Incident.

Many crews, I'm sure, experienced the odd snag with Stirling undercarriages at some stages or other. Here is what happened at 1651 HCU Waterbeach one night in June 1942.

I was the Screen pilot of a Freshman trip and had just taken off with full bomb load when the undercarriages refused to retract: We tried all possible remedies but it wouldn't budge and we were diverted to the Wash to jettison our bombs.

We managed to stagger to 2000 ft and proceeded to the dropping area where greatly relieved we felt the bombs go - the engines were getting a bit over-strained with the drag. Immediately flak opened up on us from all directions, coloured streams hosepiping into the sky and criss-crossing all around us: the Wash was obviously occupied by warships, probably escorting a convoy, and not very pleased at having bombs dropped on them even though safe. The navigator fired the colours of the day off as fast as he could load the cartridges into the Very Pistol but it made no difference and the firing continued. At this height on a moonlit night we were sitting ducks and the only remedy was to put the nose down and dive out to sea, which was the direction we were heading anyway.

After what seemed an eternity, we cleared the convoy which we could now see in the moonlight, and being down to near sea level we flew south parallel to the coast climbing again to height before crossing the coast at another spot. We saw an aircraft approaching us which was identified as a Beaufighter but we had no more Very cartridges left; all we could do was to flash our navigation lights on and off and hope for the best. He had probably been alerted by all the firing in the Wash and had been sent along to investigate. Fortunately he wasn't quite as trigger happy as the Navy and I'm glad to say left us in peace - it wouldn't have been the first time a Stirling had been mistaken for a German Condor.

We landed at Base without further incident and were rather shattered to find our aircraft had collected over fifty holes, one of them apparently made by an Oerlikan shell, but luckily no one was injured and nothing vital hit.

It transpired afterwards that the Navy had reported the convoy in position in the Wash but this information for some reason had not filtered down to Station level in time.

A Captain from the Admiralty came to Waterbeach the next day to interview the crew and was gracious enough to offer the Navy's apologies; we could read between the lines what a responsibility the Navy had for these convoys and how alert they had to be etc. etc. He didn't say so in so many words, but the implication was that the Navy shot first and asked the questions afterwards, and this we supposed was understandable under the circumstances. He departed with the words "It was a good job our gunners were firing over open sights." whatever that was meant to infer.

T.F.U. Defford

In January 1943 I was posted to Telecommunications Flying Unit, Defford near Worcester. This was the sharp end of the Telecommunications Research Establishment at Malvern, known briefly as T.R.E., where all the various radar devices for the RAF were thought up in pursuance of the war and tested out by the flying unit at Defford. T.R.E. moved from Swanage on the South coast after the Bruneval raid had captured large chunks of the German Wurtzberg - their early warning system and it was thought that they might retaliate. Malvern Boys Public School was taken over and T.R.E. moved in with their equipment and scientists, known as Boffins, some well known names among them including Bernard Lovell later Sir Bernard of Joddrell Bank fame.

T.F.U. Defford consisted of two wings, Defensive (Fighters etc.) and Offensive (Bombers and Coastal Command), and being a Bomber type I was posted to the latter - this account deals only with this wing.

We had a variety of aircraft including the Lancaster Mks. I, II, III, Halifax Mks. I, II, Stirlings Mks. I, III, Wellingtons Mks. Ic, II, III, Blenheim Mk. IV, Hudson, Mosquito and a few others, and the pilots were expected to fly all of these. We had no dual - just a demonstration circuit and Pilot's Notes - so we were a bit vulnerable if anything went wrong. Fortunately emergencies were rather rare and accidents few. The Boffins flew on most of our flights as well as Specialist Navigation Officers and occasionally Signals Officers. A lot of the testing was on H2S, warning devices for air gunners, airborne search radar for Coastal Command. We also did early trials on G.C.A. and equipment for locating dinghies - one pilot earning himself a well-merited A.F.C. by volunteering to parachute at night in mid-winter into the Irish Sea.

Security at Defford was very tight and RAF Police were everywhere; aircrew needed special passes signed by the Station Commander to enter the aircraft, and aircraft were not permitted to land elsewhere or stay away overnight without his authority. On one occasion I had to fly a Lancaster to Wyton for the A.O.C. 8 Group to carry out some tests on a new stabilised H2S. Air Commodore Bennett, as he then was, flew the aircraft himself with me as a passenger and the Group Navigation Officer working the radar. After an hour's flying over Nottingham and Leicester (for some reason these two cities were usually the targets for H2S testing - probably a good picture on the screen) Bennett landed and he and the navigator seemed pleased with the project. As there was a party in the Mess that night and I had done a tour of ops previously at Wyton I boldly asked the A.C.O. if he wouldn't like to do further testing the next day. After all if you don't ask......... He might well have said "yes, bring the aircraft back tomorrow" and that would have served me right. But instead he said "I presume you want to go to the party?" and when I replied "yes I did" he went to the nearest telephone and spoke to the C.O. at Defford and told him he was very pleased with the equipment and would like to try it out again the next day, and he would accept responsibility for the aircraft staying overnight. Then he turned to me and said "There you are Boggis, enjoy your evening. 0900 hours take-off, don't be late". A pretty reasonable gesture I thought.

While on the subject of security I must mention an incident involving the U.S.A.F. By the end of 1943 we had two Flying Fortresses attached to Defford, equipped with H2S and flown by their own crews. Supposedly they were subject to the same security regulations as we were. When the Americans started up their Pathfinder Force they threw an Inaugural party at Alconbury and several of us went from Defford, but not allowed to fly there we went by car. Imagine our surprise on arrival to see both the Defford B17's on the airfield, complete with their radar domes for all to see. Then walking along a corridor in one of the buildings we passed the skipper of one of these B17's with an American nurse on his arm. Someone asked him where his navigator was and he said "Down at the radar section" (few people knew the Americans had radar in those days). The nurse said "Gee, you got radar here?" and he replied "Sure, Honey". But to his credit he told her he couldn't show her it.

Later we discovered that the Americans had filled these two aircraft with nurses from their hospital near Malvern and flown them up to Alconbury. Goodness knows how they smuggled them into the base at Defford, let alone into the aircraft!

One of our pilots had an unfortunate accident: half way down the runway on take-off he found he had got "George" in, tried to overpower it but was not successful and ended up going through the fence that surrounded Station Headquarters and came to rest outside the Station Commander's office. No one was injured and the aircraft was only slightly damaged, repairable on the Unit.

The C.O. rushed out of his office and into the aircraft, grabbed the first person he saw, who happened to be a civilian Boffin and shouted at him "What happened?" and this fellow, despite being a bit shaken, replied with commendable sang-froid "I don't know - Why don't you ask the pilot?" The outcome was that the pilot, in due course, was sent to the Brighton Disciplinary course for two weeks, which we all took a dim view of, especially as he had been an acting Squadron Leader in Bomber Command with a DSO and DFC. He came back from it none the worse for wear with horrific stories of what went on there, and amazingly without too much bitterness. These discip. courses, I feel, were never intended for this sort of thing and I don't think it would have happened in Bomber Command; but Defford was not in Bomber Command and these things were viewed differently on non-operational stations.

We were always rather apprehensive in case we did something silly like a taxiing accident. Sure enough an incident did occur to me - I was taxiing a Stirling to the hangar when the brakes failed and although I quickly switched all engines off the aircraft slowly rolled down the gentle slope to the hangar doors. Visions of Brighton loomed large before me, particularly as the propeller boss of one engine just touched the hangar door. The dent on the boss was insignificant and luck was on my side as the Engineering Officer who saw the incident quickly had the boss replaced and we thought no one would be any the wiser. But people talked of course and several days later the acting C.O. of my Wing sent for me and asked why I had not reported this incident and I should consider myself lucky that I was not up before the Station Commander. However he said he was not going to pursue it further and that was the end of the matter. Sad to say he died heroically a year later when shot down flying a Stirling at Arnhem.

Flying back on one occasion from an experimental sortie I thought I would see how a Lancaster would cope, firstly on two engines, and then on one engine. I was at 20,000 feet and with two fans feathered the aircraft could just maintain height (this was the Merlin engined type): with three feathered I had to put it into a gentle glide path to keep up the airspeed. I was most impressed with the performance. What the Boffins thought of some of our antics I can't imagine but I reckon they were pretty long-suffering.

Kirkbean — Peter Boggis.

Acknowledgement.
The story "Naval Incident" by Peter Boggis is reproduced by kind permission of the Editor of "Stirling Remembered" the journal of the Stirling Aircraft Association.

Flying Officer James W. Rogers, B.Sc. (Eng.), M.I.C.E. (Pilot)

Jim Rogers was born on 4th May 1924 in the coastal town of Nickerie in Dutch Guiana (now Surinam) in South America, where his father was, at that time, a consultant engineer. Whilst he was still a child the family moved back to the United Kingdom and Jim was able to complete his education at Aberdeen Grammar School. At the age of 18 years, Jim volunteered for flying duties as a pilot in the RAF, enlisting in March 1943 at A.C.R.C. in London. He completed initial ground training at No.8 I.T.W. Newquay in Cornwall and was sent to No.6 E.F.T.S. at Sywell for his grading course, to determine whether he was suitable for further training as a pilot. He was, and in his own words below he outlines his experience in Canada, culminating in his gaining his wings in mid-1944 at No.9 S.F.T.S., Centralia, Ontario, and being granted a commission.

He and his crew flew their own Liberator from Montreal to Jessore near Calcutta, arriving in early April 1945 and became members of No.357 Squadron. At that time the squadron was principally engaged in special operations under the direction of the Special Operations Executive. These they later continued from China Bay in, then Ceylon.

Towards the end of 1945, Jim was returned to the U.K. and posted to Syreston in Nottingham, where he collected a fresh crew and converted to flying transport Dakotas. After an instrument flying course at Snaith in Yorkshire, the crew moved to Melbourne, also in Yorkshire, for training in B.A.B.S techniques (Beam Approach Beacon System) and qualified to act as calibrators of B.A.B.S. installations elsewhere. They were then again posted overseas to rejoin Far East Asia Command as members of No.31 Squadron then based in Batavia, in Java. From that base they were engaged in supply operations, the evacuation of wounded and repatriation to friendly territory of Dutch Prisoners of War.

In due course Jim's crew were transferred to No.52 Squadron, based at Mingladon, in Burma, where again they continued in the support role on flights to Singapore and on long hauls to Hong Kong.

Early in 1947 Jim returned to U.K. and was demobilised in March. Wishing to follow his father's profession he obtained a place at Aberdeen University where he gained a degree in engineering. He has since practised as a Civilian Engineer. Now retired, he and his wife live in Moffat, Dumfriesshire; their family of three are now all adult. Keen on outdoor pursuits, Jim lists his hobbies as fishing, shooting and golf.

Ten Times "Roly"

In films and stories of pilot training in the RAF one always hears of the unfortunate chaps who panics on his first solo flight, usually with dire results. My short story to-day is of such an airman, a great friend of mine, who really choked-up in a very big way on his first solo flight at E.F.T.S., which scared the daylights out of him, and kept most of the rest of us in jokes for weeks after.

"Roly" (we will call him this, although this was not his real name) was a Londoner, an exceptionally pleasant fellow, and very quiet. We had both gone through grading school together, flown the necessary hours for grading, and were both deemed as suitable for pilot training.

We were sent to the prairies of Canada to do our E.F.T.S., to a small drome called De Winston just south of Calgary.

We both progressed reasonably satisfactorily, and I was sent off solo after roughly the average hours of dual had been pumped into me. I felt on top of the world, and thought nothing can stop me now. The ignorance of youth.

Then poor "Roly" was sent off to accomplish his first solo, his instructor must have felt that he was ready to do this. I will never forget the occasion, I feel De Winston will never forget it, and if "Roly" is still alive I am sure to his dying day he will never forget it.

It was just before lunch, when flying all over the drome was grinding to a halt. This was a psychological time to give a pilot cadet his first solo trip because there was less activity going on all round him.

"Roly" took off just as I was making my way to the canteen for lunch, and I decided to wait for him. In he came to land, and then I suppose the panic set in although I did not know this at the time. Before he even touched the ground there was the sound of revving up and round "Roly" went for the second time. Now as pilots know this is not bad thing if there is a sound reason for "going round again" but I could see from where I was that no obvious problem on the ground existed to cause "Roly" to abort his landing. However, I waited on, and the same thing happened again and I had a gut feeling that "Roly" was in trouble, not mechanically but mentally.

My hunger got the better of my anxiety for my friend and off I went to the canteen for my mid-day meal. Flying had all ceased by now, except for Roly doing his lonely vigil in the sky. As we sat eating, the whole mess would become silent at the sound of Roly on the approach leg then at the sound of another huge "revving-up and going-round -again exercise" a loud cheer would go up from the mess and all sorts of ribald comments would ensue.

Now, the Air Force was short of many things but it was never short of "wit", and in some time later escapades which I had as aircrew it was the wit of some of our crew, which even in the most terrifying times, was the saviour of our sanity.

As each fresh pilot cadet entered the mess we would all ask him what was the latest on "Roly". One said he had just seen the C.O. kitting himself out to go up in another plane to force "Roly" down.

Another entered to say he had just passed the Armaments Section and they were cleaning up an old anti-aircraft gun of first war vintage to shoot old "Roly" down. All the time this was going on old "Roly" was pressing on with his unintentional circuits and bumps. I often wondered what was going through the head of his instructor during this ordeal.

A fresh cadet entered then to say that he had just been speaking to the Adjutant and they had phoned for one of the West Coast Defence Fighter Squadrons to shoot "Roly" down once and for all. There were many more remarks of this nature but my memory dims. Young men can be extremely cruel in situations such as this!

Through it all chugged "Roly" and as he grew more and more frightened, his circuits grew bigger and bigger until we felt sometimes he had come down somewhere else. The cheers from the canteen greeted him every time we heard his engine approaching once again. this went on for TEN circuits till at long last, I suppose in sheer desperation or lack of fuel (I never asked him), "Roly" plumped it down on the runway. Someone who actually saw the landing said it was the nearest thing to a hop, skip and a jump exercise that he had ever witnessed being done in an aircraft. The plane was left at the end of the runway to be towed away to a hangar and "Roly" was whipped off to the sick bay.

Anyway I feel sure "Roly" couldn't have cared less. He was on the ground in one piece and as far as he was concerned that was all that mattered.

I went back to our billet in the late afternoon after flying had finished for the day and there was old "Roly" (and he really looked "old Roly"), he appeared to have aged several years, and although this was a good three hours after the events he was still as white as a ghost and his eyes were staring as if he had seen a ghost). "Roly" was stuffing all his personal things into his kit-bag.

When he saw me he said "Now don't you start, I've had enough of aircraft to last me a life-time''. He said ''I've wet myself and messed myself, (this in slightly more colourful language than I have used!) and as long as I live I will never step into another aircraft'',

''Roly'' left Flying School that afternoon. I never saw him again but if he is still around I often think of him.

Undeterred by ''Roly's'' misfortunes, I subsequently finished E.F.T.S. and although I wanted to go on to Harvards, found myself doing S.F.T.S. at a place called Centralia in Ontario on Ansons. I graduated as a pilot from Centralia feeling fairly pleased with myself, as by now several of my ''Buddies'' had fallen by the wayside, starting with old ''Roly''.

From S.F.T.S. we were posted to O.T.U. at a delightful spot called ''Boundary Bay'' in British Columbia, which involved another long train journey across the prairies and through the Rockies from London, Ontario, to Vancouver. At Boundary Bay we flew Mitchell's. We were told that some of us would stay on Mitchells and go on to Mitchell Squadrons in the Far East and others would go on to H.C.U. on Liberators.

Although I did my utmost to remain with the Mitchell contingent ''Sods Law'' saw me eventually posted to H.C.U. at Abbotsford, British Columbia, on Liberators. I was crewed up with a great bunch of fellows who had come from all over Canada. Training flights from Abbotsford were an event in themselves as the station was situated right at the foot of the Rockies and any flight inland involved climbing up to 15,000 feet just to clear the tops of the mountains. As that was in the middle of a Canadian winter we learned very quickly about icing. This I thought was a bit daft as we were all bound for India.

At the completion of our H.C.U. we were posted to Dorval at Montreal, where we were given a brand new Liberator straight off the American production lines. We spent three days there with the American Ferry Pilot who had delivered the plane, to familiarise ourselves with the aircraft (which incidentally had vast improvements on our H.C.U. versions). The two pilots also did about seven hours each on the Link-trainer on ''Letting down and landing'' procedures on the Azores Radio Range Beam which I suppose was our first major hurdle on our forthcoming ferry trip to India.

Then off we went, Montreal to Calcutta. Nothing fazed us in those days but we eventually arrived at our destination No. 357 Squadron stationed at Jessore not far from Calcutta, a very much wiser aircrew after a few hair raising experiences on route (but that's another story!).

We were reminded on arrival by our navigator, of the reply he had received at our final briefing at Dorval to his somewhat naive question

"Are there many good pin-points on route?" To be told "Yes, if you survive the Atlantic crossing, you just have to follow all the crashed Liberators on route from the Atlantic coast to India".

As I said earlier there was never any shortage of wit in the RAF.

Moffat J. M. Rogers

Sqdn. Ldr. A.G. Douglass, O.B.E., A.F.C., R.A.F. (Retd.)

16 Years With The Royal Air Force.

Graham Douglass, born in York on 29th October 1918 was educated at St. Olave's Preparatory School and St. Peter's Senior School, both in York. On leaving school he worked as a junior clerk in two firms of solicitors in York, volunteering for service in the Yeomanry Regiment of Yorkshire Hussars during the Munich crisis of 1938. Early the following year he joined the West Riding of Yorkshire Constabulary on a two year engagement hoping to qualify for entry to the Police Officer College at Hendon. On outbreak of War on 3rd September service in the Police Forces was frozen and remained so until late 1941 when officers were permitted to volunteer for aircrew duties in the Royal Air Force. This he did in November that year and was placed on deferred service until reporting to A.C.R.C. London on 2nd February 1942.

From A.C.R.C. his training as a pilot took him finally to No.6 B.F.T.S. Ponca City, Oklahoma, where he graduated with "Wings" and was commissioned on 9th April 1943. Below he tells a story of his life as a flying instructor in wartime Britain.

After the cessation of hostilities in Europe and the Far East, having found his proper niche in the world, Graham was able to extend his wartime service by eighteen months and was awarded a permanent commission in the General Duties Branch whilst serving as Flight Commander on No.207 Squadron at Stradishall in Suffolk. His subsequent career took him through the post of Personal Assistant to the Air Officer Commanding No.3 Group, Bomber Command, before completing a final squadron tour with No.90 Squadron at RAF Marham in Norfolk, flying B29 Superfortresses. This tour culminated on a very satisfactory note his crew having competed successfully in the open competition for the Laurence Minot Navigation and Bombing Trophy and subsequently being selected to lead the fly past over Buckingham Palace to celebrate the Victory of the Battle of Britain.

Promotion to Squadron Leader followed and a posting to the Organisation Staff of the Headquarters of the 2nd Tactical Air Force in Germany. A year at the Staff College at Bracknell then ensued to be followed by a tour of almost four years as the Squadron Leader Operations at Headquarters No.3 Group, Bomber Command. While in that post, in addition to the management of day to day operations and training, the force of Valiant "V" Bombers was brought from inception to operational readiness. There were periods of intense activity during the reinforcement of Cyprus and Malta for operations against Egypt in the Suez crisis and again during the two episodes of nuclear bomb tests in the Pacific when the passage of all aircraft overseas were controlled from the 3 Group Operations Centre.

At the conclusion of his tour at No.3 Group H.Q. Graham elected to take early retirement from the RAF at the age of forty, since further promotion prospects were virtually nil in a Service being drastically shrunken by changes in defence policy. During his service Graham flew sixteen different types of aircraft including the jet powered Meteors and Canberras.

Shortly after leaving the R.A.F. Graham obtained an appointment as Senior Technical Officer and Pilot to the Committee for Aerial Photography of the University of Cambridge. He remained in that post for twenty years gaining between 300 and 400 flying hours each year. He retired on his 63rd birthday - looking back with satisfaction on almost forty worthwhile years in aviation - his gift from the Royal Air Force.

Now retired Graham and his wife live in Dalbeattie; they have an adult family of one son and a daughter and, happily, a grand-daughter aged eight of whom they see a great deal. On Graham's final retirement from aviation his wife remarked "Well, I've played second fiddle to an aeroplane for almost forty years, it's my turn now!".

How the Mighty Were Fallen

"What did you do in the War, Daddy,
How did you help us to win?"
"Circuits and bumps all day, laddie
And how to get out of a spin."

After six long weeks of waiting at No.31 P.D.U. Moncton, New Brunswick, and a further period kicking one's heels at Harrogate in Yorkshire, most of us were prepared to accept any posting which promised action of any kind. Thus it was that I willingly accepted a posting to No.10 Flying Instructors School at Woodley, near Reading, to qualify as a flying instructor. The carrot that was dangled in persuasion was the promise that after training the period spent instructing would be limited to six months after which one would be given free choice to join any of the Operational Commands.

Promises, promises; in fact, I commenced training at Woodley early in July 1943 and having qualified as a "B" category Q.F.I. was posted to No.15 E.F.T.S. at Kingstown on the fringe of Carlisle, where all training was carried out in Tiger Moths. There I remained until the end of December 1944 when I was finally posted to No.6 P.A.F.U. at Little Rissington for twin-engined training, en-route to Bomber Command, without my having any say in the matter!

In 1943 no one could predict how long the war in Europe was to last and RAF policy was to create a large reserve of aircrews of all categories, after all, the menace of Japan still also had to be faced. All aircrew cadets who wished to become pilots were given an opportunity to show whether they had the necessary aptitude for that role. Allowing all cadets into the mainstream of flying training had led to the whole training scheme becoming bogged down; for this reason the "grading scheme" was introduced in which would-be pilots were allowed ten hours flying instruction from which to assess their suitability. Those who did not qualify could then be re-mustered to other categories of aircrew. By 1943 virtually all the elementary flying schools in Britain were devoting almost all their efforts to the grading scheme.

For the first six months my duties at Carlisle were entirely devoted to giving ab-initio flying training to cadets in the grading scheme. Instructors were expected to carry out a minimum of five and a half hours flying instruction each day, a target often not attainable during the winter months. One rest day a week was allowed but it was expected that some portion of that day would be devoted to practice flying exercises such as aerobatics or cross-country flights which did not feature in ab-initio training.

Whilst the truth of the jingle at the head of this article quickly became apparent the work was not without satisfaction and interest was constantly revived by the arrival of fresh intakes of pupils, all anxious to make the grade.

Early in 1944 I was transferred to work from the relief landing ground at Kirkpatrick near Annan, where the work become more varied. Periodically we took batches of newly qualified pilots and navigators from the overseas training schools for what known as "Pre-A.F.U. Training". The object was to acclimatise these newly qualified aircrew to flying conditions in Britain which can be very different from the clear skies and good visibilities pertaining in Canada and Rhodesia. On map reading exercises the navigators quickly discovered that due to the complexities of the British Rail system "Navigation by Bradshaw" did not really work.

Similarly, many of the pilots had completed their advanced training on Oxfords or Ansons and skill in handling light single-engined aircraft had largely been lost.

Delightful little aeroplane to fly that the Tiger Moth is, if mishandled during aerobatics it is quite easy to stall the engine, thus the exercise to re-start the engine in flight had to be taught. The technique is to immediately put the aircraft into a really steep dive, for the propeller will not commence to rotate until a speed of 160 mph has been attained, a speed which can seem alarmingly fast in a Moth. Some of the young pilots with a stalled engine when flying solo were a bit tentative about the steepness of the dive and would lose valuable height without re-starting the engine. A consequent forced landing followed and I have vivid memories of recovering stranded aircraft from some very quaint places indeed, where they had miraculously been put down in one piece - an acquired experience which served me well at a later date.

After I had instructed for a year, I and two other Flying Officers together with a Flight Lieutenant "G" were detailed for a visit to that Holy of Holies, the Empire Central Flying School at Hullavington in Wiltshire to be examined by the Examining Flight, usually referred to in hushed tones as "The Trappers". On a fine September morning we set course from Kingstown flying in box formation, with "G" in the lead. The three F.O.'s each carried one of the more experienced Pre-A.F.U. pilots in the rear seat, supposedly to assist with navigation; "G" carried a second Flt.Lt. an ex-staff pilot from Canada.

The Moth cruising at around 80 mph made Wiltshire seem a long way from Cumberland and the flight necessitated several stops on route. After some two hours in the air we landed at the E.F.T.S. at Sealand at the head of the Dee Estuary to be re-fuelled. From Sealand we staged again at Worcester and spent the night at RAF Pershore a few miles further south. Next morning we made an early start and arrived at Hullavington at about 10 a.m.

On landing we were immediately taken over by "the stern young men" of the Examining Flight who proceeded to wring us out on the ground (viva voce) and in the air. The experience was not so alarming as we had privately feared and I was quite charmed when, towards the end of the test, my examiner remarked that he had not flown a Moth for about three years and took over the controls. For the next few minutes he performed a series of impeccable aerobatics; he then pointed out a small town to port and said "That's Malmesbury, take us back to Hullavington and teach me instrument flying on the way!!

All four of us must have performed reasonably well as we were all raised to "A" category Q.F.I.'s. After lunch, and feeling quite proud of ourselves, we set course for base, again in box formation with "G" in the lead. We landed at the E.F.T.S. at Wolverhampton to refuel and to spend the night. Next morning the weather had deteriorated markedly and we had again to land at Sealand as the Dee Estuary, Liverpool Bay and the land to the east were shrouded in low cloud as far as the eye could see. We stayed at Sealand for a further night. The morning brought a slight improvement and at 8.15 a.m. the Chief Flying Instructor took-off into the haze to fly a local weather test. On return he delayed all flying for two hours after which he again took to the air. On landing he authorised duel instruction only in the local area. He then advised our leader that conditions should be alright for us to leave but strongly advised a return to Sealand if we should encounter worsening conditions on route.

At about 11 a.m. we took-off for base. Conditions crossing Liverpool Bay left much to be desired - very hazy with patches of low stratus appearing from time to time. We crossed the coast near Southport and continued on a NNE heading at about 1,500 feet. Patchy stratus appeared beneath us periodically and the haze made it impossible to estimate conditions ahead. We were still in loose box formation and I began to wonder whether it was wise to continue, particularly in view of the higher ground over which our course would take us. Accordingly, I moved in close to the leader and when he finally looked our way I shook my head and signalled back. In return "G" shook his head and signalled forward. I asked my passenger, Sergeant Hallsmith, who was attempting to map read, if he knew our position. He said that we had crossed the main road south of Lancaster a few minutes ago but had seen nothing to fix our position since. Some seconds later we flew straight into cloud so dense that I had difficulty in keeping the lead aircraft in sight. I asked Hallsmith if he could see our number four. He replied that he had seen him a few moments ago but could not see him now. Uncertainty as to number four's position made me wary of turning back so I continued with the leader for a few minutes more when suddenly cloud broke below us and I could see the ground not far below. I signalled "breaking away" to the leader and stuck the nose down. The clear area was not extensive and to right and left of us low stratus covered the higher ground, the way ahead was also blocked. Without further ado I selected a small field free from grazing animals in which to make a precautionary landing. As I turned to make a trial run over the field I spotted two Moths flying toward me. Their pilots obviously thought that if the field I had chosen was good enough for me it would also do for them and promptly slipped into it ahead of me. Being baulked of my approach I managed to make a second approach without getting embroiled in cloud and slipped into the field behind the other two, landing successfully. The field rose in quite a steep slope and my aircraft only ran a few yards after touch down. At least we were safely on terra firma once more but with considerable embarrassment over the episode! How were the mighty fallen indeed - three category "A" instructors stuck in a small field on the Lancashire Fells!

One of the aircraft was slightly damaged; the stub axle on the port side almost twisted off by dropping into a rabbit hole. Clearly it would need repair before it could be flown back to base. While we were debating our next move the farmer, a Mr. Francis, arrived on the scene and invited us to his home about two fields away. His wife and daughter made us very welcome and immediately started to prepare a hot meal for us of beautiful home cured ham and large brown eggs. Whilst we were enjoying this hospitality a contingent of "Dad's Army" arrived in the belief that we might be the enemy. At last accepting our identity as genuine they left us in peace to be visited a few minutes later by the local sergeant of police who had been alerted by the ever vigilant Observer Corps. Finally satisfied as to our identity the sergeant also left.

Fortunately Mr. Francis had a telephone and "G" was able to phone Sealand to report what had happened. He got more than an earful from the Squadron Leader C. F. I. for our failing to comply with his instructions, finally being told to wait by the phone whilst he advised Carlisle of our predicament. He also complained to our C. F. I. that we had failed to follow his advice!

After some time Carlisle eventually rang back with instructions. A truck with engineers was being dispatched and we were to wait for clear conditions before returning. Guards would be arranged for the aircraft and we were to report to the RAF staging post at Morecambe for accommodation and meals. "G" was also advised that our number four, Flying Officer Sanderson, had indeed turned back and had landed safely at RAF Warton, on the Ribble Estuary, a base occupied by the American Air Force.

A wait of some four hours then ensued before the truck arrived with two mechanics on board and also our civilian deputy chief engineer. Repairs to the stub axle commenced at once and were completed just before light failed, when a contingent of G.I.'s arrived in two jeeps from Warton, as over-night guards for the aircraft. The "Chief" pronounced all three aircraft serviceable and we all climbed into the back of the truck for an uncomfortable journey to Morecambe in the dark. On arrival we were told that we were to go to the ''Waldorf'' for the night, and that meals for visiting aircrew were provided at ''Roger's Restaurant'' where we would get breakfast. The name ''Waldorf'' conjured up the vision of a hotel along the sea front, in fact it turned out to be a back street disused cinema! We were met there by a rather scruffy corporal of dubious sobriety who announced ''officers sleep in the gallery, other ranks on the ground floor''. As we entered the building through black-out curtains I noticed six bodies covered in rather dirty grey blankets, presumably asleep on the floor of the dimly lit foyer. I asked what they were and the corporal grunted ''Fire Picket''.

There were no beds or bedding in the gallery and the seats were uninvitingly hard. Fortunately the aviators still had on their flying kit which provided some comfort as we draped ourselves awkwardly along the seats. I don't believe anyone slept very much and in the cold light of morning one member observed as he struggled up ''Cor, I've got a back like a venetian blind!''. The ''ablutions'' proved to be the cinema toilet which had seen better days and cleanliness. ''Roger's Restaurant'' also was something of a disappointment, turning out to be a clap-board building on the outskirts of the town, ''Caf'' would have described it better. The only bright thing was the weather which had miraculously cleared overnight. As we all piled into the truck to return to our aircraft I felt that the hospitality of RAF Morecambe left much to be desired.

After carefully examining the down hill run of our small field for possible snags we decided to send our passengers home in the truck as the available run for take-off was barely enough. As the one with some experience of getting Moths out of awkward places it was agreed that I should go first. We manhandled the aircraft to the top of the slope tucking the tails virtually into the boundary hedge. The engineers chocked the wheels and swung the props and then stood by. We all three gave our engines a thorough warm up and breathing a silent prayer to the God of Aviation, I waved the chocks away and opened the throttle wide. The dry stone wall at the foot of the slope seemed horribly close but getting the tail up quickly and probably assisted by the down slope I gained flying speed and lifted off with about thirty yards to spare. Watching from above I saw the others take-off safely and without further ado set course for home.

On arriving at Carlisle ''G'' remarked ''Well, if you want to write a book about it you had better call it ''Through darkest Lancashire with "G"''.

Looking back over the period I spent in Training Command I have never regretted it as an experience; the increased confidence, knowledge and skill which it imparted stood me in good stead throughout almost forty years as a pilot. How much my work contributed to the war effort is difficult to judge; few of the successful pupils I taught on their grading course can have qualified for operational flying, though some of the Pre-A.F.U. pilots and navigators almost certainly did so. Possibly, another contribution may have stemmed from the young Army officers who had volunteered as glider pilots prior to the invasion of Europe and came to us for initial air experience and training. Throughout the period of hostilities it was impossible not to feel a sense of "dodging the column" and I was once unwise enough to mention this reservation to my flight commander, Flt.Lt. David Crook, D.F.C. David was one of the most charming men one could wish to meet and also one of the most decisive. As a member of No. 609 Auxiliary Squadron David had fought right through the "battle" on Spitfires with several confirmed kills. His reaction to my remarks was immediate and characteristic; brusquely, "Look, if the RAF says you instruct you instruct, now, go and get on with it".

It is with deep regret that I have to record that David was killed later whilst re-training on Spitfires for the P.R. role - almost unbelievable in a pilot of his quality.

Dalbeattie A.G. Douglass

Flight Lieutenant John W.H. Elder, M. B. E. (Pilot)

From 1950 until 1982 Dr. Elder, M.B.,B.Chir., was in general practice in Annan. During the war years he interrupted his medical studies and volunteered for air crew duties in the R.A.F. being assessed for training as a pilot after being enrolled at A.C.R.C. St. John's Wood, London, in August 1942. His keen interest in the Royal Air Force manifested itself whilst at Trinity Hall, Cambridge, when he joined the University Air Squadron in October 1941. Since demobilisation in November 1945 he was for a short time a member of the R.A.F.V.R. and since 1947 an active member of the R.A.F.A., serving for a period as Chairman of the Annandale Branch and for the past thirty years as Branch Secretary.

Born in Glasgow in March 1922, John Elder was educated firstly at St. Ninian's School in Moffat, (now Dowding House Residential Home) and at Charterhouse. From thence to Cambridge University and, post war, St. Thomas's Hospital, London. Qualifying as a pilot in February 1944 after training in Canada, he was employed as an instructor and staff pilot at various training schools in that country. In a covering note to his article, Dr. Elder is a little self-deprecating about his active role. For this there is no need; without the tails of Training Command there could have been no operational teeth.

Now retired in Annan, Dr. Elder lists his interests as large scale gardening, antiques and philately.

Royal Air Force Career

Cambridge University Air Squadron October 1941 - July 1942. Promoted to Corporal! An instructor had a white ribbon, the Polar Medal, the only one I have seen. At Camp at RAF Wyton, I had a short trip in a Stirling. August 1942, ACRC St. John's Wood, London, now an L.A.C. Offered choice of three Grading Schools so put 15 EFTS Carlisle last as this was the posting I wanted. I got it and was able to cycle home to Annan. Soloed on Tiger Moth after about 12 hours. Postings then alternated between Heaton Park, Manchester and Brighton (the Grand and Metropole Hotel). Sent to Canada on H.M.T. Andes in which I was very seasick. We docked at Halifax on Christmas Eve 1942. I remember particularly the bright lights and the cheerful ladies who supplied us with apples on the train to 31 RAF Depot Moncton, New Brunswick.

The next stop was USNAS, Grosse Ile, Michigan (Towers Scheme). I found the Stearman biplane very heavy after a Tiger Moth. One of the exercises was to land in a circle from 500 feet over trees without use of engine or crafty side-slips. When talking to my instructor, a ground crew man presented me with a handful of twigs which he had found in my undercart. I was quite relieved to be posted away to 7 EFTS, Windsor, Ontario and then to 32 EFTS Bowden, Alberta in October 1943. We flew Cornells and I had the advantage over the others of extra hours. The next posting was to 36 SFTS Penhold, Alberta on Oxfords. On my first solo night cross-country, I forgot to put the switch from half-charge to full charge. I did not have enough power to send regular position reports to base so asked an "Alpha" aircraft receiving me to contact base. This was apparently successful.

I became a Sergeant with the Flying Badge w.e.f. February 1944. I was commissioned and posted to No.2 Flying Instructors School at Pearce, Alberta. I failed to master the Cessna Crane, a very light twin-engined job which I had great difficulty in landing but found the instructing side to my liking. I was taken off the course and sent to Mount Hope, Hamilton - No.33 ANS as a staff-pilot in May 1944. We had Anson Mk. I's with wind-up wheels. Our usual routine was two three-hour day or night flights with U/T Navigators. While at Hamilton I met my future wife Dorothy. I also visited my brother whose Squadron was at USNAS Squantum, Boston, Mass. They took me on practice dive bombing over the sea - a frightening experience. I remember there was a heat wave at ground level but freezing cold at 10,000 feet.

At Mount Hope I remember on solo low-levels being off course and crossing Malden Airport (now Toronto Airport) and an army artillery range at very low altitude - I saw live shells bursting.

The next posting was to No.2 ANS Charlottetown, Prince Edward Island as Mount Hope was being closed. Here I met the Anson Mk.5, a lovely aircraft, streamlined with portholes, (the Mk.I looked like a flying conservatory), constant-speed props and a proper retractable U/C. Apart from routine flights with pupil navigators and WOP's I logged flights labelled variously Met, Coastal Command and Sealed Orders (I think the last were to transport Squadron Leaders with documents).

We did aerial photography, square searches and bombing which made life more interesting than before. I remember a Free French bomb aimer yelling "I zee it, I zee it, bomb gone". We did hit the target once from 5,500 feet with a 7lbs. bomb. I was delighted to become a member of the "Target Buster Club" but the ground crew who had to repair the target were not so pleased. I have fond memories of fried oysters and Cona coffee in the break between the night flights. I also had a minor prang, nose up in the snow after landing. Fortunately the previous pilot had reported that the port wheel brake was grabbing - I heard no more about it!

In April 1945 I moved to 14 SFTS Kingston, Ontario where I flew Harvard Mk.2s and Lysander Mk.3s towing targets behind the latter.

In May 1945 I returned in a BOAC Liberator (Dorval - Goose Bay - Prestwick). There was a Ship Recognition course at Harrogate before going to Bawdsey Manor, Suffolk (the home of radar). I had volunteered for a Filter Officers' course not knowing what it was! The theory and practice of radar was extremely interesting. Next stop was the underground control centre at Raigmore, Inverness - billeted at RAF Dalcross.

The final posting was Sopley, Hants where I presided over a table upon which a number of WAAF plotters put counters, height indications etc. and I put arrows purporting to show the track of the aircraft. I was also Fire Officer and something to do with drains! I recall an "empty" foam extinguisher going off in the back of the truck - some foam hit me. Travelling through Ringwood in a 15 cwt van I saw a wheel going ahead of us along the road - it was one of our rear ones. I was demobbed from Sopley in November 1945 with the substantive rank of Flt.Lt.

I returned to medical studies at St. Thomas's Hospital and joined the RAFVR in August 1947; back to Tiger Moths at 18 RFS, Fair Oaks, Woking. After completing Annual Training in June 1948, I asked the Air Ministry to release me because of pressure of work. In October 1947 I joined the RAF Association (Surbiton Branch) then Wokingham and Woodley. I joined my father's practice in Annan in 1950 and retired in 1982, the same year I received the MBE in the Birthday List.

I am still in the RAFA after transfer to the Lockerbie Branch (now Annandale). After a short spell as Chairman, I became Branch Secretary and have remained so for over 30 years.

Annan — John W.H. Elder.

Flying Officer Jack Geekie
(A National Service Pilot.)

Jack Geekie, born in Dundee in 1928, is a product of Aberdeen Grammar School and Art College. Called for National Service at the age of twenty he was determined to fly with the Royal Air Force. He achieved his ambition, undergoing flying training at RAF Feltwell in Norfolk and going on to become a jet fighter pilot flying Meteors with No. 263 Squadron at RAF Wattisham in Suffolk.

After a short service engagement he left the RAF in August 1952 to take up the profession of school master. Married with two adult sons he lists his hobbies as fishing, philately, model engineering and D.I.Y. He gives a graphic account of his indoctrination to service life.

Survival in an Alien Environment

The night train from Scotland deposited me on Warrington station at dawn on a cold, wet, Monday morning in August 1948. I was twenty years old, finished, after three years, with Art College and determined to fly with the RAF. On presenting myself at the Guard Room at R.A.F. Padgate I was told to come back after nine o'clock! A good start to my RAF career - the RAF was shut!

By Wednesday about a hundred of us had been partially kitted out and looked something like airmen. We were escorted to Hornchurch for three days of aptitude tests, medicals and interviews. I was offered and accepted, with alacrity, Pilot (National Service). On our return to Padgate I was told to pack my kit and report to the Guard Room to pick up a railway warrant - no explanations, just do it! the warrant said Liverpool, report to R.T.O. at the Liver Buildings. Arrival at Liverpool led me to the docks and the Marine Steam Packet. I was stunned to see RAF uniforms everywhere, not 'rookies' like me, L.A.C.'s, Corporals, Sgts, Flt/Sgts, even a W.O. , about a third of them with half wing brevets and 'gongs' galore. I must be in the wrong place - but I wasn't! We were all bound for RAF Jurby, on the North West tip of the Isle of Man, to become No.64 P course at I.T.W. Conversation was difficult but I learned that my course-mates had come from the Aircrew Educational Centre (A.C.E's) at St. Athen where, for the past three months, they had lived and worked together, before re-mustering as cadet pilots - and I was the only National Serviceman amongst them. I discovered that National Serviceman were regarded as the lowest of the low. Nothing personal, you understand!

We were billeted in wooden huts, complete with anthracite stove, linoleum and floor pads. I'm sure my later enjoyment in ice skating emanated from those days of sliding over the highly polished floor on felt pads. That first night, in what was to be our home for the next three months, was not a pleasant one. I was ignorant, confused, lonely, unable even to speak their language, trapped on this strange, hostile island.

Our first task next day was the removal of all badges of rank - I didn't have much to do - replacing them with cadet pilot wreaths, sewn on where the stripes had been. Brevets and medal ribbons remained, of course. To say my learning processes were about to accelerate is an understatement. I had the greatest difficulty accepting my course-mates, with the service background and experience that they had, were prepared to participate so enthusiastically in the two ''bull'' nights per week. Our course leader, one Bob Bendeaux, was a Flt/Sgt. air gunner with a D.F.M., won over Peenemunde in a Halifax, a married man with a family, yet, there he was on his knees polishing his bed space, or scraping one of the hut's broom handles with a razor blade to make it white before wrapping it in newspaper to keep it that way. They expected me to shape up and not handicap their chances. One example of my cupidity shows how much I had to learn. We were issued with flying kit - I never discovered why, there were no aircraft at Jurby - RAF psychology, I suppose. Back at the billet I opened the large cardboard boxes containing flying boots, gloves, etc., carelessly tossing the boxes into the centre of the hut. After admiring the clothing for a bit I was surprised to see no evidence of the discarded boxes. Attached to the walls of the hut above each bed space was a small shelf meant to hold a big pack and a small pack. My packs were on the shelf, but they didn't look like everyone else's, mine were standing easy, or resting, while all others were rigidly square, neat and tidy. They had been lined with cardboard - some of it mine! I was advised to visit an adjacent hut and 'find' enough cardboard to ensure my packs matched those of my room-mates.

Most of our lecturers were very good. They were National Service graduates, like me, who, unlike me, chose to stick to their specialisations. I was impressed with the efficiency of the educational system used in the services, it certainly worked. There was an exception, an RAF Regiment Sgt., he was reputed to be stupid, cruel, with a chip on his shoulder the size of Snaefell, about aircrew. He was to instruct us on the finer points of the .45 service revolver, which was to be our personal weapon. He looked normal to me when he started his lecture, his delivery suggested he had learned it all beforehand and was reciting it like a piece of poetry. He was stressing how important it was never to accept a weapon from anyone unless it had been broken open, as he said this he turned the gun in his hand holding it by the barrel, offered it to me. Like a fool I held out my hand, whereupon he hit my hand very hard with the butt. My hand then hit the desk almost as hard. His mirth was unbounded. I had been hurt mentally and physically, but I'd learned a lesson. Three weeks later staff played hockey against the cadets. I was delighted to see our weapons instructor playing against us for the staff. We clashed early on, and he retired to the sick bay with a broken nose - a complete accident, of course. The depth of my concern was evident to all, but he knew I'd evened the score.

Pay parades were a great disappointment. I was an A.C.2 cadet pilot, I saluted for ten shillings one week and a pound the next, while my room-mates continued to receive pay commensurate with their ranks! Was there no justice? After eight weeks exams thinned our numbers. Those of us left became officer cadet pilots and a new factor was introduced to the equation. We were now to be continually assessed for O.Q. (Officer Qualities!) and at the end of flying school - still more than a year away - some of us would emerge as pilot officers, the rest would be Sgt. pilots. This system was guaranteed to ensure maximum effort from the ex-Halton boys and re-mustered aircrew alike. Life was improving for me, and I'd discovered a way to make it even better, I was selected to play hockey for Command. This got me off the island and into the real world, and all expenses were paid! Just before Christmas our final exams at I.T.W. had to be overcome. There were sad faces on those who hadn't made it, we had lost almost half our original number, they were all R.T.D'd but we were in high spirits, despite the odds we were off to flying school. No.3 F.T.S, to be exact, at R.A.F. Feltwell, deep in the heart of Norfolk, where for the next year we would learn to fly. I left the Isle of Man with no regrets but many disturbing memories.

Lockerbie J. F. Geekie

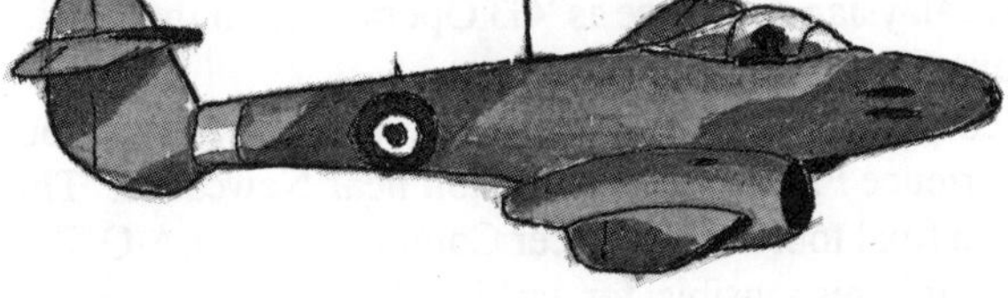

Flight Lieutenant Tim Hannay, R.A.F. (Rtd.)
(Jet Fighter and Helicopter Pilot)

Born in Edinburgh in September 1929, Tim Hannay comes from an active service family. His father, who served in the first World War, was a regular officer in the Cameron Highlanders in which regiment he attained the rank of Lieutenant Colonel. Colonel Hannay was one of the few army officers to serve also in alternating tours of duty in the Royal Air Force in which he held the rank of Squadron Leader. In this capacity in 1938 he was the first army officer to command a RAF squadron, No.53 at RAF Odiham in Hampshire.

From such a background it is not surprising that Tim should elect to serve as a regular officer in the RAF. Educated at Glen Almond Public School in Perthshire, Tim completed National Service in the army between 1947 and 1949, before entering Edinburgh University to read history in which he graduated in 1954. Whilst in University he was a member of the University Air Squadron and gained the rank of Pilot Officer in the R.A.F.V.R.

Volunteering for service in the Royal Air Force in 1954 he was accepted for further training as a pilot in the rank of Pilot Officer. After qualifying as a service pilot he gained a permanent commission and entered Fighter Command in which he flew Vampires, Meteors and Hunter jet fighters, serving on No.257, 19, and 209 squadrons.

Following his service with Fighter Command, he transferred from fixed-wing aircraft to fly helicopters. Training on Sycamores, he progressed to Whirlwind helicopters with No.225 Squadron, forming part of No.38 Group, Transport Command, a group with special responsibility for army co-operation. It was whilst training with 225 Squadron in 1963 that he underwent the "special training" which is the subject of his witty article subscribed below.

Having gained experience in the Far East serving in both Malaya and Borneo with No.225 Squadron and with No.72 Squadron flying Wessex Helicopters, between 1966 and 1969 he was seconded for service with the Royal Malaysian Air Force as 'G3 Operations' at the Tactical Air Force Operations Centre in Kuala Lumpar.

After secondment he returned to the U.K. and completed a tour with No.11 Air Experience Flight based at Ouston near Newcastle. This tour was followed by a final tour as the Officer Commanding M.A.O.T., again in 38 Group, a unit responsible for tasking helicopter operations and exercises both widely in Europe and in support of ground forces in Northern Ireland.

In 1975, Tim retired from the active list and took up an administrative appointment with Dumfries Health Board, a post he still holds. He and his wife live at Balmaclellan, near New Galloway, they have two grown up sons and two further boys still of school age.

Monsieur le Commandant

The last helicopter flew onto HMS Albion just after 11am as the ship edged in towards the North African coast opposite El Adem.

No.225 Squadron was to re-inforce the Far East Air Force in Sarawak, where confrontation with Indonesia was beginning to look as if it might just turn into a full scale war.

We had been on Desert Express, one of a series of "express" exercises in which 38 Group gave tactical and logistic support to the Army's "Fire" Brigade. We had flown out from RAF Odiham a month before. Odiham, Vichy, Nice, Rome, Reggio, Malta, Tripoli (RAF Idris) Benghazi, El Adem. It had all the sound of a 1930's flight to Cairo. The Whirlwind, even with internal overload tanks was not exactly long range and didn't take kindly to this sort of flying. Much to our disgust and envy two crews arrived only three days before embarking on Albion having had a splendid holiday in Rome and Naples!

The Pilots and Groundcrew were to fly back to Odiham, have two weeks leave then out to Sarawak to pick up the aircraft from the carrier. The heavy backup equipment would hopefully arrive soon afterwards.

Having had only a week of my embarkation leave I got a message to report to the Station Commander as soon as possible. Hell, what I had done now! "You're off to Paris, Hannay" ....."Er, Paris, Sir?" "Yes Hannay, Paris, France." "Yes Sir". "You are to do the two weeks Guided Weapon Course with Sud Aviation. F.E.A.F. are going to modify four aircraft to take the SS11 Air to Ground Guided Weapon. You will do the course and then convert more pilots when you get to the Far East." I decided not to ask 'Why me?' I suspected that would become clear later! But two weeks in Paris on Her Majesty, whatever the drawbacks, was not to be sniffed at. A quick briefing at MOD (Air) mainly drawing a sizeable wad of francs and I was off.

The Sud Aviation Guided Weapon School was run by a splendid retired Lt. Colonel of Cavalry, 'Monsieur le Commandant'. (In France a large number of light tanks were armed with the SS11). Always immaculate in the sort of tweed suits more often seen in Edinburgh and Inverness than Paris, he was a martinet and I sweated blood on the simulator and in absorbing the drills and technicalities. The SS11 was wire guided with a range of about 4000 yards. A control box was mounted on the left hand cockpit combing (helicopters are captained from the right hand seat) together with another box with a miniature stick at elbow height where the co-pilot's controls would have been. Four missiles were carried, two on each side attached to the fuselage, level with the cockpit. Basically you selected a missile, pressed 'fire' and after a count of one acquired control through the little control column which worked in the normal sense. A flare was mounted on the rear of the missile, the effect of which after about 300 yards was exactly that of a blip of light moving across a flat picture. (The 3d effect goes after 250-300 yards.) The trick was smoothness, count off the seconds of flight and never, never let the missile fall below the target.

At last the day came to fire the only missile that Her Majesty's Government, budget conscious as ever, had allocated for the defence of the Empire. A beautiful day, we drove en mass, Monsieur Le Commandant, staff, pupil, to the great range at Chalons Sur Marne, scene of one of the devastating battles of 1914-18. Everything may stop for tea in U.K., but in France it stops for lunch, or did. I politely declined the wine, but the Commandant was becoming expansive and insisted. I did not need much encouragement and felt I must keep my end up. By the time we had toasted the L'armme de L'air, the Royal Air Force and the auld alliance - I had made it clear I was a Scot - my confidence was boundless and the whole thing was going to be a piece of cake.

As we drove into the range I felt my confidence ebbing. It took a final sickening plunge as we arrived on the firing point. I could not believe my eyes, to left and right were about 30 AMX tanks line abreast, all with SS11's mounted on their turrets banging away like mad. In the centre was a solitary tripod with the firing mechanism and a ground launch SS11 just in front. This the Commandant proudly gestured was my "point de tirer".

As I got ready an ominous hush seemed to descend on the range and I heard the Commandant explaining to a ring of tank crews that I was a 'pilot anglaise' who had in two weeks already reached a standard only equalled by tank controllers in three months. I knew then that disaster was inevitable.

The target, an old tank was about 3000 yards away on the side of a hill. I pressed the firing button. Launch was good, acquisition smooth. I heard the Commandant exhale with a soft satisfied whistle. I was so tense I had stopped breathing and a large bead of sweat trickled slowly into my eye. In brushing it aside I must have eased forward on the control column. When I looked up the blob of light was well below the target. I eased back, nothing, I pulled back, nothing, I took it to the back stop. Suddenly the missile reared up at 30°- it must have got into ground effect - went dead over the target and soared on and up over the hill. My last thought was - if it lands outside the range will they court martial me? - Monsieur le Commandant never spoke to me again.

As I look at my log book, thirty years on, I see that during that year I trained six squadron pilots and we fired thirty-three practice missiles in Malaya and Sarawak. We also fired some live rounds so that the Army could get an idea of their use and effect. We never fired one in anger, but the Royal Navy did. A group of TNKU (Tentera National Kalimantan Utara) - Guerillas! - got holed up in a remote cave on an escarpment in the third division of Sarawak. A Navy Wessex put two missiles straight into the cave and finished the lot. Monsieur le Commandant would have been very proud.

Balmaclellan — Tim Hannay Ex 225 Sqn Pilot.

George Thomas Manson.
(Master Pilot)

Tom Manson was born in Edinburgh on 3rd September 1921 and spent some of his childhood years in Canada to which country his parents emigrated in 1922. In 1932 the family returned to Scotland and Tom completed his education at Dunoon Grammar School and Camphill, Paisley. In 1936 Tom started a five year apprenticeship in marine engineering with the firm of Wm. Simons, Shipbuilders of Renfrew. On completing his apprenticeship Tom volunteered for aircrew duties with the Royal Air Force and was called up to A.C.R.C. London in January 1942. Selected for training as a pilot he completed his initial training at Newquay in Cornwall before passing through his grading course at No.7 E.F.T.S., RAF Desford in Leicestershire. Qualifying for further training he crossed the Atlantic again to join No.33 E.F.T.S. at Caron, Saskatchewan. Advanced training on Harvards followed at 37 S.F.T.S., Calgary, Alberta, where he received his wings and sergeant's rank.

After a spell at the General Reconnaissance School at Charlottetown, Prince Edward Island, Tom returned to the U.K. After a brief visit back to his first E.F.T.S. at Desford, where he renewed his experience of flying conditions in this country, he was sent for advanced flying training on Oxfords at No.14 P(AFU), Fraserburgh, on the extreme north-east coast of Aberdeenshire.

On completion of A.F.U. training Tom was posted to Africa where, at Dar-es-Salaam, on the coast of Tanzania, he joined No.259 Squadron as a second pilot on Catalina flying boats. The Catalinas were engaged in long flights over Indian Ocean on anti-submarine patrols and convoy escort duties. In due time Tom was transferred to No.209 Squadron, based at Mombassa, where he converted on to Sunderland Flying Boats, continuing the same duties. Finally moving to Koggala in (then) Ceylon, Tom returned from the Far East in 1946 and has the superb sang-froid to describe his wartime experience as 'rather humdrum'.

Tom elected to remain with the Royal Air Force long term and below outlines a history of a flying career that many will envy, flying in all twenty-eight different types of service aircraft. His services as a helicopter pilot on No.194 Squadron operating in Malaya call for special mention. Having recently lifted their 1,000th casualty in the Federation, Her Majesty approved the issue of a badge for the squadron. Equipped with both Dragonfly and Sycamore helicopters the squadron chose a design picturing the dragonfly which is thus perpetuated into RAF Heraldry. As may be seen from the newspaper cutting reproduced at the foot of his article, Tom Manson also scored a century in evacuating more than a hundred casualties whilst in Malaya. For his valuable work on 194 Squadron Tom was mentioned in Dispatches.

Characteristically, also missing from Tom's account of post-war flying is the part he played in the search for a Canberra bomber and its crew which had crashed among the White Mount Peaks near Braemar. Flying from Leuchars at first light Tom and his navigator, Stephen Cawthorne, located the crashed aircraft on Cairn Taggart (3,430ft). Landing on the snow and ice covered slope Tom had to keep his main rotor turning to prevent his aircraft sliding down the mountain side, whilst Stephen Cawthorne ascertained that the crew of the Canberra had been killed in the crash. Tom then made contact with the search and rescue teams and airlifted them to the scene; finally the two bodies were airlifted down to a shooting lodge on the Royal Estate. Tom's efforts with No.275 Squadron from Leuchars earned him the Queen's Commendation.

Tom continued his very worthwhile service in the air until 1961 when he then transferred to the Air Traffic Control Branch in which he served until retirement late in 1966. He settled in Glasgow as a Clerical Officer in the Ministry of Labour. Later he transferred to National Savings from which Department he retired as a Higher Clerical Officer in 1982. Now fully retired he and his wife are residents of Dowding House in Moffat from where he continues his chief interests of golf and travel.

A Valuable post-war Career.

Returning from the Far East in '46 I signed on and was posted to 201 (F.B.) Squadron at Calshot. A couple of months on the Berlin Airlift was a highlight. We were stationed in Hamburg at the Blohm and Voss seaplane factory and took off from the Elbe, landing in the American sector at Lake Havel. Next to B & V were submarine pens - feet thick, some of which had caved in with subs still in them. I like to think that some of my Dumfries and Galloway Aircrew friends did this accurate bombing. In fact I'm sure of it.

After a short spell at 57 (F.B.) M.U. at Wig Bay by Stranraer, and on the run-down of Flying Boats I was posted to 2 Ferry Pool at Aston Down in 1949. Having to contend with an undercarriage was a problem for a time. This was an interesting job flying most of the types in service. One could ferry four different types in a day and normally ten to fifteen in month.

After two years I was posted to 45 M.U. Kinloss as the M.U.'s test pilot. We held all the RAF's Spitfires, plus some Harvards, Valettas, Lincolns and Canberras.

In the early part of '53 I was selected for Helicopter training at Westlands, Yeovil. Posted to Malaya on Casevac (Casualty evacuation) work was a very rewarding job. An instance is that, returning from the Siam border I stopped at Ipoh airport for fuel and while having a coffee was informed of an ambush on a patrol 15 miles into the jungle. There were 3 dead and 5 injured and within an hour the wounded were being treated in hospital. There is little doubt that this versatile machine saved at least some of their lives as it could have taken days to carry them out.

The Casevacs were a great variety, Gunshot, Fevers, Accidents on Bamboo, meeting with Crocodiles; one who had leeches on his 'willie' which had turned septic - not a pretty sight! One patrol found some Aborigines; one woman was in a bad way delivering her baby. She was picked out and treated in hospital. I wondered what she thought of it all, having spent her life in the jungle. Operating with the Ghurkas and their Iban trackers, also the 22nd S.A.S. was an eye-opener, they seemed fearless and to help in a small way was rewarding.

Returning to the U.K. December '55, I thought life would be a bit of a let down but a posting to Air Sea Rescue was as interesting in a far different environment. Searching for missing and ditched aircraft, our main purpose, a lot of our time was also spent on lost climbers and hill walkers. It is sad that nearly forty years on, a lot of them are still ill clad and do not plan their trips, putting other at risk. One party of hikers lost above Glen Doll in January were not found until the Spring thaw.

Lighter moments included spotting a yacht, flying a red item of clothing at the mast. It transpired that the engine had packed in and, as it was drifting on to rocks, we alerted a fishing boat which towed it into harbour. The gentleman owner turned up that evening at the Station in a beautiful Bentley, with a bottle of Scotch and a request that the story should go no further, as his wife might not appreciate this sortie with his secretary. Silence was bought not so much by the whisky, but the two laps allowed round the airfield at the wheel of the car!

Severe winters can be a busy time, apart from those lost on the hills. we dropped food to isolated places and evacuated difficult births cases. I saw a lot of our own country from the helicopter, all the islands of the West Coast and as far as St. Kilda. I've seen a bit of the world, but those islands at sunrise and sunset are as memorable as anything you could wish to see.

In 1958 I was off again, first to Cyprus then El Adem, Libya, on

Desert casevac. A fairly quiet time but still able to be useful, the odd aircraft missing, people lost, numerous injured from land mines and ammunition during their 'Steptoe' operations. After this tour I returned to the U.K. and took up Air Traffic Duties until retiring at last in 1966.

Moffat | Tom Manson.

RESCUERS WIN A BADGE

THE QUEEN has approved a badge for 194 (Helicopter) Squadron, R.A.F., which recently lifted its 1,000th casualty in the Federation.

The squadron, commanded by Squadron-Leader C. R. Turner, was formed in 1942. It is now equipped with Dragonfly and Sycamore helicopters.

The badge will bear a drawing of a dragonfly, a kris and the Latin motto "Surrigere Colligere" — to arise and pick up.

Flight/Sgt. G. Manson, one of two members of the squadron who have already scored "centuries" in casualty evacuations, once used his helicopter as an ambulance to lift a maternity case.

Air Commodore Sir Hector Monro, A.E., M.P. (Pilot)

Sir Hector Monro was born in Edinburgh on 4th October 1922, but was brought up in Langholm in the Dumfries and Galloway Region, and which he regards as his home town. He was educated at Canford School in Dorset, progressing to the University of Cambridge, where he was a member of the University Air Squadron from where he joined the R.A.F.V.R. in 1940.

Initial training was continued in the RAF at Booker near High Wycombe, before Sir Hector was sent to the United States Naval Station at Pensacola, Florida, for advanced training and conversion to flying boats. When qualified he served initially with Atlantic Ferry Command before joining Coastal Command in the U.K. and taking Operational Training at Invergordon on the Cromarty Firth. He joined No.240 Squadron flying Catalina flying boats and was for a time based in Madras flying over the Indian Ocean. He also operated in the U.K. from bases at Stranraer and Oban. He then converted to Sunderland flying boats and joined No.209 Squadron.

During 1945 and 1946, Sir Hector was based in Hong Kong, flying regularly between there and Japan, Singapore and Australia. On the cessation of hostilities in the Far East he was firstly engaged in flying prisoners of war back from Singapore to Ceylon; he was also one of the first pilots to fly through Rangoon to Hong Kong.

Demobilised from Hong Kong in July 1946 Sir Hector returned to Langholm and immediately became a member of No.603 (City of Edinburgh) Auxiliary Squadron flying Spitfires from Turnhouse. He gained the Air Efficiency Medal in 1953, In addition to the flying boats of his wartime service Sir Hector has flown Harvards, Ansons, Dakotas and jet propelled Meteors. He has maintained a close interest in RAF activities and has taken part in training exercises with current operational squadrons. He has flown many types of light aircraft and still maintains his private flying licence.

Sir Hector has held the rank of Honorary Air Commodore for the past ten years and in 1990 was appointed Honorary Inspector General of the Royal Auxiliary Air Force on the retirement of Air Chief Marshall Sir John Barraclough from that appointment.

Sir Hector and Lady Monro now live at Kirtlebridge near Annan. He has had a distinguished career in politics being first elected to Parliament as Member for Dumfriesshire in 1964, the seat that he has held continuously since that date. Sir Hector was Minister for Sport from 1979 to 1981 - the year that he gained his knighthood. In the present government Sir Hector again holds an appointment in the Scottish Office as Minister for Agriculture and Environment; his long involvement in farming as his peacetime occupation most amply fits him for such an appointment.

Sir Hector's close interest in sport is also borne out by his personal involvement; he has played Rugby for Langholm, for some seasons as Captain, and has been President of the Scottish Rugby Union. He was also Manager of the Scottish Fifteen which toured Australia and Canada. He lists his other hobbies as 'Country sports, flying, vintage sports cars, golf, cricket etc.'

Below Sir Hector tells an amusing story of an experience when in charge of a Catalina on Lough Erne in Northern Ireland, which ended happily - but only just!

On Water.

It is a known fact that aeroplanes are happiest when flying, but they have at times to move over the ground - seaplanes over water. Aircraft moving over the ground have the ability to be stable because of the friction with terra-firma, but with seaplanes it is a different kettle of fish (no pun intended). When taxiing over water there are other hazards to contend with such as the sea itself, which does not give a great deal of stability, currents and wind.

In 1944 Hector Monro was a young RAF Officer stationed in Northern Ireland with Coastal Command and he was converting from Catalinas to Sunderlands and training a new crew who had little experience on Sunderlands and none at all on Catalinas.

He relates the following incident which happened on Lough Erne, when putting the fresh crew through its paces on the Catalina, and which, luckily had a fortunate outcome.

"....Overconfidence or foolhardiness, however, encouraged me to say we would taxi along... and save considerable time. It was quite a task showing the crew what they had to do...especially explaining to the flight engineer, Bill May, how to start the twin Wasps from his isolated position in the tower.

....Eventually we started the engines and were off, with myself climbing about the boat giving directions and leaving Eddie Edmonds, my second pilot at the controls. He had started as a corporal pilot before the war, had over 3500 hours as a flying instructor, and was desperate to get onto an operational squadron.

Flying boats weathercock quickly into a moderate wind, and as we taxied across wind through the rows of moored boats, I was quite happy that when we were about fifty yards off the jetty she would swing to starboard into wind and coast up to the buoy another 200 yards ahead......

Maybe it was Ireland. Maybe it was bad luck, but suddenly the wind died completely. Our speed increased and the Catalina just would not turn into a non-existent wind. As the jetty approached, I rapidly opened up the port engine until the throttle was right through the gate. With a crescendo of noise and spray she came round, lifting the port wing tip float over the jetty by six inches or so.

We made the buoy with a chastened Captain covered in sweat. I had been within six inches of a court-martial or worse, though the crew were impressed and spoke of 'cutting it fine'.

But my everlasting thanks go to the marine-craft section, the only witness of a near disaster. Never a word to anyone, and certainly not the Station Commander, Group Captain John Barraclough, now Air Chief Marshal Sir John Barraclough, and a fellow Honorary Air Commodore in the Royal Auxiliary Air Force!"

Kirtlebridge — Air Commodore Sir Hector Monro.

Sergeant Bertie Moss
(Pilot, "L" Squadron, Glider Pilot Regiment)

Bertie Moss, born in Nottingham in December 1925, was educated at Nottingham High School where he was a member of the Officers' Training Corps. Keen to see some action, at the age of 17, he volunteered to serve in his County Regiment with no thought of becoming a pilot at that stage. Opportunity to transfer to the Glider Pilot Regiment occurred and this he did. When qualified he piloted large troop carrying gliders, Hotspurs, Horsas and Waccos, a very far cry from the light Tiger Moths on which he had learned to fly.

Demobilised in 1947, he took employment with the Gas Corporation and subsequently British Gas, in which he made a career in general management, marketing and public relations. Now retired, he and his wife live in Kippford, a delightful village on the Urr Estuary, boasting a thriving yachting marina. They have a daughter, and a son who is a senior consultant at Doncaster Royal Infirmary. Bertie lists his hobbies as "Dogs in Animal Welfare" world wide correspondence, gardening and bridge.

Below, Bertie describes an incident in his flying training which seems entirely apposite for a future glider pilot - after all, they had to land without any engines, often in the most inappropriate places!

The Making of a Glider Pilot.

At the age of 17 years, I, like many thousands of other enthusiastic young men, volunteered for the Army. My home town being Nottingham, the County Regiment was the Notts. and Derby's, better known as the Sherwood Foresters.

Soon I was off to Lincoln barracks for basic training. Long marches with full pack and weapons in unyielding army boots (definitely not as described in Helen Shapiro's hit) was not my idea of the best way to serve King and Country! Even after becoming a somewhat hardened N.C.O. Instructor such endless marching remained abhorrent.

Imagine therefore my response to an item on Regimental Orders asking for volunteers for Glider Pilots. No more marching. The prospect of being carried by air into action must be the answer to any foot soldier's prayer. After the usual aircrew selection procedures I was posted to Fargo Camp on Salisbury Plain, the bleakest place imaginable where training consisted of unimaginable 'bull' inhuman assault courses and.... yes...you've guessed it, even longer and faster route marches.

Eventually the purgatory came to an end, the survivors being sent for pilot training, in my case to E.F.T.S. , RAF Burnaston, near Derby. It was during this training that I experienced one of the more exciting events of my Army career, since despite the keen volunteering, I had an easy war.

What happened was this - having flown solo (what a wonderful thrill) I was doing routine circuits and bumps, when I thought it would be great to fly over the family home and show off a bit. Not, one would have thought, too demanding since the distance between Derby and Nottingham is only about 15 miles, with the river Trent and a main railway line to guide the way.

Now this may be difficult for Pathfinder types to understand, but I got completely lost. After what seemed hours I started to look for a suitable field to come down in, but like the proverbial policeman ''there's never one there when you want one''.

By now things were getting a bit desperate, all the best fields seemed to be occupied by cows, which despite being 'buzzed' to clear a way, just stood and looked unconcernedly at my plight. The fuel gauge looked most unhealthy - it was decision time. There was an empty field, it looked pathetically inadequate, but it would have to do.

I decided to get down on the first and only attempt, if I went round again it would surely only get worse. As a safety measure and to avoid the temptation of having another go I switched off the engine - this was it.

I sideslipped to virtually zero feet (clever stuff), just cleared the first hedge and plopped down to my one and only three point landing. the boundary hedge was fast approaching, but full right rudder brought the Tiger Moth alongside the hedge, and at last to a standstill. It was perhaps just as well not to have tried to go round again since telegraph wires, which I hadn't seen, blocked the way.

The farmer came up to see if all was well and seemed more surprised to see a soldier, not an airman, climbing out of the cockpit, than the landing on his property.

I phoned the Duty Officer from the farmhouse and had some difficulty in explaining that the Tiger Moth was in a field in Staffordshire!! Luckily the officer was a decent type whose price for his understanding was a dozen eggs, a rare commodity at that time, which the farmer very kindly supplied.

I had mentioned to the Duty Officer that there could be problems with the take-off because of the size of the field, and his cool response was ''if an Army pilot can get it down, a real pilot would have no problem in getting it up''. The Tiger Moth was eventually returned to RAF Burnaston - by trailer!

My navigation continued to be neglected, after all, what is the point when you know a real navigator will see that you are towed to your destination.

Incidentally, a comrade of mine named Banjo Bannerman wasn't so hot either, he got lost doing a cross country exercises and landed on a golf course to ask for directions.

Weren't we lucky we learned on Tiger Moths!

Kippford — Bertie Moss.

Flying Officer Robert (Bob) Pate.
(Pilot)

Robert M. Pate otherwise known as "Bob" was born in Hamilton in Lanarkshire in 1923. There he spent his childhood and youth. In 1940, after taking his 'Highers' at Hamilton Academy he took up work in an insurance office in Glasgow.

By April, 1942 he had volunteered for the RAF at Moffat Street in Glasgow; May found him in Edinburgh being processed for aircrew. He was recommended for training as Observer and sent home. This was a sample of the time wasting that was to be typical of his service in the RAF.

However by the beginning of 1943 he was well and truly into the RAF proper. There he learned to find his way round central London in the blackout, but apart from the Zoo, Abbey Road and Lord's Cricket ground he would have been lost in daylight.

Next movement was to Babbacombe, Torquay. This was much more rewarding and work started in earnest. He thoroughly enjoyed his stay in Babbacombe. The hard physical training plus the "Hygiene and Sanitation" etc. resulted in a feeling of glowing health.

There was only one fly in the ointment. That was known as F.W. 190. It had a habit of coming over unannounced. On one occasion a bomb rendered his billet uninhabitable and himself a bit woozy. For the next two or three days (he does not know how long.) his memory shows gaps. He remembers throwing joists aside and pulling a woman out of a bombed house. He remembers kicking the door of the First Aid Post with the woman in his arms. Next he remembers working in a bombed Sunday School full of little orphans. More gaps, then being on parade at a totally different billet one or two days later being thanked by the C.O. for helping to clear up the Officers Mess, which had also been bombed. The awful thing was that although he was badly concussed and knew so little about what was going on, nobody around him noticed.

On to 7 EFTS for Grading School. At the end of the course he was asked what he wanted to be. He had changed his mind and wanted to be a Bomb-Aimer. Accordingly he was recommended for Observer (Radio). Next thing was that he was posted to 6 BFTS, Ponca City, for training as a pilot. His first escape there was from a mid-air collision. Although trapped in the cockpit he survived because the planes were stuck together. Once again he had concussion.

Hazards and death in flying duties come not only from enemy action but also from accidents, inexperience and natural phenomena. One such hazard which can occur in piston engined aircraft is the formation of ice in the throat of the carburettor, given the right combination of humidity and air temperature. In particularly bad conditions even the use of the alternative warm air supply from the engine may be insufficient to combat this hazard as Bob found when making a night cross-country flight in an advanced trainer, AT6 (Texan), as his account now relates.

Ice is not nice

"It all started with what was just another briefing session for night flying in the month of March. The trainee pilots were each given a destination for a solo cross-country flight and it was up to them to get there and back using their own navigation skills, with no-one to hold their hand. Before they set off they were all briefed on the sort of weather to expect, especially the wind direction and speed. From this the pilot had to plot out the track on his chart and, using the above information, work out the dead-reckoning course to set to keep on that track. On the chart he had to mark out where he anticipated to be at certain intervals of time. With a bit of luck this could be fairly accurate. Map reading at night could sometimes be rather tricky however, as having a light bright enough to read the chart inside, meant some loss of vision outside.

As my dead-reckoning navigation had been very good, I had no qualms about my ability to cope. After half an hour however I was beginning to have second thoughts. Visibility was bad enough at the best of times but this time nothing that I expected to see was visible. I decided to persevere and hoped that some landmark might appear.

It was shortly after this that the engine started to splutter and very quickly cut out altogether. My height was 8,000 feet. The first thing was to set the trim for maximum gliding range. Then I waggled the throttle back and forth. To no avail. Next I had a look over the side. It was as black as the Earl of Hell's waistcoat down below. Undoing the safety belt was the next stage before moving on to the very important one of tightening my parachute harness. The sudden tightening of harness during a drop could cause consternation.

During all this time I made sure the carburettor heating system was switched on. I weakened the mixture fully and operated the throttle. I did the same with the mixture at fully rich position. These were usual tricks to try to make the engine backfire and blow the ice out of the carburettor. Still no avail.

All this time the aircraft was getting lower. I had already decided that if it went anything below 2,000 feet, it was going to be without Robert. As the height got nearer that crucial position I pushed back the canopy and, as my safety belt was already undone, prepared to abandon ship. Heaving myself up I managed to get my feet on the seat. Then against a considerable but not impossible wind got my left leg over the edge of the cockpit. The wind forced me to hold myself tight down against the canopy. My foot had just found a hold and I was ready to hurl myself down and back, when the engine coughed a couple of times and started up again. It was indeed fortunate my leg was on the port side and so missed the flames from the exhaust.

As my rat-like philosophy is to desert only a sinking ship, I climbed back in again. The aircraft played a few tricks while my big boots and legs were negotiating the control column. To hang with safety belts, I concentrated on nursing the aircraft back up to a safe height again. The carburettor heat was working. I could now relax and look about me. And a fat lot of good that did me. Where was I? There was the rub. I could not see anything that looked like anywhere. The realisation came that I was slightly unsure of my position (i.e. lost). How was I to get back to base?

The obvious thing to do was to make a square search. I went down to 6,000ft and started so many minutes this way, make a 90 degree turn. So many minutes that way - a 90 degree turn. And so on. Eventually I spotted a junction of railway lines. Fixing the shape in my mind, I went up to 10,000 feet and stooged around while I tried to find the shape on my map. I did indeed find a suitable shape but it was nowhere near where I was supposed to be. It was something, I decided on a course which should have me meet the Arkansas River. After all it is big enough, but where would I hit it?

Sure enough I did meet the river, once there, it was a case of port or starboard. I decided on starboard. About this time another problem was beginning to bother me, namely fuel or rather the lack of it. With one thing and another I had been out somewhat longer that I was supposed to be. There were places with aerodromes on the river bank at reasonable intervals and I decided to play for safety and set down at the first one. As luck would have it one did appear on the horizon and I headed for it. On making my approach I was more than agreeably surprised to recognise.my own airfield!! Touching down I was safely home just 2 hours and 48 minutes after taking off.

Apart from the icing which happened without warning, the wind I had been given at the briefing session was 50mph out. Others were not as fortunate as I was. They did manage to land, but at other airfields.

Later in my career landing at night without engines did not particularly bother me. I did not have any engines. Come to think of it, I did not have a parachute either!"

Newton Stewart — Bob Pate

When Bob's course at 6 BFTS in Oklahoma qualified for "Wings", these were presented by Group Captain Donaldson. The ceremony ended with a march past to the tune "Beat me Daddie Eight to the Bar"!

Back home came more messing about wasting time and having his morale get steadily worse. What had it all been for? In Harrogate he got so fed up with "Skiving" that he volunteered to work on the food supplies wagon. There were little breaks at 24 EFTS Sealand and 16 EFTS Derby to lighten things.

In the fiasco at Arnhem in September the Glider Pilot Regiment lost 229 pilots killed and 469 taken prisoner. This was a shattering blow to such a small unit. More landings were due to take place and there was no time to train soldiers to be pilots. The RAF had plenty to spare and transferred 1,500 pilots to the Regiment.

In the U.K. about 1,000 pilots were to be used, the rest being sent to the Far East. Bob was reserve on three drafts to the Far East before joining "L" Squadron in the U.K. Having been in reserve his Squadron was not included in Operation "Varsity" but moved into front line for the next operation code name "Arena". As the war wound down very rapidly, this operation was cancelled at the last minute.

Bob stayed on in the GPR until December 1945, when he was transferred back into the RAF. After demobilisation, he took up training as a teacher, finishing up as Headmaster of a large primary school.

He joined the Royal Observer Corps and later on commanded a Squadron in the ATC. As it gradually became too difficult to do both jobs properly, he gave up his commission in the ATC because he felt that the ROC was the more important. Later he commanded 25 Group in the ROC, with the rank of Observer Commander.

Our Belgian Friends

Commandant Marcel Wouters.

A Belgian Patriot and Hero of the Resistance.

In 1936 Belgium adopted a policy of neutrality in the event of a European war; both Britain and France accepted this policy and gave a unilateral promise of support should Belgium be attacked. In October 1937 Germany also undertook to respect Belgian territory, which promise was re-affirmed by the German Ambassador to Belgium on 26th August 1939. The subsequent invasion by Germany on 10th May 1940 showed how utterly worthless were her undertakings. The Belgian armed forces resisted bravely until, on 28th May, his country now almost over-run by the enemy and subject to a merciless bombing offensive from the air, King Leopold III capitulated - an action not wholly supported by his Government, then in Ostend.

In a country racially divided, reduced to chaos by refugees fleeing from both east and west, the Germans adopted a policy in victory of divide and rule. Despite the presence of numerous collaborators, the efforts of the Germans to split the country, the existance of pro-Rexist and pro-Government factions, the vast majority of the Belgian people remained loyal to their country and patriotism was never more clearly demonstrated than by the men and women of the Resistance Movement. Every member of the Resistance faced appalling dangers from the enemy which was also reflected on wives and families. Such a one was the late Commandant Marcel Wouters. His own graphic account (Belgium Twice Under Invading German Boots and Britain Twice Our Allies) vividly describes the work of the Resistance not least of which was the assistance rendered to allied airmen shot down over Belgium. The famous 'Comete' escape line earned the undying gratitude of thousands that it saved from capture and assisted to return to the United Kingdom.

At the time of the invasion of his country, Marcel Wouters was a cavalry officer serving in the Belgian Army. He became a leader in the Resistance in which he served with the utmost gallantry. Our Branch Chairman, in his then capacity as Chairman of the British Legion, Annan Branch, visited Belgium where he renewed war-time friendships, made contact with members of the Wartime Resistance and with many Belgian airmen who had flown with the RAF during the war. A close friendship developed between Donald Irving and Marcel Wouters and it was with enthusiasm that our branch members, in April 1989, invited Marcel to become an Associate Member of the A.C.A., Dumfries and Galloway Branch. Marcel's charming letter of acceptance is reproduced with his article. A bonus accuring from Donald's visits to Belgium is that we are proud to have as members a number of Belgian airmen who flew with us in the war.

Sadly, Marcel Wouters is no longer with us and to maintain our links with the Belgian Resistance Movement it was decided, in the summer of 1991, to invite his son Georges Wouters to take up associate membership with us. This he accepted with gratitude as a fitting gesture to his late father's heroism. A retired Superintendent of Police in Brussels, Georges has given assistance to relatives and friends in the U.K. to trace Resistance members who gave help to the RAF during the war. Tragically, in the summer of 1992, Georges was killed in a traffic accident, so the direct link with the Wouters family is now broken. There is, however, a further memorial. In the Spring of 1992, Georges sent us a most telling account of his family's sufferings in occupied Belgium entitled "I Was Only Eight Years Old At The Time". This account follows that of his father.

UNION NATIONALE DES
CROIX DE GUERRE BELGES
ASSOCIATION SANS BUT LUCRATIF
C.C.P. 341.45
(Annexe au Moniteur Belge
du 29 septembre 1956, no 3590)
SIEGE SOCIAL
RUE DU LUXEMBOURG, 33
1040 BRUXELLES
TEL: 02/512.21.00
C.C.P. 000-0034145-01

NATIONAAL VERBOND DER
BELGISCHE OORLOGSKRUISEN
VERENIGING ZONDER WINSTGEVEND DOEL
Postcheck 341.45
(Bijvoegsel aan het Belgisch Staatsblad
van 29 september 1956, nr 3590)
SOCIALE ZETEL
LUXEMBURGSTRAAT, 33
1040 BRUSSEL
TEL: 02/512.21.00
P.C.R. 000-0034145-01

Home address:
8th May 89 - memorable day for all soldiers of W.W.II.
Commandant e.r. Marcel Wouters,
Avenue des Faons 18,
1189 UCCLE-Bruxelles, Belgium.

My dear Scottish Comrade,

Your letter of the 17th April 89 have made a Happy Belgian once more. How nice this gesture from You and Your Committee, surely I suspect my good Friend, Your Chairman, Donald Irving of Annan.

I accept to be an Honorary Associate Member of Your Branch, it is a great Honour for me, to be a brother-in-arms with the R.A.F. me as an old Horseman also of the Resistance.

Thank you all, so much!

About your suggestion to build up a report concerning our escape-lines, secret inquires services during NAZI occupation in Belgium, I think, I will be able to do that. We Belgians, we know that U.K. people consider us as great Allies, for certain, that high respect from Scotland.

An idea is born, I shall write to my friend Donald to obtain his views. Next November I hope to come over to Scotland again. It depends from the date of the annual big re-union of my Scottish Regiment, 52nd Div. R.E.C.C.E. (L) Regiment, met in September 1944, of which I am an Honorary Live Member too. I hope to come over to Annan and Dumfries, where I hope to see again, the sister of a RAF boy, lying in the British Cemetery (with other men of the crew) at Heverlee-Louvain.

You may know about all what we were doing to save our unlucky RAF friends shot down in Belgium, what happened in full darkness to put and keep you out of German hands or traitors.

Faithfully yours,

I remain a Friend of that Scottish people. In Comradeship Too.

Marcel Wouters.

(Belgium)

Belgium Twice Under Invading German Boots And Brtain Twice Our Allies.

1914 - The pin-helmeted Germans came through Belgium as murderers, brutish terrorists, killing many innocent civilians, women and children included in this carnage: even old worthies throughout the country, in such towns on the River Meuse, such as Andenne, Dinant, Tamines, Spontin, Surice etc. Houses were burnt to the gound in a large area of Dinant, and at Leuven the University was completely destroyed. There were 350 innocent victims, the youngest only three weeks old, the eldest 88 years old in Dinant. The onslaught on the town was occasioned because the French regular army stopped there and was attacked by the Boche. It was here that a young French Lieutenant was wounded, his name Charles de Gaulle.

At the end of October the Boche advance was halted in Flanders Field on the River Yzer, by the Belgian Army, who were in sufficient numbers to effect this. The front line extended to the English sector at Ypres, where the 'Poppy History' was born. For years the Allies held fast with them going on the offensive in September and October 1918. Then came the glorious day of Amistice. We will never forget the criminal gas attacks at Ypres and north of this area.

1939 - Poland was attacked and subsequently occupied by the Boche on 1st September. Britain and France declared war against Germany on the 3rd September 1939. All Belgian borders came under surveillance by the Belgian Army. The biggest envisaged danger was from the Siegfried Line.

On the 10th January 1940 two Boche majors were captured by my armoured squadron and found to have plans on them for the invasion of Belgium, the Netherlands and Luxembourg. The plan showed the Boche intended to drop paratroopers at the rear of the Maginot Line, and also showed that a concerted rush to Sedan was planned.

On the 10th May 1940, the sons of the 1914/18 bandits came back, more refined in torture and repulsive practices. They said they were going to protect us from the British.

After 18 days of fierce fighting the Germans were the victors. The Belgian Army fought hard to help us protect the retreating B.E.F. We were at the base from which 33,000 British soldiers returned safely to England. We did our loyal duty for our Allies.

France capitulated on the 18th June 1940. The voice of that 1914 French Lieutenant, now a Colonel, broadcast from England, "We lost a great battle, but not the war. Immense forces are still available, we shall later put the Germans out".

Then, from Mr (Cigar) Churchill, "We will never capitulate and we will fight on the beaches, in the towns, on the land, everywhere. Maybe we lost all the battles, except the last one. Britannia rules the waves."

The Germans stood on the rocks in France, their eyes on the Channel. There in the sunshine, seemingly only a stones's throw away, lay "la Fiere Albion" (alias Britain). But the Boche had a problem for high in the sky above their heads flew those wretched wasps and in the blue they traced the letters R.A.F.

"What do we do?" asked the Boche of themselves; any invasion had to be a success, failure could not be afforded. But 'Channel water' came in flames and the RAF wasps were not seizable by the Germans, though the Luftwaffe tried. Result - Luftwaffe 0 - R.A.F. 4.

Everyone on the Continent understood the invasion of England would be a very hard job, and hope rose in all hearts. Here at last was first halt in the German battle successes. They understood that even taking the shortest route to England had all the substance of a fable.

Then came the famous 'Battle of Britain'. Belgian pilots who took part numbered 29, seven of whom were killed in action and others wounded. This saw the beginning of the Belgian R.A.F. During the war nearly 600 Belgians fought with the RAF with about the same number of ground staff.

In occupied Belgium more than 700 Allied pilots and others aircrew were saved by our escape services. The lucky boys who came to England know it was a very good what the Belgians did. We are very proud of this assistance from little Belgium to a great Great Britain.

What about the Resistance and the Escape Lines? This organisation was beginning before the Krauts tried to cross the Channel. Once we saw written on a wall, in chalk, "Jerries be careful, the Tommies are ready, and the fishes too." Also the meseages, R.A.F. (Resistance all Forces) still snapping at your buttocks.

I remember from the BBC in London, broadcasting as 'Radio Belgique', each day, in French and Flemish. The voice over the ether wished us courage and the message that the Boche would eventually be caught and made to answer for their crimes. Listening to the BBC was strictly forbidden, but we needed these words, and we were faithfull followers in spite of the danger.

For four years we stood in the Resistance, serving our land, day by day and throughout the nights too. Germans police were very hard and brutal to us. Our duty was to be, and remain, good patriots. We never regretted what we did.

We wondered why the Germans came to our land...to protect us? Against whom, against what? Most of our soldiers, N.C.O.'s and Officers were in 1940 taken to Germany as P.O.W.'s. Supposed dissidents were sent to prisons and concentration camps.

I was captured twice by the Germans, and because of my Flemish origin and good knowledge of the German language, found it easy to escape. Very early in the war I joined the Resistance Movement, especially the secret inquiries and escape lines section. My home was at Leopoldsburg, an old garrison town in the N.E. corner of Belgium, and a training centre for the Belgium Army. It was occupied by the invaders, the Wermacht and the Marines. It was in December 1942 that I was arested by the Boche police, but on the way to the concentration camp I managed to glide away in the darkness to freedom. The Feldgendarme who had arrested me was a repulsive man, and before my escape I swore I would find him after the war. We were in possession of so many names of Nazi criminals. His home was in Madgeburg. After the war I was on my way to Berlin, and the train stopped at Madgeburg, but there was no question of me stepping out for it was situated in the Russian sector. Bandit Neumann, if he was still alive, was now protected by the Ivans!! It was such a pity, I missed my boxing match with a K.O. for that pig.

After my escape I did clandestine work as a secret agent. All messages were sent on microfilm or by courier. 'Lizzies' (Lysander aircraft) were used, also by S.A.S. and S.O.E. (dropped agents). Messages were also sent by wireless operators. Information was transmitted about railway traffic movements, 'feldpostnummers', military occupation areas, sabotage operations being planned, addresses of dangerous collaborators, places where Allied aircrew waited for evacuation, all in code of course.

What happened under you, the Allied aircrews, when your bombers flew over France, Holland, and Belgium? We were always alert to help shot down crews, and we were very proud of our well organised escape lines. I modestly say we did a good job, the successful results spoke for themselves. The aircrews who survived after being shot down over Belgium and other occupied territories are the best witnesses to tell you, fellow fliers, through which routes, often in full darkness and with the aid of helping clandestine hands, they were returned to Britain after so many dangers endured. A great many of these courageous patriots paid with their lives for helping RAF personnel. They were either summarily shot or sent to concentration camps. They did this work fully knowing the risks they ran, as did the RAF men on their missions over Europe. All brave men indeed and will always merit honour and the highest respect. When one fell another came to replace him, another link in the chain to ultimate freedom.

I read a book 'Ticket to Freedom' written by an R.A.F. flier who was shot down in France. Three months later he was back in England. He described his odyssey in France and Belgium. In Brussels he found the 'Comete' (Committee) Line. He tells how he retains the highest possible regard for members of the Resistance he met. From them he obtained civilian clothes and false papers, and given bed, food, money and train tickets and the promise of medical assistance if wounded. On his journey to Spain he was watched by friendly caring eyes and advised by the ladies who worked in the background. This airman author wrote the word Resistance always with a capital letter. Many years ago an honourable Scottish lady, through an ex-RAF man, asked for information from our Branch of old Resistance members. Her brother had been a member of the crew of a Lancaster which left a British airfield on 2nd September 1942. It was shot down in flames by flak near Liege in Belgium on the 3rd September, eactly three years after war was declared. The only information I received from this lady was that the graves of these young RAF men were situated at Heverlee/Leuven, not far from that famous German night fighter airfield during the occupation. This was really a 'death dealing triangle' of Beauvechain, Brustem (St. Trond) and Gilze-Tyen (Holland).

I found the three graves of the airmen killed that sad night. The Lancaster had been shot down by flak over Liege and crashed 20 miles to the west of this city, only 100 yards from the houses in the village of Abee. All high explosive bombs were still on board the plane. Four of the crew had bailed out, one left Belgium by the underground movement at the end of September 1942 and eventually reached England safely. The others were picked up by the Belgian Resistance, but tragically the Resistance members and the three aircrew were denounced and handed over to the Luftwaffe Police by a traitor who was a burgomaster. He was shot dead in full daylight by one of our Resistance members.

I spoke to two witnesses that sad night and they showed me the exact place where the Lancaster crashed. There was a crater and young trees were growing in it as though a silent tribute to three brave young men who fought, just as we did, for freedom and justice. We worked to help our Allies, and, at the same time to punish the hated Boche at every opportunity.

To Aircrew Association Members, have I any memories? Yes, the raid on Pennemunde - the aim to destroy the V. weapons which was successful thus retarding Hilter's plan. The attack on the prison at Amiens, the object to liberate 200 political prisoners.

May 1942 - the first attack on Cologne with 1000 bombers. That night, I tell you, the German soldiers did not sleep. We were so satisfied to hear all those planes passing overhead. Cologne was on fire. The RAF lost 71 bombers, and nearly 500 aircrew. A lot were saved and returned to England.

The complete destruction of the camp at Beverlo (Leopoldsburg in Belgium, where my garrison was stationed before the war) happened on the night of 24th May 1944.

I had noted the presence of the SS Panzer division Hitlerjugend there, resting. I specially asked for the RAF to do the bombing (no Americans) for an important reason. There were two nearby camps full of political prisoners, and I was afraid mistakes may be made by the Americans. The RAF completely destroyed the Beverlo camp, killing 3,500 German marines, but missed an SS division because a few days earlier the Germans started out for France. I think the Boche had a smell of the landing of the Allied troops.

At last, perhaps the most important raid, the attack on the gigantic blockhouse in which was prepared the V3, the German styled 'terror bomb', Hitler's last chance.

This was situated 10 kilomeetres from St. Omer in France, in the forest of Watten, the bunker being Eperlesques. On April 27th 1944 this was completely destroyed by a new British invention, the penetration bomb which went deep into the ground before exploding. Now the V3 no longer existed and Britain was saved from possible destruction, thanks to the 'Tallboy' bomb. There are still the remains of 1,600 victims of that bombing inside the bunker. A great many airmen gave their lives in the WWII, to save the world from catastrophe, and among them is the brother of the late President of the U.S.A., John Kennedy, who is buried in French soil, his plane having exploded in mid-air.

I Was Only 8 Years Old At The Time.

My father was a dedicated soldier, a true patriot who put his country, Belgium , first. But what agonies this caused my mother and myself.

My father was a very good Resistance member, both when in action and engaged in Intelligence work. This put his family in grave danger. We were nearly sent to a concentration camp and my mother suffered from the after effects of her imprisonment by the Gestapo.

My father was in the Maquis from 1941 to 1944. In 1943 my mother was beaten up by the Gestapo and was in a pitiful state. I did not know when exactly she was deported. She was arrested one morning when I was at school and it wasn't till I came home at mid-day that neighbours gave me the news. I then remembered what my mother had told me "If there is a vase of flowers in the window don't ring the bell but get yourself off to Sterrebeck. Don't go direct to grandfather's house, go to his neighbour, Monsieur Jules". This was about 100 kilometres to be covered and I was eight years old.

I went through the village of Heppen and I was hungry. Farms stood along the route. At the first of these I was fortunate in avoiding a kick on the backside, at the second I was given a large slice of bread and butter. The farmer asked me where I was going and I answered, "To Brussels". The farmer, dumbfounded, then called his wife and she asked me why was I going there. My instincts as a child told me that a second slice of bread and butter might be in the offing for the journey so I replied, "The Germans are after me". The farmer asked me if I knew the way and I answered "Yes, via Beeringen, Diest, Leuven and Steerebeck".

They gave me a second slice of bread and butter and some milk. They kept me there for a further half hour, plying me with questions. I did not have the slightest idea of what happened to my father and mother.

I set off again with my slices of bread and butter and a sausage, after expressing thanks to the couple. I had just gone through Beeringen when a car stopped beside me. My instant reaction was run as fast as I could, but a priest got out of it and asked me if he could drop me off somewhere. I learned later that the priest had been told about me by the farmer.

Cars fascinated me. I had never been in one and the priest seemed to be a nice person. I told him I was going to Diest, "So am I" he answered. That bucked me up because it meant I didn't have to cover all the kilometres on foot. Once we got to Diest, we chatted about all sorts of things, including school. The priest reproached me for not having chosen the 'common school', (Catholic Community School). I told him I didn't like the teacher. "Your teacher was not a 'brother', but if you like, there are 'Fathers' and we're going to Rotselaer to have something to eat with the Fathers. Between Diest and Louvain hė took me to a magnificient home of the Fathers of the Belgian Congo. One of the Fathers explained that I couldn't go to Steerebeck because no doubt the Germans would be waiting for me there. I was in a distressed state and spent weeks in bed. It was like being an orphan. I remember attending a school in Hasselt for some time. Then one day my mother came back. She stood there looking very thin but smiling and we went back to Bourg-Leopold.

The bombing attacks on Germany became more and more frequent and my mother had probably heard of a possible attack on Bourg-Leopold. She had the cellar re-inforced with beams. She must have received this message from my father - "Tongues of flame are going to fall on your head, bombs are going to fall at Whitsun." And sure enough, bombs were dropped on Bourg-Leopold at Whitsun. 3,800 Germans were killed. This was the biggest number of Germans killed in Belgium during the war and the bombing last half an hour. The weather was hot and it was awful to see lorries going past our house loaded with corpses. Most of them were naked and the stench were intorable. The ammunition in the dump kept exploding for a week. No one dared go out because the Germans were furious.

Nevertheless we attended mass at Whitsun after the bombing. We first gave thanks to God because the British arrived instead of the Americans because the latter were not too fussy, and we also gave thanks for still being alive.

Belgium — Georges Wouters.

GLOSSARY 0F SERVICE TERMS

A.C.	Army Co-operation
A/C1	Aircraftsman 1st Class
A/C2	Aircraftsman 2nd Class
ACRC	Aircrew receiving centre
AFC	Air Flying Cross
AFU	Advanced Flying Unit
Bale Out	Leave aircraft by parachute
Bought it	Killed, dead
Box barrage	Concentration of A/A fire in space
Browned off	Fed up
CFI	Chief Flying Instructor
Chop	Killed
'Chute	Parachute
Circuits and Bumps	Flying around airfield and landing
Coned	Aircraft lit up by searchlights
CO	Commanding Officer
Corkscrew	Taking evasive action
Ditched	Emergency descent on to water
Dicey	Dangerous
DFC	Distinguished Flying Cross
DFM	Distinguished Flying Medal
ETA	Estimated Time of Arrival
EFTS	Elementary Flying Training School
Flak	Anti-aircraft fire
Gardening	Sea mine laying by aircraft
Gee	Radio Navigational Aid
George	Automatic Pilot
GPR	Glider Pilot Regiment
Happy Valley	Heavily Defended Ruhr Valley
H2S	Airborne Radar Navigational Aid
HCU	Heavy Conversion Unit
LAC	Leading Aircraftsman
Legs	Stages of Complete Flight
Line shoot	Tall Story
NCO	Non commissioned officer
Ops.	Operations

GLOSSARY (contd)

Orbit	Circle Round
OTU	Operational Training Unit
Pathfinder	Aircraft ahead of main force to mark target
Piece of cake	Easy
Prang	To damage, destroy or crash
ROC	Royal Observer Corps
SFTS	Service Flying Training School
Skipper	Captain of aircraft (usually the pilot)
Solo	Fly alone, generally for the first time
W/Op	Wireless Operator
W/T	Wireless Telegraphy
Wimpey	Wellington Bomber